SignalR Real-time Application Cookbook

Use SignalR to create real-time, bidirectional, and asynchronous applications based on standard web technologies

Roberto Vespa

BIRMINGHAM - MUMBAI

SignalR Real-time Application Cookbook

Copyright © 2014 Packt Publishing

All rights reserved. No part of this book may be reproduced, stored in a retrieval system, or transmitted in any form or by any means, without the prior written permission of the publisher, except in the case of brief quotations embedded in critical articles or reviews.

Every effort has been made in the preparation of this book to ensure the accuracy of the information presented. However, the information contained in this book is sold without warranty, either express or implied. Neither the author, nor Packt Publishing, and its dealers and distributors will be held liable for any damages caused or alleged to be caused directly or indirectly by this book.

Packt Publishing has endeavored to provide trademark information about all of the companies and products mentioned in this book by the appropriate use of capitals. However, Packt Publishing cannot guarantee the accuracy of this information.

First published: April 2014

Production Reference: 1160414

Published by Packt Publishing Ltd.
Livery Place
35 Livery Street
Birmingham B3 2PB, UK.

ISBN 978-1-78328-595-2

www.packtpub.com

Cover Image by Aniket Sawant (aniket_sawant_photography@hotmail.com)

Credits

Author

Roberto Vespa

Reviewers

Sriram Cherukumilli

Robin Karlsson

Duncan Mole

Emanuele Rabino

Richard Seroter

Commisioning Editor

Saleem Ahmed

Acquisition Editor

Rebecca Youe

Content Development Editor

Dayan Hyames

Technical Editors

Dennis John

Sebastian Rodrigues

Copy Editors

Dipti Kapadia

Aditya Nair

Kirti Pai

Stuti Srivastava

Project Coordinator

Swati Kumari

Proofreaders

Simran Bhogal

Linda Morris

Indexer

Hemangini Bari

Production Coordinators

Pooja Chiplunkar

Manu Joseph

Cover Work

Manu Joseph

About the Author

Roberto Vespa has been passionate about programming computers since he was at high school, and he always wanted to do that for a living.

He has a degree in Electronic Engineering obtained in Italy, and has been working in the Information Technology industry since 1995, consulting on many different projects and for several customers. He is a software developer and architect with strong experience on the Windows platform, and in particular on the .NET Framework since Version 1.0, and on web technologies. He has always been working across a broad spectrum of responsibilities from distributed applications to complex user interfaces, from architecture and designing solutions to debugging server and client code, and from native Windows clients to web user interfaces.

He loves to learn, share, and communicate about technology. He wrote technical articles for an Italian magazine in the past, and now puts his effort into looking at the latest advances in programming or in contributing to open source projects such as ElmahR, a real-time error monitoring web dashboard built on top of SignalR. You can find out more about it at `http://elmahr.apphb.com/`.

Since 2011, he has been working in Switzerland where he lives with his wife, Cecilia, and their cats.

You can follow him on Twitter at `@wasp_twit`.

Roberto's blogs are at `http://www.robychechi.it/roby`.

Acknowledgments

I would like to thank Packt Publishing for the opportunity they gave me to write this book. This has been my first time as a writer and, for sure, it has been a challenging task, but their support has been constant and fundamental in making it possible. I would like to thank my colleague Duncan Moles and my old friend Emanuele "Lele" Rabino for accepting to review my first drafts. Their helpful advice comes from their skills and expertise. My gratitude goes also to Jean-Luc Marbot, Roberto Forno, Atif Aziz, and Gustavo Perez Leon. I learned so much from them in the last couple of years, and they have been very important to me during my adventure in Switzerland.

My biggest thanks go to my intercontinental family, without whom this book would not have been possible: my parents and brother in Italy, who have always supported and loved me; and my adoptive family in Paraguay, who received me as if I had always been one of them. And, of course I would like to thank my wife, Cecilia, who's at the center of my life: I love you.

About the Reviewers

Sriram Cherukumilli is a developer/architect with experience in architecture, design, and development across all application tiers with emphasis on enterprise real-time backend systems. He works at Argo Data Resources on Windows Workflow Foundation 4.5-based workflow management applications that abstract developer-specific and platform-specific details to present business-friendly orchestration services to build workflows across the company's different verticals. Sriram holds a Bachelor's degree in Engineering and a Master's degree in Information Technology. Before working at Argo, Sriram worked with many .NET SOA-based enterprise software systems at EMSI, Yahoo! Inc, and Verizon.

I would like to thank Packt Publishing for providing me with this opportunity.

Robin Karlsson is a Tech Lead and System Developer at Teleopti, with more than 10 years' experience of development in product companies in the HR area. The team at Teleopti successfully switched from a proprietary solution to a SignalR-based solution to enable monitoring the contact center performance in a web-based solution.

Duncan Mole is an experienced .NET architect/developer, and C# specialist with a focus on real-time, reactive programming. In recent years, Duncan has worked for a variety of investment banks and financial institutions, delivering solutions involving push-style messaging models on a variety of technologies such as SignalR.

Emanuele Rabino is a freelance developer specialized and passionate about everything related to the world of web development.

After working for many years on enterprise projects, using the ASP.NET stack in all its forms, he has been driving the development of e-commerce solutions using HTML5 and full-stack JavaScript environments.

Richard Seroter is the head of product management for CenturyLink Cloud, a Microsoft MVP, an instructor for the developer-centric training company Pluralsight, an InfoQ.com editor for cloud computing, and the author of multiple books on application integration strategies. He is a recognized public speaker and has spoken at events around the world. Richard maintains a regularly updated blog on the topics of architecture and solution design (http://seroter.wordpress.com), and can be found on Twitter as @rseroter.

www.PacktPub.com

Support files, eBooks, discount offers and more

You might want to visit www.PacktPub.com for support files and downloads related to your book.

Did you know that Packt offers eBook versions of every book published, with PDF and ePub files available? You can upgrade to the eBook version at www.PacktPub.com and as a print book customer, you are entitled to a discount on the eBook copy. Get in touch with us at service@packtpub.com for more details.

At www.PacktPub.com, you can also read a collection of free technical articles, sign up for a range of free newsletters and receive exclusive discounts and offers on Packt books and eBooks.

http://PacktLib.PacktPub.com

Do you need instant solutions to your IT questions? PacktLib is Packt's online digital book library. Here, you can access, read and search across Packt's entire library of books.

Why Subscribe?

- ▶ Fully searchable across every book published by Packt
- ▶ Copy and paste, print and bookmark content
- ▶ On demand and accessible via web browser

Free Access for Packt account holders

If you have an account with Packt at www.PacktPub.com, you can use this to access PacktLib today and view nine entirely free books. Simply use your login credentials for immediate access.

Table of Contents

Preface

The World Wide Web has been with us for the past 20 years and has become a fundamental part of our lives. Its distributed architecture has proven to be efficient and scalable. Thanks to it, nowadays, an incredible amount of information and services is available to all of us. We just have to connect, look for what we need, and pull it onto our devices to use it. However, it's also true that many scenarios would be more efficient if services themselves were able to determine the information that we need and then push it towards us at the right time. The contrast between these two ways of distributing content is clear and important, and according to the specific goals, there might be a clear advantage in using one or the other.

We already have several networking and application technologies that are ideal to build push systems, but the World Wide Web and its enabling protocol, HTTP, were not born for that. Traditional applications based on HTTP offer a request/response model where it's always the client's responsibility to initiate a connection, and it's always the client who has to ask the server for something. The server will send back the appropriate response on the same connection opened by the client to perform the request, and then, it will terminate the connection. According to this model, there is usually no natural way for the server to send any piece of information without a previous specific incoming request. Nevertheless, it would be a shame to miss the opportunity to leverage such a ubiquitous protocol in order to enable push scenarios for all its users.

This is how the Web has lately started to move towards enabling push scenarios, first with a series of technology tricks (Long Polling, Forever Frame, and Server-Sent Events) applied over the traditional HTTP/HTML stack, and then with the rise of a proper technology that introduces a way to establish persistent connections between clients and servers, which can then be used for fully bidirectional communications: WebSocket. Modern browsers and web servers bring full support to the latter option, while older systems can recur to the former tricks. So, now we have several ways to deliver a solution, but also the problem of having to decide which technology to use, or maybe the need to replicate our solution using all these techniques together to reach every potential user.

Enter SignalR! SignalR is a very interesting library that leverages all the strategies that we previously mentioned to deliver a real-time push platform. It enables a two-way communication model between the client and the server, and it achieves this goal simply by leveraging what HTTP and HTML5 have to offer. SignalR looks like magic because it transparently adapts itself to the available environment (the HTTP server and the web browser) and transforms a normally transient HTTP connection into a virtually persistent connection. The messaging API offered by SignalR succeeds in abstracting the low-level networking strategies, chosen according to what's supported by the involved counterparts, and offers us a simple and generic way to write code that remains unaware of the underlying complexity.

We briefly mentioned what SignalR does and how it does it, but the actual goal of this book is not to dig deep into the mechanics SignalR is built on top of. This is a practical, hands-on guide that provides you with a number of clear, step-by-step recipes that will gradually enable you to add SignalR as an innovative, effective, and useful item in your toolbox. It will move from simple examples down to complex use cases, going through a comprehensive overview of the library.

Although most of the recipes will give some information on how SignalR works behind the scenes to enable the proposed solution, these explanations shall not be too detailed. You should not expect otherwise from this book. The book will not go into deep architectural details. It will just provide you with a decent level of explanations to help the reader understand what is going on, while keeping the focus on bringing practical and synthetic solutions to specific questions.

In each recipe, we will be picking a problem and showing you a SignalR-based solution, or, if you prefer, we'll be choosing a specific feature from SignalR and matching it to the class of scenarios it helps tackle. This way you will gradually learn how to perform a set of common tasks, which the last chapter will combine to build complex applications.

At the time of writing this book, SignalR reached Version 2, and this is the one that we'll be using for our discussion. If you need to use Version 1, this book could still be used as a general reference. However, there are some differences that you would have to take care of, especially in areas related to hosting and bootstrapping a SignalR-based application. That said, these differences will not be treated throughout the text, and no particular attention will be paid to the older version.

You might also have to pay attention to the fast evolution of the minor version number of SignalR and of all its dependencies. SignalR is available on NuGet. It's constantly updated, and the same happens to the components that it depends on, such as jQuery or Newtonsoft. Json. This means that the actual version numbers that you might reference while writing your code are likely to be different from the ones you will find listed here. The recipes have been constantly revised, and have been updated to what's available at the time of the final technical reviews (February, 2014). You will have to take care of any further update that might be released later and act manually to fix any mismatch. This will probably result in having to change some JavaScript reference to a later version, or to add some `assemblyRedirect` directive in your configuration files to remap an older version of a required assembly to a newer one. Once done with that, the code will still be valid and fully working.

It's worth mentioning that SignalR is an open source project whose source code can be found at `https://github.com/SignalR/SignalR`.

Whenever there's anything unclear and you really need to shed some light on it, you can inspect its code and find the answers by yourself. It's a very clean and well-organized code base, and you should not get scared by the idea of going through it. The official documentation can be found at `http://www.asp.net/signalr`.

What this book covers

Chapter 1, Understanding the Basics, covers the basic steps to add the server and client portions of a SignalR application in the context of different hosting technologies. We will be writing the simplest code possible, and we'll perform the minimal steps that are required to have everything up and running.

Chapter 2, Using Hubs, illustrates the Hubs API from a server-side point of view.

Chapter 3, Using the JavaScript Hubs Client API, introduces the Hubs API from a client-side point of view, using the JavaScript client library.

Chapter 4, Using the .NET Hubs Client API, explains the Hubs API from a client-side point of view, using the .NET client library this time.

Chapter 5, Using a Persistent Connection, moves to the more low-level persistent connection API, illustrating its peculiar features and differences when compared to Hubs.

Chapter 6, Handling Connections, illustrates some advanced features that we can leverage to optimize and customize the way we handle the existing connections.

Chapter 7, Analyzing Advanced Scenarios, digs into more infrastructural features made available to fine-tune and extend SignalR's behaviors.

Chapter 8, Building Complex Applications, is all about full-fledged examples, illustrating how SignalR can be used as the foundation technology to solve real-world, bidirectional messaging problems.

Appendix A, Creating Web Projects, explains the steps to create each one of the various types of ASP.NET projects that we created in Visual Studio, in case you are not yet used to it.

Appendix B, Insights, discusses the different transport strategies that SignalR chooses to provide a logical persistent connection, according to the environment it runs on. It also talks about the basic concepts of asynchronous programming.

What you need for this book

All the code samples have been prepared and tested using Microsoft Visual Studio 2013, which brings the highest integration with Version 2 of SignalR with it. Microsoft Visual Studio 2012 could be used too, and you would be able to reach the same final result, but the experience inside the IDE might be slightly different. Again, the book will not try to fill any gap between the two environments, and it will explicitly only target the 2013 version.

Who this book is for

This book can be read by different types of developers.

Beginners will be able to learn all the fundamental concepts of SignalR, quickly becoming productive in a usually difficult arena that real-time, bidirectional communication normally is.

In this book, experienced programmers will find a handy and useful collection of ready-made solutions to common use cases, which they will then be able to enhance as needed. They will be able to use it as a quick reference to the most important SignalR features. No previous practical experience either in SignalR or real-time communication in general is required.

Conventions

In this book, you will find a number of styles of text that distinguish between different kinds of information. Here are some examples of these styles, and an explanation of their meaning.

Code words in text, database table names, folder names, filenames, file extensions, pathnames, dummy URLs, user input, and Twitter handles are shown as follows: "To add a friendly name, we can use the `HubName` attribute."

A block of code is set as follows:

```
public class Startup
{
    public void Configuration(IAppBuilder app)
    {
        app.MapSignalR();
    }
}
```

When we wish to draw your attention to a particular part of a code block, the relevant lines or items are set in bold:

```
public class Startup
{
    public void Configuration(IAppBuilder app)
    {
        app.MapSignalR();
    }
}
```

Any command-line input or output is written as follows:

```
signalr.exe ghp
```

New terms and **important words** are shown in bold. Words that you see on the screen, in menus or dialog boxes for example, appear in the text like this: "Clicking on the **Ok** button creates a new file."

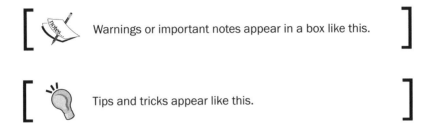

> Warnings or important notes appear in a box like this.

> Tips and tricks appear like this.

Reader feedback

Feedback from our readers is always welcome. Let us know what you think about this book—what you liked or may have disliked. Reader feedback is important for us to develop titles that you really get the most out of.

To send us general feedback, simply send an e-mail to feedback@packtpub.com, and mention the book title via the subject of your message.

If there is a topic that you have expertise in and you are interested in either writing or contributing to a book, see our author guide on www.packtpub.com/authors.

Customer support

Now that you are the proud owner of a Packt book, we have a number of things to help you to get the most from your purchase.

Downloading the example code

You can download the example code files for all Packt books you have purchased from your account at http://www.packtpub.com. If you purchased this book elsewhere, you can visit http://www.packtpub.com/support and register to have the files e-mailed directly to you.

Errata

Although we have taken every care to ensure the accuracy of our content, mistakes do happen. If you find a mistake in one of our books—maybe a mistake in the text or the code—we would be grateful if you would report this to us. By doing so, you can save other readers from frustration and help us improve subsequent versions of this book. If you find any errata, please report them by visiting http://www.packtpub.com/submit-errata, selecting your book, clicking on the **errata submission form** link, and entering the details of your errata. Once your errata are verified, your submission will be accepted and the errata will be uploaded on our website, or added to any list of existing errata, under the Errata section of that title. Any existing errata can be viewed by selecting your title from http://www.packtpub.com/support.

Piracy

Piracy of copyright material on the Internet is an ongoing problem across all media. At Packt, we take the protection of our copyright and licenses very seriously. If you come across any illegal copies of our works, in any form, on the Internet, please provide us with the location address or website name immediately so that we can pursue a remedy.

Please contact us at copyright@packtpub.com with a link to the suspected pirated material.

We appreciate your help in protecting our authors, and our ability to bring you valuable content.

Questions

You can contact us at questions@packtpub.com if you are having a problem with any aspect of the book, and we will do our best to address it.

1
Understanding the Basics

In this chapter, we will cover:

- ▶ Adding a Hub to an ASP.NET project
- ▶ Adding a Hub to a self-hosting application
- ▶ Connecting to a Hub from a JavaScript client
- ▶ Connecting to a Hub from a .NET application

Introduction

SignalR is an amazing framework that delivers a real-time and bidirectional messaging platform. SignalR provides several options to reach its goal, but in this chapter we'll start simple and use the most basic API to set up a persistent and real-time channel: Hubs. A Hub is a special class that SignalR will expose to all the connected clients, allowing them to make **Remote Procedure Calls** (**RPC**) to it. Inside the Hub, the developer will also have a set of special objects to use in order to perform calls back onto the connected clients.

There is a very important detail to highlight: SignalR is composed of a server-side library and a set of client-side libraries. In every working solution, you will always need to use both; you will need to expose the server-side endpoints and connect to them using the most appropriate client library. SignalR will do the rest, and you will experience a very natural, simple, and bidirectional programming model.

All the recipes in this chapter will be classic "Hello World" applications. Nothing fancy or exciting will be happening, but all of them will clearly illustrate what can be achieved and how. The *Adding a Hub to an ASP.NET project* and *Adding a Hub to a self-hosting application* recipes will show you how to prepare a server portion of a SignalR application using the Hub type in different hosting contexts, whereas the *Connecting to a Hub from a JavaScript client* and *Connecting to a Hub from a .NET application* recipes will illustrate how to write client-side code to connect to it from different types of client processes. Each recipe has the goal to be fully functional, therefore all of them will in some way provide at least some hints about the missing counterparts. Server-side recipes will have minimal client code in place, and client-side ones will either contain a basic Hub to connect to or refer to one created earlier, but for all of them, the focus will remain on the actual topic of the recipe.

Adding a Hub to an ASP.NET project

SignalR sets a clear separation between the actual messaging runtime and the hosting environment. Although the host could be any plain old .NET-based process, the most natural context where you can add a SignalR Hub is inside an ASP.NET project, which is the topic of this recipe. Later in this chapter, we'll see how to host it in a different context.

This recipe will concentrate on the server-side; however, some minimal client-side code will also be added to be able to fully demonstrate a complete, although trivial, client-server connection.

Getting ready

There are three main types of ASP.NET projects:

- ▸ A Web Forms application
- ▸ An MVC application
- ▸ A website

The process of creating them is a fairly common task, so we are going to skip the details. If you want more information, you can refer to the *Appendix A, Creating Web Projects* at the end of the book and check how to generate them step by step. In this recipe, we will be covering all of them at once, highlighting the points where there's some difference across those types.

 In order to show a complete sample for all three cases, the code that comes with this book will contain three separate projects, called `Recipe01_WF` (for the Web Forms sample), `Recipe01_MVC` (for the MVC project), and `Recipe01_WS` (for the website).

Before proceeding, please pick one of them and create your project in Visual Studio 2013.

How to do it...

We're ready to actually start adding the SignalR bits. Let's start with the Hub with the following steps.

From the **Project** menu, select **Add New Item** (you can also use the project context menu from **Solution Explorer** or the *Ctrl + Shift + A* keyboard shortcut), click on the **Web** folder, and then select the **SignalR Hub Class (v2)** template; specify EchoHub as the name and click on **OK** as shown in the following screenshot. Make sure you have selected the **v2** Version because we want to target **SignalR 2.0**.

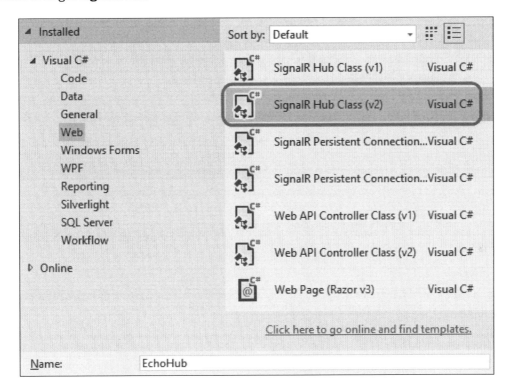

Visual Studio will add a new file called EchoHub.cs with some boilerplate code inside.

1. Let's edit the file content to make it look like the following code snippet:

```
using System.Diagnostics;
using Microsoft.AspNet.SignalR;
using Microsoft.AspNet.SignalR.Hubs;
namespace Recipe01
```

```
    {
        [HubName("echo")]
        public class EchoHub : Hub
        {
            public void Say(string message)
            {
                Trace.WriteLine(message);
            }
        }
    }
```

Downloading the example code

You can download the example code files for all Packt books you have purchased from your account at `http://www.packtpub.com`. If you purchased this book elsewhere, you can visit `http://www.packtpub.com/support` and register to have the files e-mailed directly to you.

The following lists the important points here:

- The necessary `using` directives are listed at the top of the file.
- The `EchoHub` class is derived from `Hub`, which comes from `Microsoft.AspNet.SignalR.Hubs` and makes the server-side SignalR API available to our class.
- The class is marked with the `HubName` attribute, which allows us to give the Hub a friendly name to be used by the clients; if we don't use the `HubName` attribute, the Hub name will be the same as the class name (in this case, it would be `EchoHub`).
- Our Hub contains a method called `Say()`. This is just a sample method we'll use to show how to expose Hub endpoints. On every call, it will just output the value of the `message` parameter in the debugger **Output** window, or in any **trace listener** we may want to configure.

The class namespace is not so important. Here, I'm choosing the same name as the project name; it's the recommended way, but it does not have to be like that.

2. From the **Project** menu, select **Add New Item** again, click on the **Web** folder, and then select the **OWIN Startup class** template. Specify `Startup` as the name and click on **OK**, as shown in the following screenshot:

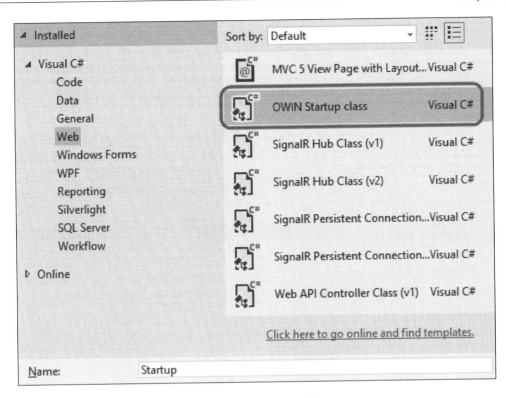

Visual Studio will add a new file called `Startup.cs` with some code inside it.

3. Let's edit the file content to make it look like the following:

```
using Microsoft.Owin;
using Owin;
[assembly: OwinStartup(typeof(Recipe01.Startup))]
namespace Recipe01
{
    public class Startup
    {
        public void Configuration(IAppBuilder app)
        {
            app.MapSignalR();
        }
    }
}
```

The following lists the important points here:

▸ SignalR 2.0 uses **Open Web Interface** (**OWIN**) for .NET as the standard interface between .NET web servers and web applications, enabling a level of indirection and abstraction that keeps your project from directly tying to any specific hosting platform. This is the technical foundation that actually enables SignalR to be hosted from both web applications and traditional .NET processes, as we'll see later.

▸ Every OWIN application must have a `Startup` class that follows specific conventions. In particular, a `Configuration()` method with the signature shown in the preceding code must be made available.

▸ The assembly-level attribute `OwinStartup` is there to declare that our `Startup` class will be used to bootstrap every OWIN-based asset contained in all the loaded assemblies; there are other ways to declare the right `Startup` class to load, but we'll see them in the future recipes.

▸ Inside the `Configuration()` method, we start up SignalR using an appropriate extension method (`MapSignalR()`) made available by the SignalR *core* inside the `Owin` namespace; a call to the `MapSignalR()` method will expose an endpoint called `/signalr`, which the clients will use to connect to the server.

We're done! Our first SignalR Hub is ready to be called. However, as already mentioned, in order to see it in action, we need a client. Let's build one inside our web application using the JavaScript SignalR client.

Let's add a web page that we'll use as the place to put our basic client to test our Hub. This is where the recipe differs across the different project types. The most natural choices are as follows:

▸ **Web form for a Web Forms application**: From the **Project** menu, select **Add New Item**, click on the **Web** folder, select the **Web Form** template (specifying, for example, `index.aspx` as the name), and click on **OK**.

▸ **Razor View for an MVC application**: Let's first add a default controller named `HomeController` and then a view for its `Index` default action, which will be called `index.cshtml`. Please refer to the *Appendix A, Creating Web Projects* if you want more details about these steps.

▸ **HTML page for a website**: From the **Project** menu, select **Add New Item**, click on the **Web** folder, select the **HTML Page** template (specifying, for example, `index.html` as the name), and click on **OK**.

Visual Studio will create the specified file with some basic HTML content. Those files will slightly differ according to the type you picked earlier, but for now we're just interested in the content of the `<head>` section, which we'll modify to make it look like the following code:

```
<script src="Scripts/jquery-2.1.0.js"></script>
<script src="Scripts/jquery.signalR-2.0.2.js"></script>
```

```
<script src="/signalr/hubs"></script>
<script>
    $(function () {
        var hub = $.connection.echo;
        $.connection.hub
            .start()
            .done(function () {
                hub.server.say('Hello SignalR!');
            });
    });
</script>
```

We basically kept what was there and then we just added a few `<script>` blocks. We'll go into detail about this portion in the *Connecting to a Hub from a JavaScript client* recipe. So, for any questions you might have about this code, please hold on for a while! The only thing we anticipate here is that the special `/signalr/hubs` endpoint does not correspond to any file that you'll find in the project; nevertheless, it's correct and will be explained later on.

We can now launch the application from Visual Studio: a browser window will open, the page will be loaded, and the `Say()` method of the `EchoHub` class will be executed as soon as the page is completely loaded in the browser. We can prove this by observing the effect of the `Trace.WriteLine(message);` line of code on the **Output** debug window, where the message will be printed.

How it works...

Let's review the main points of what we just did:

- We added a `Hub` class. Any class available in the project that is derived from `Hub` is automatically discovered and exposed when SignalR is initialized calling `MapSignalR` in the `Startup` class.

- The client page established a connection to our `EchoHub` using the JavaScript SignalR client library.

- When the connection is ready, we make a remote call to the `Say()` method exposed by our `EchoHub`.

- SignalR coordinates the two sides using the most appropriate connection strategy (more on that in future recipes), taking into account which is the HTTP server hosting the application and which web browser is used to run the client page; it gives us the feeling of a direct connection towards our server-side Hub, allowing us to call methods on it directly (the line `hub.server.say('Hello SignalR!');`).

There's more...

So far, we did not experience anything really special. We just performed a client-to-server call, which could have been done with plain old HTTP techniques. Nevertheless, we just laid the foundation for any SignalR Hub-based web application.

Adding a Hub to a self-hosting application

SignalR can be considered as a web framework because it's based on web technologies, such as HTTP and HTML5, but it can actually be used in the context of classic standalone processes without any relationship to browsers or web servers. This is possible thanks to the .NET client library for the client part, and to the self-hosting capabilities for the server part. The latter, in particular, is the subject of this recipe. It enables scenarios where the server-side portion of a SignalR application can live inside any hosting process, without requiring it to be an ASP.NET web application. In this recipe, we'll see how to host SignalR inside a simple **console application**, but any other .NET process would do. This way, we have a chance to use SignalR in scenarios where we do not have a proper web server available, or where thinking about an *embedded* SignalR makes sense.

Getting ready

Let's create a console application using the following steps:

1. Navigate to **File | New Project**.
2. Navigate to **Installed | Visual C#** in the dialog box and select the **Windows** folder.
3. On the central panel of the dialog box, select **Console Application**, give it a name (`Recipe02`, in this case), and click on **OK**.

Visual Studio will add a `Program.cs` file containing the startup code for our application to the new project that we just created in Visual Studio 2013. For this recipe, we will add all our code to this file just after the `Program` class, whose `static Main()` method we'll be filling at the end of the recipe.

How to do it...

We're ready to actually start building our SignalR server. Visual Studio simplifies the process for web applications or websites, offering a series of code templates for `Hub` or `Startup` classes that we used in the previous recipe. But, for more general Windows applications, those templates are not available, and we'll have to undergo a slightly longer process. First, we'll need to add a reference to SignalR 2.0, which we can be easily found on NuGet, using the following steps:

1. Select the `Recipe02` project, and under the **Project** menu, click on the **Manage NuGet Packages...** entry.

2. From the corresponding dialog box, let's do a search for the online packages using `signalr self host` as a filter condition. We should be presented with a results list like the following:

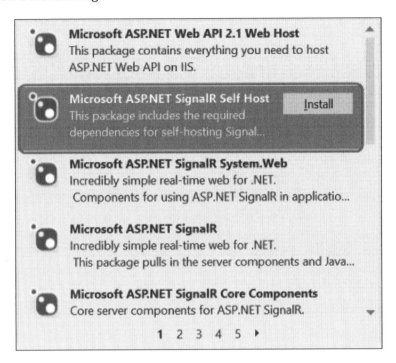

3. Let's select the **Microsoft ASP.NET SignalR Self Host** package and then click on the **Install** button; this action will download and install all the packages we need to proceed with our application.

4. We are ready to add some code. Let's start with our Hub by opening the `Program.cs` file and adding the following code just outside of the existing `Program` class:

```
[HubName("echo")]
public class EchoHub : Hub
{
    public void Say(string message)
    {
        Trace.WriteLine(message);
    }
}
```

In order to compile the previous code, we'll have to add the following `using` directives at the top of the file:

```
using System.Diagnostics;
using Microsoft.AspNet.SignalR;
using Microsoft.AspNet.SignalR.Hubs;
```

The following lists the important points here:

- The class `EchoHub` is derived from `Hub`, which comes from `Microsoft.AspNet.SignalR.Hubs`, and makes the server-side SignalR API available to our class.

- The class is marked with the `HubName` attribute, which allows us to give the Hub a friendly name to be used from the clients; if we don't use the `HubName` attribute, the Hub name will be the same as the class name (in this case, it would be `EchoHub`).

- Our Hub contains a method called `Say()`. This is just a sample method we'll use to show how to expose Hub endpoints. On every call, it will just output the value of the `message` parameter in the debugger **Output** window, or in any trace listener we may want to configure.

Let's proceed with the rest of the code.

5. Now we need to add a `Startup` class, as shown in the following code, to correctly bootstrap our SignalR Hub:

```
class Startup
{
    public void Configuration(IAppBuilder app)
    {
        app.MapSignalR();
    }
}
```

The `MapSignalR` call will expose an endpoint called `/signalr` that the clients will use to connect to the server. In order to compile the code, we'll have to add the following `using` directive at the top of the file:

```
using Owin;
```

6. We're almost done. We just need to start up everything inside the `Main()` method mentioned earlier, which we now modify to make it look like the following code snippet:

```
static void Main(string[] args)
{
    using (WebApp.Start<Startup>("http://localhost:1968"))
```

```
        {
            Console.WriteLine("Server running!");
            Console.ReadLine();
        }
    }
}
```

In order to compile the code, we'll have to add the following `using` directives at the top of the file:

```
using System;
using Microsoft.Owin.Hosting;
```

The following lists the important points here:

- By calling `WebApp.Start<Startup>("http://localhost:1968")`, we are telling the self-hosting subsystem that it has to use our `Startup` class to initiate a SignalR endpoint and make it listen to the supplied URL. The chosen port (`1968`) is a random one. You could pick any other, provided you check your firewall when deploying your solution.

- The resulting endpoint will of course expose the SignalR protocol, therefore only connections to it from a SignalR client would make sense and actually work.

- When the initialization call has been completed, we print a message and then wait for someone to press *Enter*; this is important to keep our console application alive. Without it, the process would immediately end and the server would go away.

Our self-hosting process is now ready to be used. When launched, it will wait for clients to connect and call the `Say()` method on the `EchoHub` Hub. At each call, we would notice a **Hello SignalR!** message printed on the **Output** debug window by the `Trace.WriteLine(message);` call inside the `Say()` method.

We did not write any client code, but in self-hosting scenarios, it's not so common to have any client portion at all. Therefore, we'll end this recipe here. In the *Connecting to a Hub from a .NET application* recipe at the end of this chapter, we will be writing a standalone .NET client, and we'll be using it to connect to this server.

Connecting to a Hub from a JavaScript client

After having illustrated the two different ways we have to expose a server-side Hub let's now move on and see the client-side code in more detail.

During the *Adding a Hub to an ASP.NET project* recipe, we quickly used the JavaScript client library in order to demonstrate that our Hub was fully functional, but we did not go much into detail about it because we were concentrating on the server-side code. This recipe will fill this gap and give more clarity on how a JavaScript client is written. However, in order to make it fully functional, we will need a server-side portion; therefore, we'll be adding a basic Hub the same way we did for the *Adding a Hub to an ASP.NET project* recipe. Any specific detail about how to do it will be skipped because it's just an accessory to the real goal of this recipe, and we will just list the necessary steps. For any further clarification about that part, you can check the *Adding a Hub to an ASP.NET project* recipe.

Getting ready

Let's create a website where we'll be hosting our client. This is a common task, so we are going to skip the details. If you want more information about this, you can refer to *Appendix A, Creating Web Projects* at the end of the book.

How to do it...

We're ready to actually start adding what we need to build our SignalR client. We need to use the following steps:

1. As we did in the *Adding a Hub to an ASP.NET project* recipe, we'll add a Hub called `EchoHub` and a `Startup` class. Here, we'll skip all the related details for brevity. Just make sure that the project ends up containing the same server-side code. These actions will download and add all the SignalR-related references, including the JavaScript client libraries.

2. Let's add a web page to which we'll add our client. From the **Project** menu, select **Add New Item**, click on the **Web** folder, select the **HTML Page** template (specifying, for example, `index.html` as the name), and click on **OK**.

Visual Studio will create the specified file with some basic HTML content; let's edit it to make it look like the following:

```
<!DOCTYPE html>
<html xmlns="http://www.w3.org/1999/xhtml">
<head>
    <title></title>
```

```
<script src="Scripts/jquery-2.1.0.js"></script>
<script src="Scripts/jquery.signalR-2.0.2.js"></script>
<script src="/signalr/hubs"></script>
<script>
    $(function () {
        var hub = $.connection.echo;
        $.connection.hub
            .start()
            .done(function () {
                hub.server.say('Hello SignalR!');
            });
    });
</script>
</head>
<body>
</body>
</html>
```

We basically kept what was there and just added the highlighted `<script>` blocks that you can see in the previous code.

We can now launch the application from Visual Studio; a browser window will open and the `index.html` page will be loaded. Then we'll observe the code reaching the `Trace.WriteLine(message);` line inside the `Say()` method of the `EchoHub` class as soon as the page is completely loaded in the browser.

How it works...

Let's concentrate on our client page. The details are as follows:

▶ The first relevant portion of code are the first two `<script>` blocks, where we reference `jquery` and `jquery.signalR` as JavaScript libraries. jQuery is necessary because the SignalR JavaScript client is actually a jQuery plugin, as the actual name of the library makes clear.

▶ Our libraries are taken from the `/scripts` folder, where they have been placed by one of the NuGet packages installed as soon as we added our Hub. This package is actually called **Microsoft ASP.NET SignalR JavaScript Client** and can be installed in any ASP.NET application, even if the application does not contain any Hub. We'll see how this can be useful in future recipes, where we will be trying to connect to Hubs hosted in a different web application from the one containing the client.

▶ The third `<script>` block refers to a dynamic endpoint (`/signalr/hubs`) exposed by the server portion because of the `MapSignalR` call from the `Startup` class, already explained in the previous recipes. It actually generates JavaScript code on the fly according to the available Hubs. In practice, the JavaScript proxies for our Hubs (in this case, the `EchoHub` Hub) are built *on the fly* by the server-side portion of SignalR as soon as this endpoint is hit, and they're sent to the client as JavaScript source code.

▶ The last `<script>` block is where we actually connect to our Hub. Let's dig more into it. The details are as follows:

- ❑ Our code is written inside a classic jQuery `$(...);` call, which actually ensures that our code is called when the page is fully loaded.

- ❑ We first take a reference to our `echo` Hub, which is exposed by the `$.connection.echo` property generated by the dynamic endpoint that we just described.

- ❑ Then we call the `start()` method exposed by the `$.connection.hub` member, which performs the actual connection to our server.

- ❑ The `start()` call is asynchronous, and we have to make sure it has actually been completed before using any Hub; that's easy because `start()` returns a **promise** object containing a `done()` method to which we can pass a callback function, where we put our Hub-related code. This way, we are sure that SignalR will call our code when the Hub proxy is fully initialized and ready to be used.

- ❑ Inside our callback function, we can use our Hub instance; in particular, it's the `server` member from which we are able to call any method exposed by the Hub. The `hub.server.say('Hello SignalR!');` line of code will actually call the `Say()` method on our server-side Hub.

- ❑ Note that `say` is written in lowercase here. Regardless of the actual name on the server-side Hub, in a JavaScript context, SignalR automatically generates camel case names in order to provide a more idiomatic JavaScript API.

When launching the application from Visual Studio, a browser window will open, the page will be loaded, and the `Say()` method of the `EchoHub` class will execute as soon as the page is completely loaded.

Connecting to a Hub from a .NET application

In the context of the *Adding a Hub to a self-hosting application* recipe, we already mentioned that SignalR can be used in the context of a generic standalone process, and we detailed how this can be leveraged for the server-side portion of an application. Thanks to the .NET client library, we can apply the same reasoning on the client side, enabling traditional Windows applications to connect to any SignalR server. In this recipe, we'll learn how to use the .NET SignalR client inside a simple console application. For the server portion to connect to, we'll make use of what we did in the *Adding a Hub to a self-hosting application* recipe, so please make sure you have the code from that recipe ready and fully working before proceeding.

Getting ready

Let's create a console application using the following steps:

1. Navigate to **File | New Project**.
2. Navigate to **Installed | Visual C#** in the dialog box and select the **Windows** folder.
3. On the central panel of the dialog box, select **Console Application**, give it a name (Recipe04, in this case), and click on **OK**.

Visual Studio will add a `Program.cs` file containing the startup code for our application. For this recipe, we will add all our code to this file, which contains the following lines:

```
namespace Recipe04
{
    class Program
    {
        static void Main(string[] args)
        {
        }
    }
}
```

How to do it...

We're ready to actually start building our SignalR client. Visual Studio simplifies the process for web applications or websites, which are normally supposed to contain both server- and client-side portions; hence, the action of adding a Hub through the corresponding Visual Studio code template actually includes the JavaScript client portion too. When building a purely .NET client, we do not have a specific code template to use, and we have to resort to NuGet to import the appropriate package. This is done using the following steps:

1. Select the Recipe04 project, and under the **Project** menu, click on the **Manage NuGet Packages...** entry.

2. From the corresponding dialog box, perform a search for the online packages using `signalr client` as the filter expression. We should obtain a results list like the following:

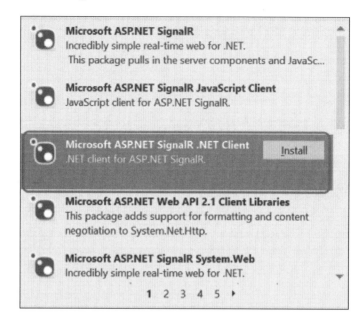

3. Select the **Microsoft ASP.NET SignalR .NET Client** package and then click on the **Install** button. This action will download and install all the packages that we need to proceed with our application.

4. We are ready to add some code. Let's open the `Program.cs` file and modify the `Main()` method's body as follows:

```
using System;
using Microsoft.AspNet.SignalR.Client;

namespace Recipe04
{
    class Program
    {
        static void Main(string[] args)
        {
            var url = "http://localhost:1968";
            var connection = new HubConnection(url);
            var hub = connection.CreateHubProxy("echo");
            connection.Start().Wait();
```

```
            hub.Invoke("Say", "Hello SignalR!");

            Console.ReadLine();
        }
    }
}
```

How it works...

▶ Starting from the inside of the `Main()` method, the first line defines the address to which our client will try to connect to, and the second line actually instantiates a `connection` object pointing to that address; our client will expect to find a SignalR server listening at that position.

▶ Then we use the `connection` object to create a proxy for the `EchoHub` Hub that we used so far when building our servers (the third line). In this recipe, we are using the one that we created in the *Adding a Hub to a self-hosting application* recipe, so we know from its code that it will be listening on port `1968`, and it will expose our `EchoHub` Hub with the friendly name `echo`, which we supply as a parameter to the `CreateHubProxy()` method that will provide us with a proxy pointing to it.

▶ We are now ready to perform the connection using the `Start()` method. Its return value is a `task`-derived object, which means its execution will be asynchronous; indeed, we are not allowed to use a Hub until the connection process has properly completed. That's why in this example we use the `Wait()` method to block our code until the connection is effectively ready.

▶ When we are done with the `Wait()` call, we can safely address any method on our Hub proxy. We know that `EchoHub` exposes a `Say()` method, so we call it using `Invoke`, to which we pass the name of the method to call (`Say()`) and the list of the expected parameters (in this case, just one for the `"Hello SignalR!"` message argument).

▶ The `Console.Readline()` method is there to prevent the process from exiting immediately.

That's it. If we now launch the `Recipe 02` console application first and then the one we just built in this recipe (either from Visual Studio directly or from a console window), we should see the server application happily printing `Hello SignalR!` on the screen because of the call from our client.

 Pay attention; you have to keep the application's `Recipe02` project open while Recipe04 is running. If you just debug `Recipe02` and then stop the debugger to launch `Recipe04`, `Recipe02` will be killed. There are several ways to achieve the right workflow. One of the simplest is to make `Recipe02` the active project, start it without debugging (*Ctrl + F5*), and then make `Recipe04` active and launch it, with or without debugging.

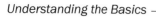

This recipe has completed our first showcase of SignalR features, and it allowed us to understand the basics of how it works and the general structure of any SignalR-based application. We also learned about the different types of hosting we can use and about the two client libraries available out of the box.

2
Using Hubs

In this chapter, we will cover:

- ▶ Adding a method to a Hub and counting the calls to it
- ▶ Calling back the caller from a Hub's method
- ▶ Broadcasting to all connected clients
- ▶ Adding a connection to a group
- ▶ Removing a connection from a group
- ▶ Broadcasting to all connected clients except the caller
- ▶ Broadcasting to all clients except the specified ones
- ▶ Broadcasting to all clients in a group except the caller
- ▶ Broadcasting from outside a Hub
- ▶ Using the return value of a Hub method

Introduction

SignalR's main goal is to deliver a real-time experience over HTTP, where both clients and servers can participate in a conversation as senders and listeners at the same time (known as **full-duplex communication**). A client initiates the flow by starting a new connection, but after that, both types of actors are equally capable of sending and receiving bits of the conversation.

In order to deliver such an experience, SignalR comes with two distinct APIs: one called **persistent connection**, which we can consider to be the low-level API, and one called **Hubs**, which is built on top of the former and brings a higher-level set of concepts and an easier and straightforward experience for the developer. We'll talk about Hubs first as we want to make our way through the SignalR features, starting from the simplest to use to the more sophisticated.

A Hub can be seen as a set of methods exposed by a server that any client can connect to, in order to perform actions on that server or to retrieve data from it. If you are familiar with the MVC pattern, it looks like a controller because it offers a way to expose the server-side functionalities through methods whose names we are free to define as we prefer. The usual way to exploit this capability is to use names related to our business logic, and SignalR's Hubs are no different; they enable us to do so on top of a bidirectional communication framework.

Previously, I decided to define a Hub as a set of methods and not just an object or a type (which it is technically), because I wanted to highlight the fact that, when connected to it, we should not expect to have any strong reference or link to a particular instance of a Hub. The Hub life cycle is not under our control; we should avoid putting any instance state in it and expect it to be kept across all the calls. If we keep these concepts in mind, we will be in a better position to write good SignalR code.

In the same way, a client has no power to select a specific Hub instance to talk to. A server should avoid talking to specific clients, and talk to specific sets of clients instead. A Hub should refer to clients according to the following sets that are offered by the SignalR platform:

- The caller
- Every connected client
- Every connected client but the caller
- Every client belonging to a specific group (more on what a group is will be covered later on)
- Exclusion lists that could be passed to most of the previous sets to identify exceptions

There are some other variants of this schema; however, in general, these should be the targets of any server-side calls. The main reason for this choice is scalability; the less state about the connected clients we have to maintain on the server, the more concurrent clients SignalR can serve.

This is the guiding principle that we should try to follow, although there might be the need for slightly different approaches. This is also a simplified description of the problems and of the features around SignalR. The implications could be complex and they are not in the scope of this book. The discussion will try to stay as much as possible on the general case; therefore, the recipes in this chapter will adhere to some general guidelines about how to write good standard clients and good standard hubs. You might have to review and adapt them in case your requirements happen to be more complex.

This chapter will be about how to create Hubs, how to add methods to them, and how a Hub can interact with its connected clients. We will also briefly describe the client-side code necessary to have fully working recipes, but for more detail about the client bits, please refer to *Chapter 3, Using the JavaScript Hubs Client API* and *Chapter 4, Using the .NET Hubs Client API*.

For the following recipes, we will always start from empty web application projects, and we'll use simple HTML pages to host the client code. Creating such a project is a fairly common task, so we are going to skip the details about it. If you want more information, you can refer to *Appendix A*, *Creating Web Projects*, at the end of the book. The same strategy will apply when creating recurring assets such as a `Startup` class or a Hub. We will just briefly mention the need for them. You could go back to *Chapter 1*, *Understanding the Basics*, for some more information about the steps required in Visual Studio to get there.

For clarity in the explanation, we may sometimes introduce some intermediate variables in the code to make any related explanation clearer. Of course, you'd want to remove them from your production code and refactor them to a more streamlined version.

Adding a method to a Hub and counting the calls to it

This first recipe of the chapter is very simple, and in a way similar to the others we saw in *Chapter 1*, *Understanding the Basics*; however, the focus will be lesser on the process and the parts involved and more on specific Hub features. We'll learn a simple way to count how many times a Hub method is called by the connected clients.

Getting ready

Before writing the code of this recipe, we need to create a new empty web application, which we'll call `Recipe05`.

How to do it...

We're ready to actually start adding our SignalR bits by performing the following steps:

1. Let's add a Hub called `EchoHub`. Behind the scenes, this action references a NuGet package called Microsoft.AspNet.SignalR, which then brings a few more packages.

2. Then we add an OWIN Startup class named `Startup`, which contains just a simple `app.MapSignalR()` bootstrap call inside the `Configuration()` method.

3. It is important to highlight the fact that it is recommended to add a Hub to the project before adding the `Startup` class, because the first action adds more package references to the project, and one of them (Microsoft.AspNet.SignalR.Core) contains the definition of the `MapSignalR()` extension method that we need to call from inside the `Startup` class.

4. Let's edit the Hub file content to make it look like the following code:

```
using System.Diagnostics;
using Microsoft.AspNet.SignalR;
```

```
using Microsoft.AspNet.SignalR.Hubs;

namespace Recipe05
{
    [HubName("echo")]
    public class EchoHub : Hub
    {
        private static int _calls = 0;
        public void Hello()
        {
            Trace.WriteLine(string.Format("Calls: {0}",
                ++_calls));
        }
    }
}
```

What's important here? We need to make sure that the following steps are performed:

▶ The class `EchoHub` is derived from `Hub`, which comes from `Microsoft.AspNet.SignalR.Hubs`, and makes the server-side SignalR API available to our class

▶ The class is marked with the `HubName` attribute, which allows us to give the Hub a friendly name to be used by the clients; if we don't use the `HubName` attribute, the Hub name will be the same as the class name (in this case, it would be `EchoHub`)

▶ We added a `static int _calls` field and used it to count how many times our exposed method will be called by any client

▶ We exposed a public method called `Hello()` to increment the `_calls` static field on every call to it and then output its value into the debugger **Output** window, or in any Trace listener that we may want to configure

What we are expecting from the preceding code is a pretty naive way to count how many times the `Hello()` method is called. As mentioned in the introduction, we cannot assume anything about any specific instance of `EchoHub` being around (the actual default implementation will always create a new instance per call). The best way to count the calls across the clients is to use an external reference accessible by all the Hub instances, which will maintain the state across calls, for example, a static member as we do here. This is not a good strategy for production environments though, because static fields do not survive application recycles and this strategy does not scale horizontally in case of web farms. Still, this is just fine for the introductory goal of this recipe.

Let's move on with the client portion; to build that, we create an HTML page calling it `index.html` and add the following code to it:

```
<!DOCTYPE html>
<html xmlns="http://www.w3.org/1999/xhtml">
<head>
```

```
<title>Recipe05</title>
<script src="Scripts/jquery-2.1.0.js"></script>
<script src="Scripts/jquery.signalR-2.0.2.js"></script>
<script src="/signalr/hubs"></script>
<script>
    $(function () {
        var hub = $.connection.echo;

        $.connection.hub
            .start()
            .done(function () {
                $('#send').click(function () {
                    hub.server.hello();
                });
            });
    });
</script>
</head>
<body>
    <button id="send">Send</button>
</body>
</html>
```

We basically kept what was there after the Visual Studio wizard execution, and then we added the `<script>` blocks to reference SignalR to address the dynamic hubs endpoint (`/signalr/hubs`), and eventually perform a connection to the server and a subsequent call to the exposed `Hello()` method. We explained these steps in greater detail in *Chapter 1, Understanding the Basics*, and we'll dig more into all the client-side steps in *Chapter 3, Using the JavaScript Hubs Client API* and *Chapter 4, Using the .NET Hub's Client API*. These will be recurring steps across the remaining recipes of this chapter.

We can now launch the application from Visual Studio. A browser window will open and the `index.html` page will be loaded. By clicking on the **Send** button on the page, the client will invoke the `Hello()` method of the `EchoHub` class on the client-side proxy, and the server-side code will reach the `Trace.WriteLine(...);` line inside the `Hello()` method of the `EchoHub` class. The `_calls` field will be incremented at every call, and we can verify that by either clicking on the button multiple times or by opening more browser windows pointing at the same address as the first one, and clicking on the **Send** button for all of them.

How it works...

The following are the most relevant points about what we just built:

► Any public method exposed by a `Hub` class can be reached by any SignalR client

► When any client calls a Hub method, a Hub instance is made available and the code from the called method is executed

▶ In order to count the method calls across clients, we cannot rely on a specific instance of EchoHub being around all the time; so, for this example, we use the simplistic strategy of incrementing a static field

See also

If you are interested in more resilient ways to solve the problem of counting without having to worry about application recycles and horizontal scalability, please check out *Chapter 7, Analyzing Advanced Scenarios*.

Calling back the caller from a Hub's method

With this recipe, we are actually starting to look at more interesting and real-time SignalR features. We will see how a Hub can call back into a client that just performed a remote method call.

Getting ready

Before starting with this recipe, we need to create a new empty web application, which we'll call Recipe06.

How to do it...

Let's start building the server-side portion of this recipe using the following steps:

1. We must first add a Hub called EchoHub.
2. We must then add an OWIN Startup class named Startup, containing just a simple app.MapSignalR(); bootstrap call inside the Configuration() method.
3. Let's make the Hub's content look like the following:

```
using System;
using Microsoft.AspNet.SignalR;
using Microsoft.AspNet.SignalR.Hubs;

namespace Recipe06
{
    [HubName("echo")]
    public class EchoHub : Hub
    {
        public void Hello()
        {
            var msg = string.Format("Greetings {0}, it's
```

```
                {1:F}!",
                Context.ConnectionId,
                DateTime.Now);
            var caller = Clients.Caller;
            caller.greetings(msg);
        }
    }
}
```

What's important here? We need to make sure that the following steps are performed:

- Inside the `Hello()` method, we build a message (msg) using the current time and a property exposed by the `Context` member of the Hub type called `ConnectionId`. This unique identifier is automatically assigned by SignalR to every new connection. Each connection belongs to a specific connected client, and we can assume for now that such a connection stays around until the client goes away. Things are actually more complex than this, but we'll talk about it in future recipes.

- `Context` is of type `HubCallerContext`, and exposes a set of properties related to the current connection, such as the just mentioned `ConnectionId`, query string parameters, cookies, and more.

- When msg is ready, we use the `Clients` member from the Hub type, which gives us access to the universe of the connected clients. From there, we take a reference to the `Caller` member, representing the calling client from which the `Hello()` method has been contacted.

- We finally call the `greetings()` method on the `caller` variable, supplying the msg we just built. We expect this call to be performed on the caller from which the server-side `Hello()` method has been hit.

This code illustrates how we can use `Context` to access information about the connection (we can not only find details about the SignalR connection identifier, but also about HTTP headers or the query string), and how to access the current caller from it.

The other interesting part about `caller` is that it's a dynamic object, meaning we can try to call whatever method we want on it as the code will pass any compile-time check and the call will be resolved at runtime by SignalR. The call will succeed only if a method with the same name and expecting the same parameters is found by SignalR on the client-side hub proxy, no matter which client library we are using (in this case, the JavaScript one), otherwise it will silently fail. You can get more information about dynamic programming in .NET at `http://msdn.microsoft.com/en-us/magazine/gg598922.aspx`, while you can get specific introduction about a dynamic method resolution strategy at `http://msdn.microsoft.com/library/ee658247`.

Finally, the execution of the dynamic call is performed asynchronously. The server-side code will not be blocked while waiting for the actual execution of the code on the client; instead, it will exit immediately, relinquishing the control of the code flow back to the caller. Asynchronism is a very important feature of SignalR. Every time there is any code that implies network activity (connection-related operations, client-to-server calls, and server-to-client calls), the execution of that code is asynchronous. This introduces some complexity, but it's an absolutely necessary feature in order to achieve the astonishing performance characteristics of this library.

The whole asynchronous strategy in SignalR is built around the **Task-based Asynchronous Pattern** (**TAP**). You can get an overview about it at `http://msdn.microsoft.com/en-us/library/hh873175(v=vs.110).aspx`.

Let's now create an HTML client page called `index.html`, which contains the following code:

```html
<!DOCTYPE html>
<html xmlns="http://www.w3.org/1999/xhtml">
<head>
    <title>Recipe06</title>
    <script src="Scripts/jquery-2.1.0.js"></script>
    <script src="Scripts/jquery.signalR-2.0.2.js"></script>
    <script src="/signalr/hubs"></script>
    <script>
        $(function () {
            var hub = $.connection.echo;

            hub.client.greetings = function (message) {
                $('#message').html(message);
            };

            $.connection.hub
                .start()
                .done(function () {
                    $('#send').click(function () {
                        hub.server.hello();
                    });
                });
        });
    </script>

</head>
<body>
    <button id="send">Say Hello!</button>
    <p id="message"></p>
</body>
</html>
```

What's important here? We need to make sure that we perform the following steps:

- We have the usual references to the jQuery and SignalR libraries, and to the SignalR dynamic hubs endpoint, which from now on we'll take for granted.

- We take a reference to the echo hub, and from there we access the client member to extend it with a function called greetings(), whose name and signature are matching the method that the Hub is trying to call back; the function will just update a p element on the page with the received message.

- We then start the connection, and when it's ready (the done callback), we hook the click event of the send button to the action of calling the Hello() method on the echo hub proxy through the server member; more detail about starting a connection can be found in *Chapter 3, Using the JavaScript Hubs Client API*.

- It's important that the client member is filled with any callback function before starting the connection.

- We decide to hook the click event on the button just inside the done callback to make sure we cannot call the Hello() method before the connection being established.

Now run the application, navigate to index.html and click on the **Say Hello!** button. We should see something like what is shown in the following screenshot:

Every time we click on the **Say Hello!** button, we'll see that the time changes, but not ConnectionId, and the page is not refreshed. On the other hand, every time we do a full refresh of the page and click on the button, we'll see a new ConnectionId displayed.

How it works...

When we ask SignalR to open a connection from the client, it gives us a persistent connection, the illusion that a permanent channel has been established between the client and the server. We can use this channel to send messages from the client to the server and the other way round. Using a Hub we can do that through an object-oriented API, which makes the connection transparent to both parts.

How the connection is physically established is a SignalR concern; it will use the best option available according to the context of the running code. However, it could well be that behind the scenes the connection is not permanent at all. We just don't have to worry about that. We'll talk more about these details in *Chapter 3*, *Using the JavaScript Hubs Client API* and *Chapter 4*, *Using the .NET Hubs Client API*.

The actual resolution of the method calls, both on the server-side Hub and on the connected clients, is actually performed by SignalR dynamically at runtime. On the server side, SignalR leverages the .NET dynamic support to do so, while on the client side, this depends on the library used. In the case of this recipe, we are using the JavaScript client library, so the actual support for dynamic objects and calls is built into the language.

Broadcasting to all connected clients

After several examples where a single client was involved at a time, we'll start looking at scenarios where multiple clients are connected at the same time, and we'll start making them interact. We will see how a Hub can call back into *all* the connected clients from the context of a single remote method call performed by just one of them. This is where SignalR becomes a more interesting and outstanding library!

Getting ready

Before proceeding, we need to create a new empty web application, which we'll call `Recipe07`.

How to do it...

As usual, we need some simple steps to get started as follows:

1. Add a Hub called `EchoHub`.
2. Add an OWIN Startup class named `Startup` with its `Configuration()` method containing just a simple `app.MapSignalR();` bootstrap call.
3. Modify the file content to make it look like the following code:

```
using System;
using Microsoft.AspNet.SignalR;
```

```
using Microsoft.AspNet.SignalR.Hubs;

namespace Recipe07
{
    [HubName("echo")]
    public class EchoHub : Hub
    {
        public void Hello()
        {
            var msg = string.Format("Greetings {0}, it's
                {1:F}!",
                Context.ConnectionId,
                DateTime.Now);
            var all = Clients.All;
            all.greetings(msg);
        }
    }
}
```

What's important here? We need to make sure that we perform the following steps:

▶ Inside the `Hello()` method, we build a message (`msg`) using the current time and the `ConnectionId` property exposed by the `Context` member from the Hub type

▶ When `msg` is ready, we use the `Clients` member from the Hub type, and from there we take a reference to the `All` member, representing all the currently connected clients

▶ We finally call the `greetings()` method on the `all` variable, supplying the `msg` we just built; we expect this call to be performed on all the connected clients, and to be triggered at every call to the `Hello()` method performed by any of them

The `All` member, like the `Caller` one we saw earlier, is a dynamic object over which we can try to call whatever method we want. The call will be resolved at runtime by SignalR, and it will reach all the connected clients with the only precondition that a method with the same name and expecting the same parameters must be available on the client-side hub proxy.

To test our hub, let's build a client HTML page, which we'll call `index.html`. Add the following code to this file:

```
<!DOCTYPE html>
<html xmlns="http://www.w3.org/1999/xhtml">
<head>
    <title>Recipe07</title>
    <script src="Scripts/jquery-2.1.0.js"></script>
    <script src="Scripts/jquery.signalR-2.0.2.js"></script>
    <script src="/signalr/hubs"></script>
```

```
<script>
    $(function () {
        var hub = $.connection.echo;

        hub.client.greetings = function (message) {
            var li = $('<li/>').html(message);
            $('#messages').append(li);
        };

        $.connection.hub
            .start()
            .done(function () {
                $('#send').click(function () {
                    hub.server.hello();
                });
            });
    });
</script>

</head>
<body>
    <button id="send">Say Hello!</button>
    <ul id="messages"></ul>
</body>
</html>
```

What's important here? We need to make sure that we perform the following steps:

▶ We take a reference to the `echo` hub, and from there we access the `client` member, to which we add a function called `greetings()` whose name and signature are matching the method that the Hub is trying to call back; the function will append every received message to a `ul` list present on the page marked with an `id` attribute whose value is `messages`

▶ We then start the connection, and when it's ready we hook the `click` event of the `send` button on the page to the action of calling the `Hello()` method on the `echo` hub proxy through its `server` member

▶ Remember, the `client` member has to be filled with the callback function(s) before starting the connection

Now we can run the application by navigating to `index.html` multiple times in different browser windows (or tabs), and then clicking on the **Say Hello!** button on each of them. We should see all the browser windows receiving the same message each time we push the button. The `Clients.All` member is effectively gives us access to the whole set of active connections, and it provides a way to broadcast method calls to all of them at once.

At every call, we'll notice that the printed time changes, but not the ConnectionId of the browser window from which the call comes, and no page refresh happens. On the other hand, every time we refresh one of the windows and click on the button, a new ConnectionId, representing that specific browser instance connection, will be shown. The following screenshot depicts this:

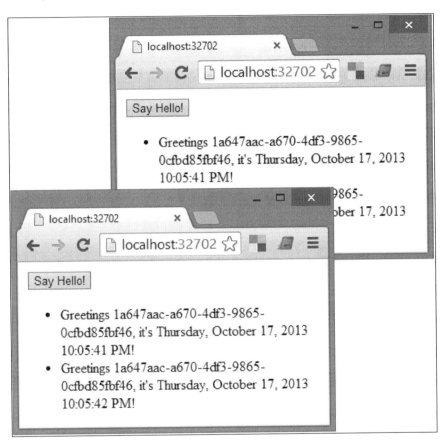

How it works...

The mechanics are the same as explained in the previous recipe, so please refer to it for more details.

Adding a connection to a group

Multiple clients can connect to a specific Hub at the same time, and the number of connections can easily increase. SignalR offers a feature called **groups** in order to define subsets of connections and use them when broadcasting to clients. We will see how a Hub can place connected clients into groups and then broadcast calls to all the connections belonging to a specific group.

Getting ready

Before writing the actual code, we need to create a new empty web application, which we'll call `Recipe08`.

How to do it...

We're ready to start building our sample. We need to perform the following steps:

1. Add a Hub called `EchoHub`.
2. Add an OWIN Startup class named `Startup` with a `Configuration()` method calling `app.MapSignalR();`.
3. Add the following to the Hub code:

```
using Microsoft.AspNet.SignalR;
using Microsoft.AspNet.SignalR.Hubs;

namespace Recipe08
{
    [HubName("echo")]
    public class EchoHub : Hub
    {
        public void Subscribe(string groupName)
        {
            Groups.Add(Context.ConnectionId, groupName);
        }
        public void Hello(string groupName)
        {
            var msg = string.Format("Welcome from {0}",
                groupName);
            Clients.Group(groupName).greetings(msg);
        }
    }
}
```

What's important here? We need to make sure that we perform the following steps:

▸ We first expose a `Subscribe()` method, which receives a `groupName` parameter, and then uses the `Add()` method of the `Groups` member inherited from `Hub` to add the `ConnectionId` of the caller to a group called after the specified argument

▸ The `Hello()` method builds a message (`msg`) and uses the `Group()` method of the `Clients` member inherited from `Hub` to broadcast a request to invoke the client-side `greetings()` method towards all the connections that joined the `groupName` group by calling the `Subscribe()` method

▸ We are allowed to dynamically call whatever method we want to because `Group()` returns a dynamic object; it works the same way we saw earlier for `Caller` or `All`

This is a very powerful API, but it's also very straightforward. You first add any connection to a certain group, and then you can access all the connections belonging to any group altogether to broadcast client-side calls towards them from the context of a server-side Hub method.

You could think about a group as a sort of topic attached to the connection. SignalR is able to efficiently target sets of connections marked with the same topic.

Let's proceed with the `index.html` client page and add the following code to it:

```html
<!DOCTYPE html>
<html xmlns="http://www.w3.org/1999/xhtml">
<head>
    <title>Recipe08</title>
    <script src="Scripts/jquery-2.1.0.js"></script>
    <script src="Scripts/jquery.signalR-2.0.2.js"></script>
    <script src="/signalr/hubs"></script>
    <script>
        $(function () {
            var hub = $.connection.echo;

            hub.client.greetings = function (message) {
                var li = $('<li/>').html(message);
                $('#messages').append(li);
            };

            $.connection.hub
                .start()
                .done(function () {
                    $('#subscribe').click(function () {
                        $(this).toggle();

                        var v = $('#group').val();
                        hub.server.subscribe(v);
```

```
                $('#send').click(function () {
                    hub.server.hello(v);
                });
                $('#send').toggle();
            });
        });
    });
    </script>

</head>
    <body>
        <label>Group:</label>
        <select id="group">
            <option value="A">A</option>
            <option value="B">B</option>
            <option value="C">C</option>
        </select>
        <button id="subscribe">Subscribe</button>
        <button id="send" style="display: none">Say Hello!</button>
        <ul id="messages"></ul>
    </body>
</html>
```

At the bottom of the file, we see some HTML markup declaring a drop-down list with three group names to choose from (A, B, and C), a button to perform the subscription, another one to say hello, and an unordered list to collect all the messages that will be received from the hub. Let's see what happens inside the `<script>` block:

▶ We take a reference to the `echo` hub, and from there, we access the `client` member to which we add a function called `greetings()` whose name and signature match the method that the Hub is trying to call back. The function will append every received message to a `ul` list present on the page and marked with an `id` attribute whose value is `messages`.

▶ We then start the connection and when it's ready, we hook the `click` event of the `subscribe` button to the action of calling the `subscribe()` method on the `echo` hub through the `server` member of the hub proxy.

▶ After calling `subscribe()`, we set up the `click` event of the `send` button to call the `Send()` method on the `echo` hub. Both `subscribe()` and `Send()` target the same destination group, but this is just the way this sample is built; of course, it does not have to be like that. The code will also take care of toggling the visibility of the two buttons with simple jQuery methods.

▶ We decide to hook the `click` event on the buttons just inside the `done` callback to ensure that we can call the `subscribe()` and `Hello()` methods only when the connection has been established (remember that starting a connection is an asynchronous operation).

We might have done the same to enable the `send` button after the asynchronous completion of the `subscribe()` call, but we'll dig more into this kind of complex workflow in the future recipes.

Now we can open `index.html` multiple times in different browser windows (or tabs), and then we can click on the **Subscribe** button after selecting one from the three available groups. After that, we'll be allowed to click on the **Say Hello!** button on any of the browser windows we have, and we'll notice the following points:

▶ Each hit on the **Say Hello!** button will send a message only to the windows that have already subscribed to the same group as the one where the button was clicked on

▶ Each window will receive messages only from other windows that have subscribed to the same group as the source window

How it works...

SignalR manages the group topics in a very smart way, which actually does not involve any state storage at the server side. It has information associated to the connection only, and this strategy allows SignalR to have great horizontal scalability. If you need to persist group associations across physical connections (think about putting users, not just connections into groups), you'll have to resort to more complex strategies, which will be analyzed in future recipes.

Adding a connection to a group is always a safe operation, as depicted by the following points:

▶ A group, if not yet existing, is automatically created when calling `Add`

▶ You do not have to check if a connection is already present inside the group, because calling `Add` multiple times for the same connection is an idempotent operation without any unexpected side effects

▶ A connection can be added to multiple groups at the same time

Removing a connection from a group

As we just saw, groups are an interesting and useful feature exposed by the Hub API. In the previous recipe, we concentrated on how to add connections to a specific group, but we did not expand on how you can remove them. This will be the subject of this recipe.

It's quite obvious that in order to remove connections from a group, we'll have to add them to it first; however, that part has already been covered by the previous recipe. Here we'll show the code to do both operations in order to deliver a fully working recipe, but we'll indulge in comments only for the removal part. For more details about adding connections to a group, please refer to the previous recipe.

Getting ready

Before proceeding, we create a new empty web application, which we'll call `Recipe09`.

How to do it...

We're ready to actually start adding our SignalR bits by performing the following steps:

1. We need a Hub called `EchoHub`.

2. We then need an OWIN Startup class named `Startup` containing just a simple `app.MapSignalR()`; call inside the `Configuration()` method to bootstrap SignalR.

3. We finally need to edit the content of the Hub with the following code:

```
using Microsoft.AspNet.SignalR;
using Microsoft.AspNet.SignalR.Hubs;

namespace Recipe09
{
    [HubName("echo")]
    public class EchoHub : Hub
    {
        public void Subscribe(string groupName)
        {
            Groups.Add(Context.ConnectionId, groupName);
        }

        public void Unsubscribe(string groupName)
        {
            Groups.Remove(Context.ConnectionId, groupName);
        }

        public void Hello(string groupName)
        {
            var msg = string.Format("Welcome from {0}",
                groupName);
            Clients.Group(groupName).greetings(msg);
        }
    }
}
```

What's important here? We need to make sure that we perform the following steps:

- The `Hello()` and `Subscribe()` methods, although important, are the same as we saw in the previous recipe, so we skip the details about them

- The `Unsubscribe()` method receives a `groupName` parameter, and then uses the `Groups` member inherited from `Hub` to remove the `ConnectionId` of the caller from the specified group, via the `Remove()` method

Basically, we are just adding the removal feature to the Hub from the *Broadcasting to all clients in a group except the caller* recipe. Let's now create an HTML client page that we'll call `index.html` and add the following code to it:

```
<!DOCTYPE html>
<html xmlns="http://www.w3.org/1999/xhtml">
<head>
    <title>Recipe09</title>
    <script src="Scripts/jquery-2.1.0.js"></script>
    <script src="Scripts/jquery.signalR-2.0.2.js"></script>
    <script src="/signalr/hubs"></script>
    <script>
        $(function () {
            var hub = $.connection.echo;

            hub.client.greetings = function (message) {
                var li = $('<li/>').html(message);
                $('#messages').append(li);
            };

            $.connection.hub
                .start()
                .done(function () {
                    var group;

                    $('#subscribe').click(function () {
                        toggler();
                        group = $('#group').val();
                        hub.server.subscribe(group);
                    });
                    $('#unsubscribe').click(function () {
                        toggler();
                        hub.server.unsubscribe(group);
                    });
```

```
                    $('#send').click(function () {
                        hub.server.hello(group);
                    });
                });

            var toggler = function () {
                $('#subscribe').toggle();
                $('#unsubscribe').toggle();
                $('#send').toggle();
            };

        });
    </script>

</head>
<body>
    <label>Group:</label>
    <select id="group">
        <option value="A">A</option>
        <option value="B">B</option>
        <option value="C">C</option>
    </select>
    <button id="subscribe">Subscribe</button>
    <button id="unsubscribe" style="display: none">Unsubscribe</
button>
    <button id="send" style="display: none">Send</button>
    <ul id="messages"></ul>
</body>
</html>
```

The preceding code again is pretty similar to the one in the *Adding a connection to a group* recipe, apart from some jQuery tricks to enable/disable buttons. The only significant addition is the call to the `unsubscribe()` method exposed by the server-side Hub, plus the fact that the selected group name is stored in a variable that is to be passed on subsequent `subscribe()`/`unsubscribe()` calls. Those are not SignalR-specific additions, and their goal should be easy to grasp.

Now we can open `index.html` multiple times in different browser windows (or tabs), and then we can click on the **Subscribe** button after selecting one of the three available groups, or the **Unsubscribe** button when subscribed. When subscribed, we can click on the **Say Hello!** button on any of the browser windows that we have and see messages going around; when unsubscribed, we won't be able to send anything, and we won't see any message popping up.

Broadcasting to all connected clients except the caller

In the previous recipes, we saw a few examples of broadcasting where the sender was always included among the receivers of the message. That was because the APIs we used always included the sender, whether we used the `Caller` member, the `All` member, or the `Group()` method. There are several scenarios though, where it does not make sense to broadcast to the caller; for example, in a live forum application, where it might be enough to broadcast each message to everybody who joined except the sender. That's why SignalR offers the `Others` member in order to send calls to everybody but the caller. Let's use it.

Getting ready

Before writing the code of this recipe, we need to create a new empty web application, which we'll call `Recipe10`.

How to do it...

This is a simple Hub. To make it work, we need to perform the following steps:

1. Add a Hub called `EchoHub`.

2. Add the usual OWIN Startup class, which we name `Startup`, containing the `Configuration()` method just calling `app.MapSignalR();` to bootstrap SignalR.

3. Add the following code to the Hub:

```csharp
using System;
using Microsoft.AspNet.SignalR;
using Microsoft.AspNet.SignalR.Hubs;

namespace Recipe10
{
    [HubName("echo")]
    public class EchoHub : Hub
    {
        public void Hello()
        {
            var msg = string.Format("Greetings {0}, it's
{1:F}!",
                Context.ConnectionId,
                DateTime.Now);
            var others = Clients.Others;
            others.greetings(msg);
        }
    }
}
```

What's important here? We need to make sure that we perform the following steps:

- Inside the `Hello()` method, we build a message (`msg`) using the current time and the `ConnectionId` properties

- When `msg` is ready, we use the `Clients` member inherited from the Hub type, and from there we take a reference to the `Others` property, representing all the currently connected clients and excluding the caller

- We finally call the `greetings()` method on the `others` variable, supplying the `msg` object we just built; we expect this call to be performed on all the connected clients except the caller, and to be triggered by each call to the `Hello()` method performed by any of them

The client page for this Hub is very simple and it's actually the same as we had in the *Broadcasting to all connected clients* recipe. Add the following code to this page:

```html
<!DOCTYPE html>
<html xmlns="http://www.w3.org/1999/xhtml">
<head>
    <title>Recipe10</title>
    <script src="Scripts/jquery-2.1.0.js"></script>
    <script src="Scripts/jquery.signalR-2.0.2.js"></script>
    <script src="/signalr/hubs"></script>
    <script>
        $(function () {
            var hub = $.connection.echo;

            hub.client.greetings = function (message) {
                var li = $('<li/>').html(message);
                $('#messages').append(li);
            };

            $.connection.hub
                .start()
                .done(function () {
                    $('#send').click(function () {
                        hub.server.hello();
                    });
                });
        });
    </script>

</head>
<body>
```

```
        <button id="send">Say Hello!</button>
        <ul id="messages"></ul>
    </body>
</html>
```

Let's now open multiple browser windows or tabs pointing to `index.html`, and then let's click on the **Say Hello!** button on them. We will see that all the browser windows receive the same message each time we click on the button, except for the one on which the button has been pressed. The `Clients.Others` member is effectively giving us access to the whole set of active connections excluding the one performing the call to the Hub from where we access it, and this gives us a way to broadcast method calls to all of them at once.

Broadcasting to all clients except the specified ones

SignalR offers a couple of ways to exclude entire sets of connections from a broadcast; here, we see how we can exclude a specific set of connected clients using their `ConnectionId` properties.

To demonstrate this feature, we need a slightly more complex sample. Let's consider a case where some of the messages should go unobserved by the specific clients we do not want to target. In such a case, we would need to inform everybody about who else is connected, and provide a way to pick some of those in order to exclude them from the next broadcast. To achieve this, we store a list of all the received connections in a static `Hashset` member inside the hub, and we send this set to every connected client when it calls a `Subscribe()` method. This set of connections will be used by the client to show a list of identifiers from which the user can select who to exclude when performing the broadcast of the message. To keep the UI simple, we'll let the user exclude just one recipient; however, the code can be easily extended to exclude several of them.

Getting ready

In order to write the code of this recipe, we need to create a new empty web application, which we'll call `Recipe11`.

How to do it...

Let's prepare the ground by performing the following steps:

1. We add a Hub called `EchoHub`.
2. We then need the OWIN Startup bootstrap class. We name it `Startup` and add the `Configuration()` method to it, containing a call to `app.MapSignalR();`.

3. The Hub should contain the following code:

```
using System;
using System.Collections.Generic;
using System.Linq;
using Microsoft.AspNet.SignalR;
using Microsoft.AspNet.SignalR.Hubs;

namespace Recipe11
{
    [HubName("echo")]
    public class EchoHub : Hub
    {
        static readonly HashSet<string> connectionIds =
            new HashSet<string>();

        public void Subscribe()
        {
            var connectionId = Context.ConnectionId;
            connectionIds.UnionWith(
            new [] { connectionId });
            Clients.All.connections(connectionIds);
        }

        public void HelloBut(string excludeConnectionId)
        {
            var msg = string.Format("Welcome {0} at {1:F}!",
                Context.ConnectionId,
                DateTime.Now);
            var allExcept =
            Clients.AllExcept(excludeConnectionId);
            allExcept.greetings(msg);
        }
    }
}
```

What's important here? We need to make sure that we perform the following steps:

▸ The class contains a static `Hashset` member to keep a unique list of all the received `ConnectionId` values.

▸ The `Subscribe()` method adds the caller's `ConnectionId` property to the `Hashset` member mentioned in the preceding point, and then broadcasts the complete list to all the connected clients (`Clients.All`) calling the `connections()` method. Please note that we do not pay any particular attention to potential concurrency problems when accessing the `connectionIds` member, but in real-world code, you definitely should.

- Inside the `HelloBut()` method, we build a message (`msg`) using the current time and `ConnectionId` property. When `msg` is ready, we reference the `Clients` member, inherited from the `Hub` type, and we call its `AllExcept()` method, which returns a set representing all the currently connected clients except the one specified by passing to it the `excludeConnectionId` argument. We store the result in the `allExcept` variable.

- We finally call the `greetings()` method on the `allExcept` variable.

The client will have to host a button to send the message and a list where it can show the available `ConnectionId` values. The user will pick one of them and the client will pass it to the `HelloBut()` call to exclude it from the subsequent broadcast.

The following sample code, like many others in the future, has to do some **Document Object Model** (**DOM**) manipulation mixed with logic specific to the sample itself. We perform DOM manipulation using jQuery, and we try to keep it at a minimum to avoid distracting you from the relevant portions. Nevertheless, some of it is necessary; therefore, please pay more attention to what's actually related to SignalR and consider the rest as just plumping code that we need in order to have things working.

Let's build our client code in an HTML page called `index.html`. Add the following code to this page:

```
<!DOCTYPE html>
<html xmlns="http://www.w3.org/1999/xhtml">
<head>
    <title>Recipe11</title>
    <script src="Scripts/jquery-2.1.0.js"></script>
    <script src="Scripts/jquery.signalR-2.0.2.js"></script>
    <script src="/signalr/hubs"></script>
    <script>
        $(function () {
            var hub = $.connection.echo,
                connectionId;

            hub.client.connections = function (ids) {
                $('#ids').empty();
                for (var i = 0, l = ids.length; i < l; i++) {
                    var id = ids[i];
                    if (id !== connectionId) {
                        $('#ids').append(
                            $('<option/>')
                                .attr('value', id)
                                .html(id));
```

```
            }
        }
        if (ids.length) $('#sender').show();
    };
    hub.client.greetings = function (message) {
        $('#messages').append($('<li/>').html(message));
    };

    $.connection.hub
        .start()
        .done(function () {
            connectionId = $.connection.hub.id;
            $('#id').html(connectionId);

            hub.server.subscribe();
            $('#send')
                .click(function () {
                    hub.server.helloBut($('#ids').val());
                });
        });
    });
</script>

</head>
    <body>
        <p id="id"></p>
        <div id="sender" style="display: none">
            <button id="send">Send to all but</button>
            <select id="ids"></select>
        </div>
        <ul id="messages"></ul>
    </body>
</html>
```

At the beginning, we prepare the `hub.client` member, adding the callback methods that the Hub will invoke (`connections()` and `greetings()`); each one of them will manipulate the content of the page accordingly. Then, we start the connection, and when done, we proceed with the following:

- We store the ID of the current connection in a variable (`connectionId = $.connection.hub.id`) used to filter out that value from the list of available connections we built inside the `connections()` callback

- We call the `subscribe()` server-side method

- We finally hook the `click` event of the `send` button to a method, which will perform the `helloBut()` calls, passing to it the connection identifier to be excluded from the broadcast and picked from the selected one in the list

We can now open `index.html` multiple times in different browser windows or tabs, and then click on the **Say Hello to all but** button. Each time we click on the button, all the browser windows will receive the same message except the one whose identifier has been selected to be excluded from the broadcast. The `Clients.AllExcept()` method is effectively giving us access to the whole set of active connections, excluding the specified ones (in this case, we always specify just one exclusion, but they could be many), and it gives us a way to broadcast method calls to all of them at once.

Broadcasting to all clients in a group except the caller

Similar to what we just did in order to exclude specific connections from the set of all the connected clients, we can provide exceptions in the context of a specific group. We can broadcast to all the connections in a given group, excluding a list of specific `ConnectionId` values that we want to omit.

Getting ready

Before writing the code of this recipe, we create a new empty web application, which we'll call `Recipe12`.

How to do it...

Let's prepare our project by performing the following steps:

1. We add a Hub called `EchoHub`.

2. Let's then add the usual OWIN Startup class named `Startup`, with a `Configuration()` method calling `app.MapSignalR()`.

3. Let's edit Hub's content using the following code:

```
using Microsoft.AspNet.SignalR;
using Microsoft.AspNet.SignalR.Hubs;

namespace Recipe12
{
    [HubName("echo")]
    public class EchoHub : Hub
    {
        public void Subscribe(string groupName)
        {
            Groups.Add(Context.ConnectionId, groupName);
        }
```

```
        public void Hello(string groupName)
        {
            var msg = string.Format("Welcome from {0}",
groupName);
            var targets = Clients.Group(groupName,
Context.ConnectionId);
            targets.greetings(msg);
        }
    }
}
```

What's important here? We need to make sure that we perform the following steps:

- We first expose a `Subscribe()` method that receives a `groupName` parameter and then uses the `Groups` member inherited from `Hub` to add `ConnectionId` of the caller inside a group called as specified, using the `Add()` method.

- The `Hello()` method builds a message (`msg`) and then it uses the `Group()` method of the `Clients` member exposed by Hub to broadcast the message to all the connections belonging to the `groupName` group; we are also supplying an additional parameter (`ConnectionId` of the caller) to exclude the calling client from the broadcast.

- The `Group()` method accepts a variable length for the list of connection identifiers to be excluded. Here, we are specifying just one value, but we can supply many of them. Also, for simplicity, we are using `ConnectionId` of the caller itself to set an exclusion, but any other connection identifier would also work.

- Since SignalR 2.0, we have a new API called `OthersInGroup`, which would have been in fact a better match for this specific case; however, the goal here was to illustrate the generic case of the exclusion of any connection from a group. Whenever you need to specifically exclude the caller, `OthersInGroup` will be your best friend.

Let's write a client to test what we wrote inside the Hub. This client is incidentally exactly the same as the `index.html` page that we wrote for the *Adding a connection to a group* recipe. Therefore, we will keep the comments to a minimum. The following code should be used:

```html
<!DOCTYPE html>
<html xmlns="http://www.w3.org/1999/xhtml">
<head>
    <title>Recipe12</title>
    <script src="Scripts/jquery-2.1.0.js"></script>
    <script src="Scripts/jquery.signalR-2.0.2.js"></script>
    <script src="/signalr/hubs"></script>
    <script>
        $(function () {
            var hub = $.connection.echo;
```

```
                hub.client.greetings = function (message) {
                    var li = $('<li/>').html(message);
                    $('#messages').append(li);
                };

                $.connection.hub
                    .start()
                    .done(function () {
                        $('#subscribe').click(function () {
                            $(this).toggle();

                            var v = $('#group').val();
                            hub.server.subscribe(v);

                            $('#send').click(function () {
                                hub.server.hello(v);
                            });
                            $('#send').toggle();
                        });
                    });
            });
        </script>

    </head>
        <body>
            <label>Group:</label>
            <select id="group">
                <option value="A">A</option>
                <option value="B">B</option>
                <option value="C">C</option>
            </select>
            <button id="subscribe">Subscribe</button>
            <button id="send" style="display: none">Say Hello!</button>
            <ul id="messages"></ul>
        </body>
    </html>
```

This client allows the user to subscribe to a specific group and to broadcast messages that will be received only by other connections subscribed to the same group as the sender. The specific exclusion logic is completely server-side based, as we already explained while commenting the code from EchoHub.

We're ready to run `index.html` multiple times in different browser windows or tabs, and we'll then click on the **Subscribe** button on each window after selecting one of the three available groups. After that, we'll be allowed to click on the **Say Hello!** button on any of the browser windows, and we'll see the following things happen:

▸ Each hit on the **Say Hello!** button will send a message only to the windows that have subscribed to the same group as the one where the button was clicked on, excluding the window of the caller.

▸ Each window will receive messages only from other windows that have subscribed to the same group as that of the target window.

Broadcasting from outside a Hub

All the recipes we illustrated so far have a common workflow as follows:

▸ A client starts a connection first

▸ The same client calls at least one method on the Hub

▸ Eventually, any sequence of client-to-server and server-to-client calls can happen

Given the precondition of starting a connection from the client, which cannot be skipped, the fact that we then need at least one client-to-server call at the beginning, before doing anything else, may not be ideal. What if we want to start a conversation directly from a Hub? There's no such limitation with SignalR. In fact, a Hub may well be the first one to call back into the clients (already connected). There are a couple of ways to do it: the first one involves connection events, which will be illustrated in *Chapter 6, Handling Connections*, while the other option is based on the fact that a Hub can be used by any server-side code outside the Hub itself. This indeed becomes a mechanism to perform server-to-client calls onto any active connection, without any client having to initiate that specific conversation with some method invocation.

Getting ready

Before describing the code, we need to create a new empty web application, which we'll call `Recipe14`.

How to do it...

We're ready to actually start adding our SignalR bits:

1. We add a Hub called `EchoHub`.
2. Let's then add an OWIN Startup class named `Startup`, containing just a simple `app.MapSignalR();` bootstrap call inside the `Configuration()` method.

3. Let's edit the file content to make it look like the following code:

```
using System;
using Microsoft.AspNet.SignalR;
using Microsoft.AspNet.SignalR.Hubs;

namespace Recipe13
{
    [HubName("echo")]
    public class EchoHub : Hub
    {
    }
}
```

As you can see, the Hub is completely empty! We just need a Hub in order to target the current active connections towards it; however, in this recipe, we do not expect clients to perform any call onto it, so no method is needed.

Let's build a client that is supposed to receive calls from the Hub without calling it first. As usual, for this chapter, this will be an HTML page called index.html. Add the following code to this page:

```
<!DOCTYPE html>
<html xmlns="http://www.w3.org/1999/xhtml">
<head>
    <title>Recipe13</title>
    <script src="Scripts/jquery-2.1.0.js"></script>
    <script src="Scripts/jquery.signalR-2.0.2.js"></script>
    <script src="/signalr/hubs"></script>
    <script>
        $(function () {
            var hub = $.connection.echo;

            hub.client.greetings = function (message) {
                $('#messages').append($('<li/>').html(message));
            };

            $.connection.hub.start();
        });
    </script>

</head>
<body>
    <ul id="messages"></ul>
</body>
</html>
```

In the preceding code, we just exposed a callback method called `greetings()` and then we connected to the remote Hub. There is no code calling onto `EchoHub` at all. So, how do we make any communication happen?

We need some server-side code that takes a reference to a Hub somehow, and use it to call back onto the active connections. We could achieve this in several ways. For this recipe, we'll write a **Razor** page that we'll call `post.cshtml`, with no JavaScript involved. The only thing happening here is a plain old HTTP POST, which will be handled at the server side, and will be used as the entry point to get a Hub context. The following code is used in the Razor page:

```
@using Microsoft.AspNet.SignalR;
@using Microsoft.AspNet.SignalR.Infrastructure;
@using Recipe13;
@{
    var message = Request.Params["message"];
    if (IsPost && message != null)
    {
        var dependencyResolver = GlobalHost.DependencyResolver;

        var connectionManager =
dependencyResolver.Resolve<IConnectionManager>();
        var hubContext =
connectionManager.GetHubContext<EchoHub>();

        var all = hubContext.Clients.All;

        all.greetings(message);
    }
}


<!DOCTYPE html>
<html xmlns="http://www.w3.org/1999/xhtml">
<head>
    <title>Recipe13</title>
</head>
<body>
    <form method="POST">
        <input type="text" name="message" value="@message" />
        <button type="submit">Send</button>
    </form>
</body>
</html>
```

The markup portion of this page just defines a form with a textbox and a button to submit it, while the first half of the page is server-side code that handles any HTTP POST received; in case it receives a valid one, it starts playing with SignalR in the following way:

- The `GlobalHost` object of SignalR is used to get a handle on the `DependencyResolver` member. This entry point allows us to interact with many services used and exposed by SignalR.

- In this specific case, we call the `Resolve()` method from `DependencyResolver` to access the `IConnectionManager` service.

- With a reference to the `IConnectionManager`, we call the generic `GetHubContext()` method on it, specifying `EchoHub` as its generic argument; in return, we get a reference to a fully valid `EchoHub` context!

- As we already did in earlier recipes, from inside any Hub method, we can now refer to the `Clients` member of the Hub context that we have got, and from there, access any of the connection sets we already know (except the one for the caller). In this case, we use the `All` member to perform a broadcast call on the client-side `greetings()` method of every connected client.

We can proceed with testing this recipe by opening a few browser tabs pointing to the `index.html` page, and then from one last tab navigating to the `post.cshtml` page. From there, we will be able to post any message to the server and see it broadcasted towards the remaining tabs pointing to the `index.html` page.

How it works...

As we saw at the beginning of this chapter, a Hub instance should be treated as a mere set of methods, and not as a specific instance with a clear identity and an associated state. In this recipe, we just introduced the concept of **Hub context**, which is a stateless façade that we can use to perform server-to-client calls. We can observe that a Hub is very much like a Hub context with just some information about the caller attached to it, and this enforces the hints about the fact that we should avoid any instance state.

From the perspective of a life cycle, a Hub is instantiated by SignalR itself on each call, and we should never try to cache any particular instance. On the other hand, a Hub context obtained by calling `GetHubContext()` can be retrieved at any time, but its creation is quite expensive. Therefore, it's recommended to cache an instance of it and reuse it whenever possible, which makes sense. Nevertheless, it's possible and legal to do otherwise. For the sake of simplicity, that's the way we did it in this recipe.

We also saw that we can ask for a valid context from outside the scope of a specific client-to-server connection, and we can use it to refer to the active connections against that Hub context in the same way as we did earlier from inside any Hub method. Thanks to the `GlobalHost` static object and the related API, we can get access to a Hub context and perform server-to-client calls without any triggering client-to-server invocations.

See also

In *Chapter 7, Analyzing Advanced Scenarios*, we'll discuss `DependencyResolver` in greater depth because that's the entry point where you can customize how services are injected into SignalR, and how we can have SignalR use whatever specific **Inversion of Control** (**IoC**) container we might already be using in our project.

Using the return value of a Hub method

So far, we examined different ways to push information from a server Hub to the connected clients; in particular, we saw how to perform a client-side call just on the caller in the *Calling back the caller from a Hub's method* recipe. All these techniques have one thing in common: the remote call is performed through the `Clients` member exposed by `Hub`. However, in the special case of communicating just with the caller, we can use a different, and in some way more natural, way to do it: have the Hub method return a value.

Getting ready

For this recipe, we need a new empty web application, which we'll call `Recipe13`.

How to do it...

We're ready to start adding our SignalR stuff, as usual. We need to perform the next set of steps:

1. Add a Hub called `EchoHub`.
2. Add an OWIN Startup class named `Startup`, containing just a simple `app.MapSignalR();` bootstrap call inside the `Configuration()` method.
3. The following code needs to be added to the Hub:

```
using System;
using Microsoft.AspNet.SignalR;
using Microsoft.AspNet.SignalR.Hubs;

namespace Recipe14
{
    [HubName("echo")]
    public class EchoHub : Hub
    {
        public string Hello()
        {
            var msg = string.Format("Greetings {0}, it's
                {1:F}!",
```

```
                    Context.ConnectionId,
                    DateTime.Now);
                return msg;
            }
        }
    }
```

What's important here? We need to make sure that we perform the following steps:

- Inside the `Hello()` method, we build a message (msg) using the `ConnectionId` property exposed by the `Context` member.

- When msg is ready, we just use it as the return value of the method: SignalR does all the necessary marshaling and transport tasks to transform this operation into an asynchronous call towards the client. We practically have the same effect that we get when we perform a remote call using the `Clients.Caller` member.

In this way, we can use a different approach, which makes things simpler in all those cases where it seems natural to think of a server-to-caller push call as the return value of a caller-to-server invocation.

Let's build a client HTML page called `index.html` to see how we can receive such a response, using the following code:

```html
<!DOCTYPE html>
<html xmlns="http://www.w3.org/1999/xhtml">
<head>
    <title>Recipe14</title>
    <script src="Scripts/jquery-2.1.0.js"></script>
    <script src="Scripts/jquery.signalR-2.0.2.js"></script>
    <script src="/signalr/hubs"></script>
    <script>
        $(function () {
            var hub = $.connection.echo;

            $.connection.hub
                .start()
                .done(function () {
                    $('#send').click(function () {
                        hub.server
                            .hello()
                            .done(function (message) {
                                $('#message').html(message);
                            });
                    });
                });
        });
    </script>
```

```
</head>
<body>
    <button id="send">Say Hello!</button>
    <p id="message"></p>
</body>
</html>
```

The client is very straightforward, and for most of its code, it's just a simplified version of many samples that we have already seen earlier in the chapter. The only difference is that we actually use the response value of the `hello()` call to manage the reception of the return value. When we open `index.html` and click on the **Say Hello!** button, we call the `hello()` method on the `server` member, and the return value is a JavaScript promise, the same type of object used as the return value of the `start()` method used to initialize a connection. That's the *de facto* standard way in JavaScript to represent an asynchronous operation, which will complete at some point in the future. When calling `done()` on the promise object and specifying a callback function as its argument, we are asking SignalR to handle the related response sometime in the future and to pass the received value to the callback. This is a simple, elegant, and idiomatic way to deal with return values of asynchronous calls, which puts the code processing the answer more in the context of the remote method asynchronously called, and not as part of the `client` member as we do when using the callback strategy.

If you want to learn more about JavaScript promises, and in particular about the Deferred API exposed by jQuery and used by SignalR, you can do that at `http://api.jquery.com/category/deferred-object/`.

There's more...

As for the method arguments of any Hub method and any client-to-server invocations, SignalR deals with the serialization and deserialization steps required when handling a return value; in fact, this mechanism is not limited to primitive types. If we just change the return type of the `hello()` method from string to dynamic, we are instantly allowed to return an instance of any serializable type we want. Even an anonymous type, that is serializable by nature, would do, allowing us to build complex return values in an elegant way without the burden of defining **Data Transfer Object** (**DTO**) types just for the sake of representing a complex value. Like magic, the client will receive a dynamic object with the same shape created inside the Hub method. The meaning of the word *dynamic* here should be adapted according to the type of the client library we are using (JavaScript or .NET).

It's worth observing that the same mechanisms are involved when we use any of the `Clients` members described earlier. Dynamic calls on those members could be supplied with any number of instances of serializable types as arguments, and the serialization/deserialization magic would kick in and do the rest.

3
Using the JavaScript Hubs Client API

In this chapter, we will cover:

- ▶ Starting a Hub connection
- ▶ Setting up connection transport strategies
- ▶ Calling a server-side Hub method
- ▶ Adding a client-side method on the proxy and calling it from the server
- ▶ Managing errors across a complex asynchronous workflow

Introduction

Now, it's time to move our attention to the client side of SignalR. We've already written the client-side code in the previous chapters and briefly described the steps we needed to build fully working recipes; however, we never went into the details. Nevertheless, the client portion of any SignalR application is as necessary and important as the server counterpart. Here, we'll explore how a SignalR client really works and concentrate on the specific characteristics of the JavaScript client library in the context of its Hubs API.

The level of abstraction used by the Hubs API lets us reason in terms of the business methods defined on our server-side Hub-derived type. As already explained earlier, we can add as many methods on a Hub as we need, and define with these an interface made up of members with names and arguments which fit our business requirements.

The JavaScript client can access this interface in two different modes as follows:

- A basic mode, where methods and events are accessed in a generic, string-based manner
- A more advanced mode based on **dynamic proxies**

The latter exposes a much easier to use and streamlined approach, and in our path from simple concepts to more advanced features, we decided to go with this one first, while the second will be the topic of a future chapter.

The Hubs API also exposes the underlying connection and what's necessary to handle it from a client-side perspective. In this chapter, we'll start talking about this.

The key enabler here is the **dynamic endpoint** (usually `/signalr/hubs`), which we already saw in the previous recipes where we used the JavaScript client library. It is able to generate a client-side proxy on the fly and contains all the methods that are declared on the available server-side Hubs. This proxy greatly simplifies the way we call the server methods, and it makes SignalR look magical. However, the generated content is nothing more than a smart JavaScript script that you can easily open in a browser's window for further investigation.

When using proxies, SignalR also allows us to augment them with a set of functions that we want the server Hub to be able to call back in order to push information to the connected clients. Each proxy exposes a member called `client` for this purpose.

The last point that we want to highlight again is the highly asynchronous architecture of this client and of SignalR in general. Asynchronism brings forth a lot of advantages in terms of performance and scalability but also some challenges. We'll see how you can set up and combine your calls when you need to implement specific sequential workflows in the context of an asynchronous API.

For the following recipes, we will always start with ASP.NET Empty Web Application projects and use simple HTML pages for the client portions. As usual, if you want more information on these steps, you can refer to the *Appendix A, Creating Web Projects,* at the end of the book. The same strategy will be applied when you create recurring assets such as a `Startup` class or a Hub. They will be briefly mentioned in this chapter and you could go back to *Chapter 1, Understanding the Basics,* to have some more information about the steps required in Visual Studio to get there.

Starting a Hub connection

In this recipe, we'll describe the first operation that is necessary in every client-side portion of a SignalR application: connecting to a server. We'll quickly see how to do it and how the asynchronous nature of SignalR is already clear since the very first step performed by any client.

Getting ready

This recipe is only about performing a connection; that's why we do not need a server-side concrete Hub yet. Therefore, there is only one simple step that we need to perform before moving to the client-side code as follows:

1. We need to add an OWIN Startup class and set it up so that the `Configuration()` method calls `app.MapSignalR();` in order to properly initiate the server-side endpoint, as we already did several times in the previous chapters. This method is contained in the **Microsoft ASP.NET SignalR System.Web** package, which we can find on NuGet. If we use the graphical UI, we should search for it and install it from there. This is depicted in the following screenshot:

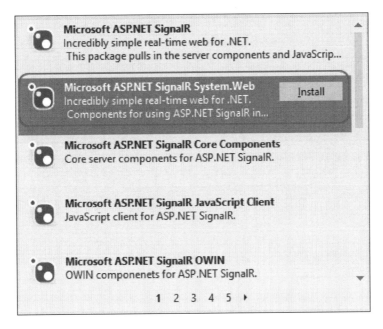

The same result can be achieved using the command line supplied by the **Package Manager Console** package.

2. When you are done, let's add an HTML page called `index.html`, where we'll build our client. We need to reference the SignalR JavaScript client, which is normally added to the project when referencing the Hub type, but in this case, we do not add any Hub-derived class. So, we have to add the **Microsoft ASP.NET SignalR JavaScript Client** NuGet package manually, as shown in the following screenshot:

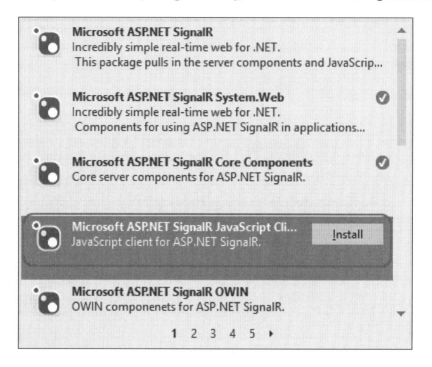

How to do it...

Now that everything is in place, let's add the necessary bits into the `<head>` section of our page. We need to perform the following steps:

1. Add a reference to jQuery (remember, the SignalR JavaScript library is a jQuery plugin, so this is a requirement) using the following code:

   ```
   <script src="Scripts/jquery-2.1.0.js"></script>
   ```

2. Add a reference to the SignalR JavaScript library using the following code:

   ```
   <script src="Scripts/jquery.signalR-2.0.2.js"></script>>
   ```

3. Add a reference to the SignalR dynamic endpoint:

   ```
   <script src="/signalr/hubs"></script>
   ```

This reference is necessary to access the Hubs API, even though we do not have any exposed Hub in this sample.

4. Add the following simple script that will help you to connect to the server:

```
<script>
        $(function () {
                var hub = $.connection.hub;
                var started = hub.start();
                started.done(function() {
                        $('#connected').html('connected!');
                });
        });
</script>
```

That's it; very simple. We first take a reference to the $.connection.hub object, which is an entry point to access the details of a connection specific to the Hubs API, and then we start the server. The start() method returns a JavaScript promise object and then starts connecting asynchronously. Thanks to the promise object, we can hook a callback that will be invoked when the connection is ready by using the done() method. Inside the callback, we refer to an HTML paragraph called connected (which must exist on the page) and set its content to the 'connected' value. We can easily verify this behavior by running the project and visiting the index.html page.

How it works...

The SignalR dynamic endpoint returns a script that, when downloaded, executes and adds the hub member to the $.connection object through which we can then asynchronously initiate a connection. There are several ways to perform this task as we'll see later in this chapter. Behind the scenes, the client and the server negotiate the better transport strategy to use. This phase occurs on the network, and as already mentioned in the past, anything requiring remote communication happens asynchronously. That's why a promise object is used to expose this specific phase in a neat and idiomatic way.

See also...

If you want to learn more about JavaScript promises in general and in particular about the Deferred API, which is exposed by jQuery and used by SignalR, you could start by visiting http://api.jquery.com/category/deferred-object/. If you want to know more about the connection strategies that we just mentioned, you can instead go straight ahead to the following recipe.

Setting up connection transport strategies

When a connection is made, a transport strategy must be put in place in order to properly move bits back and forth between the client and the server. SignalR can choose among different transport options as follows:

- **WebSocket**: This is an HTML5-related protocol that provides full duplex communication channels over a single TCP connection and is available in modern web browsers and web servers

- **Server-Sent Events**: This is a strategy based on the **EventSource** HTML5 support that allows a server to stream messages to the connected clients

- **Forever Frame**: This is a strategy based on the use of a **hidden iframe** element, where the **chunked encoding** HTTP feature is used to send an indefinitely long stream of bytes

- **Long Polling**: This is quite a basic technique that involves the opening of an HTTP connection and keeping it artificially alive to create the illusion of a persistent connection

Each one of these strategies is based on a specific underlying technology, which may or may not be available according to the specific browser used and to the capabilities of the web server in place. SignalR will try to use WebSocket whenever possible, and if it's not available, it will gracefully fall back on the remaining ones until it picks the best option for the current environment. That said, we might have good reasons to decide on a specific one or to define a custom probing sequence. In this recipe, we'll see how to do this.

For some more details about the transport options, please have a look at *Appendix B, Insights*.

Getting ready

As for the previous recipe, this one does not need a server-side concrete Hub yet. We just need to perform the following steps:

1. Add an OWIN Startup class and set it up so that the `Configuration()` method calls `app.MapSignalR();` in order to properly initiate the server-side endpoint. This method is contained in the **Microsoft ASP.NET SignalR System.Web** package, which we can find on NuGet.

2. Reference the **Microsoft ASP.NET SignalR JavaScript Client** package, which is normally added to the project when referencing the Hub type. However, because we do not have any Hub here, we have to do it manually from NuGet.

For more details about these steps, you can check the previous recipe.

How to do it...

Let's proceed with the client code by performing the following steps:

1. We first add the needed JavaScript references as follows:

```
<script src="Scripts/jquery-2.1.0.js"></script>
<script src="Scripts/jquery.signalR-2.0.2.js"></script>
<script src="/signalr/hubs"></script>
```

2. We then add the following connection code:

```
<script>
    var hub = $.connection.hub;

        var started = hub.start({
            transport: [
                'webSockets',
                'longPolling',
                'serverSentEvents',
                'foreverFrame'
            ]
        });

        started.done(function () {
            $('#connected')
                .html('connected, transport: ' +
                hub.transport.name);
        });
</script>
```

The preceding code is very similar to the code in the previous recipe, but the `start()` method is given a `transport` option that lists a specific sequence of connection strategies, which will be used by SignalR to pick the best one available. We can change the order, remove any of these, or even specify just one, in which case we can pass a simple string instead of an array of strings. When the connection is ready, we can get the current transport strategy by querying the `hub.transport.name` value. If we tried to print this value just after the start call, we would get an undefined value because the transport is available only when the connection is asynchronously established.

Not every strategy may be available to a specific combination of the server and client technologies. A specific description of all the cases is outside the scope of this book, and it would become obsolete quite quickly. For the current list of specific cases, you can visit `http://www.asp.net/signalr/overview/signalr-20/getting-started-with-signalr-20/supported-platforms`. However, you might have to periodically check the list or look for a more up-to-date one in the future.

Calling a server-side Hub method

After learning how to perform a connection and customize the transport strategy, let's move to the natural next step: calling a server-side Hub method. As we have done so far in this chapter, we'll use the SignalR dynamic proxy generation feature that allows us to perform client-to-server calls in a more natural way. The alternate available approach will be illustrated in the future recipes.

This recipe and the remaining ones of this chapter have a clear goal of illustrating the client-side code in a very detailed way, and that's because we have several important features to explain. For this reason, we'll show the code and comment on it step by step, instead of going directly to its final version and commenting on it afterwards.

How to do it...

Let's proceed to the code, starting with the server side. Perform the following steps:

1. We first need to add a Hub, which we call `EchoHub`, and add the following code to it:

   ```
   using Microsoft.AspNet.SignalR;
   using Microsoft.AspNet.SignalR.Hubs;

   [HubName("echo")]
   public class EchoHub : Hub
   {
       public string Say(string message)
       {
           return message;
       }
   }
   ```

   The content is trivial; it contains just a `Say()` method that returns the supplied string.

2. Add an OWIN Startup class where the `Configuration()` method just calls `app.MapSignalR();` in order to initiate SignalR properly. We have already done this step several times. You can refer to the previous recipes for more insight.

3. We then move to the client portion. In order to get there, we need to add an HTML page, which we'll call `index.html`.

4. We add the needed JavaScript references to the HTML page as follows:

   ```
   <script src="Scripts/jquery-2.1.0.js"></script>
   <script src="Scripts/jquery.signalR-2.0.2.js"></script>
   <script src="/signalr/hubs"></script>
   ```

5. Now we can add the client code, and we'll do this step by step to illustrate every single piece of code. We start by adding an empty script block as follows:

```
<script>
...
</script>
```

6. Inside this block, we add a jQuery **document ready** call (using the well-known shorthand version):

```
$(function() {
...
});
```

This is to guarantee that we operate only when the DOM of the page is properly loaded. It's not always necessary, but it's generally a good practice.

7. Inside the document ready call, we take a reference to the hub object as shown in the following line of code:

```
var hub = $.connection.hub;
```

With this object, which we already briefly described in the *Starting a Hub Connection* recipe, we will later be able to actually connect to the server through the Hubs API.

8. We then take a reference to the echo Hub as shown in the following line of code:

```
var echo = $.connection.echo;
```

This reference is a handle to an autogenerated proxy that points to our server-side EchoHub; its name comes from the value we supplied to the HubName attribute that we used to mark our Hub.

At this point, you might be slightly confused by the two members of $.connection: hub and echo. When the Hubs API is used, $.connection will expose each server-side Hub as a member whose name will match either the name of the concrete Hub type or the value specified by the HubName attribute. Additionally, $.connection exposes the hub member, which is not a Hub, but an entry point that we can use to manage the underlying connection and access a set of methods and properties exposed by the Hubs API itself. We need the latter to perform general purpose actions such as starting the connection, and we use the other ones to access specific Hubs.

If you use hub as the name of one of your server-side Hubs, the corresponding dynamically generated proxy will replace the general purpose hub member of $.connection, which will of course break everything!

Let's move on. We will perform the next set of steps to fill EchoHub:

1. We are ready to connect using the following line of code:

```
var started = hub.start();
```

The start() call, as already mentioned in the *Starting a Hub connection* recipe of this chapter, returns a JavaScript promise object that we'll use to set up a function to be called back when the connection is ready.

2. Let's prepare the basis for the callback that we just mentioned with the following code:

```
started.done(function() {
...
});
```

The done() method allows us to specify the actual function to be called when the connection is ready. In this way, we can guarantee that any other interaction will be performed when everything is in place; otherwise, SignalR will complain.

3. We will now fill the done() callback. We know that inside this function, we are allowed to use our Hub proxy to perform any call towards the server, as shown in the following code:

```
var call = echo.server.say("hello!");
```

The echo proxy exposes a server member on which we can call any method that is exposed by the server-side Hub. This is where we can really see the proxy generation shine because each Hub method has been made available by the dynamic endpoint. The return value of any remote call is again a JavaScript promise object, as for the connection startup method, because every call going through the network is executed asynchronously. We'll use this promise to read the return value of the Hub method.

In this specific example, we call the say method exposed by EchoHub, and it's interesting to observe how we write the method call with the initial s in lower-case (say instead of Say). SignalR automatically matches the lower-case (also known as *camel case*) call on the client, which is more natural in a JavaScript environment, with the corresponding upper-case (or *Pascal case*) method definition on the server side, which is the usual way to name public methods when writing C# code.

4. We finally hook a done() callback onto the promise object that we just assigned to the call variable:

```
call.done(function(message) {
    $('#message').html(message);
});
```

The callback declares a parameter that will be set to the value returned by the server-side Hub method. In this way, we can use it to set the content of a DOM element on the page with an ID equal to message.

We wrote some pretty verbose code to illustrate the steps one by one; but of course, in real applications, we could write it in a much more synthetic way, avoiding the intermediate variables hub and echo, as shown in the following code:

```
$(function() {
    $.connection.hub
        .start()
        .done(function() {
            $.connection.echo.server
                .say("hello!")
                .done(function(message) {
                    $('#message').html(message);
                });
        });
});
```

If we visit the index.html page, we will see a **hello!** message printed on the page as a result of a process where the following actions are performed:

1. We wait for the page to be loaded.
2. We asynchronously connect to the server.
3. We wait until the connection is ready (first done() callback).
4. We asynchronously perform a remote method call.
5. We wait for the answer and when it is received (second done() callback), we print it.

Adding a client-side method on the proxy and calling it from the server

The previous recipe taught us how to call a server-side method exposed by a Hub and how to receive its return value, if any. As we already explained in *Chapter 2, Using Hubs*, SignalR really shines when we have to push information to several connected clients at the same time, and we illustrated the various APIs available to do this. In this recipe, we'll concentrate again on those strategies, and in particular on notifying the caller, but our focus will be on explaining the client-side mechanics involved when receiving server-to-client calls.

How to do it...

We need to prepare our Hub, and to do this we need to perform the following steps:

1. Add a Hub-derived type that we'll call EchoHub.
2. Add an OWIN Startup class bootstrapping SignalR with a call to app.MapSignalR(); inside its Configuration() method.

For more details on these steps, you can check the previous chapters.

Then, let's start adding the code for this specific sample by performing the next set of steps:

1. We first need to edit the server-side `EchoHub` and make it look like the following code:

```
using Microsoft.AspNet.SignalR;
using Microsoft.AspNet.SignalR.Hubs;

[HubName("echo")]
public class EchoHub : Hub
{
    public void Say(string message)
    {
        Clients.Caller.greetings(message);
    }
}
```

The content is trivial and similar to many samples that we saw in *Chapter 2, Using Hubs*. Our `Say()` method is just pushing the supplied `message` parameter back to the caller. We could have pushed it to any of the several connection sets available, which we saw earlier. If you want to change this particular aspect of this recipe, please go back to *Chapter 2, Using Hubs*, for some inspiration.

The highlighted portion of the preceding code is the invocation of the `greetings()` method. We already saw in *Chapter 2, Using Hubs*, how such a method call is dynamically resolved.

2. Let's move to the client portion. To do this, we need to add an HTML page that we'll call `index.html`.

3. We add the usual JavaScript references as follows:

```
<script src="Scripts/jquery-2.1.0.js"></script>
<script src="Scripts/jquery.signalR-2.0.2.js"></script>
<script src="/signalr/hubs"></script>
```

4. Now, let's proceed step by step with the real code. We start by adding an empty script block as follows:

```
<script>
...
</script>
```

5. As usual, we add a jQuery document ready call inside this block (using the shorthand version) as follows:

```
$(function() {
...
});
```

6. Inside the document ready call, we take a reference to both the `hub` object and the `echo` Hub proxy, whose roles have been already explained in the previous recipe. This is shown in the following code:

```
var hub  = $.connection.hub;
var echo = $.connection.echo;
```

7. This is where we start differentiating from the previous recipe. Here we use the `client` member of the `echo` object to dynamically add a `greetings()` function expecting one parameter, as shown in the following code:

```
echo.client.greetings = function(message) {
    $('#message').html(message);
};
```

This signature corresponds to that of the method invoked from inside the Hub method on the `Clients.Caller` member, as illustrated in step 1. SignalR will wire this definition when the connection starts, and it will be able to match it to the corresponding server-side call so that the invocation from inside the Hub method triggers a call to the client. The received argument will have the same value as the value that is used during the server-side invocation.

All these callback definitions must be added to the `client` member. It's interesting to note that while these definitions go all together inside this specific member of the proxy, the corresponding server-side invocations can be triggered from any of the several `Clients` members, such as `Caller` or `Others`; each one of them corresponds to a different set of connected clients as explained in *Chapter 2, Using Hubs*.

The actual body of the client-side function is not very important. It just uses jQuery to find a specific DOM element that is filled with the value carried by `message`.

8. We are ready to connect using the following line of code:

```
var started = hub.start();
```

The `start()` call returns a JavaScript `promise` object that we'll use to set up a function to be called back when the connection is ready. It's this call that wires our client-side `greetings()` function so that the server-side call matches it.

9. Let's fill the callback that we mentioned in the previous step with the following code:

```
started.done(function() {
    echo.server.say("hello!");
});
```

The `done()` method and the `server` member have already been explained in the previous recipe. What is going on here is just a simple call to the server-side `Say()` method and performed inside the `done()` callback. We ensure that it's triggered when the connection startup has been completed successfully. The `Say()` method will be called on the server, and from there the `greetings()` invocation will go back to the calling client.

Again, we wrote some pretty verbose code to illustrate these steps. The exercise of making it simpler and more synthetic is left to you!

If we now visit the `index.html` page, we will see a **hello!** message printed on the page as a result of a process where the following actions were performed:

1. We wait for the page to be loaded.
2. We asynchronously connect to the server.
3. We wait until the connection is ready (first `done()` callback).
4. We asynchronously perform a remote method call.
5. From inside the server-side method, we push back a value to the caller (`Clients.Caller` member).
6. We receive the `message` value inside the `greetings()` method that we added to the `echo.client` member and print it.

Managing errors across a complex asynchronous workflow

In this last recipe, we'll introduce one last concept to have a full view of the basic features made available by the JavaScript Hubs API: how to react to errors that occur during all the possible SignalR operational steps and states.

For some specific cases, SignalR offers a couple of native ways to deal with errors as follows:

▶   We can supply a `fail()` callback to any JavaScript `promise` object that SignalR returns. This means that we can either use `fail()` on the `promise` object returned when starting a connection to intercept errors during the connection process, or we can use `fail()` on the `promise` object returned during the remote invocation of a Hub method. By hooking a callback with these `fail()` methods, we can be notified about the exceptions that occur during either the networking portion of a remote invocation or the server-side execution of a Hub method. We should observe that for errors occurring because of networking issues, SignalR has some built-in logic to perform some retries before giving up after a certain amount of time.

▶   We can call the `error()` method on `$.connection.hub` in order to supply a callback to be invoked when an error occurs on the current connection. This handler traps both the connection startup exceptions and the method invocation exceptions; however, for those cases where the SignalR retry logic is in place, this handler always, and immediately, receives the originating error. In other words, if the retry logic succeeds at some point, the previously mentioned `fail` handlers would not be triggered but we would see the `error` handler executed in any case.

These scenarios are managed by SignalR out of the box, but there are other types of errors that are not directly handled and must be intercepted with the traditional `try...catch` blocks. Let's illustrate a sample scenario as follows:

1. We successfully connected to a remote Hub.
2. After that, for some reason, we lost our connection to the server.
3. The retry attempts performed by SignalR have already been completed with no luck, and a timeout has expired after which no more retries are performed and the connection goes in a disconnected state.
4. We try to call a Hub method anyway.

In this scenario, for each Hub method invocation at step 4, SignalR would throw an exception complaining that we have to start the connection first, and no error or fail handler would ever see this exception. So, we'd have to set up a `try...catch` block around the method call to handle it properly.

Let's get ready to illustrate these different cases with some code.

How to do it...

Let's perform the usual setup steps as follows:

1. Add an OWIN Startup class bootstrapping SignalR with a call to `app. MapSignalR();` inside its `Configuration()` method.
2. Add a Hub-derived type, which we'll call `EchoHub`.

For more details about these steps, you can check the previous chapters.

Now, the following steps need to be performed to edit the code:

1. We first need to make the `EchoHub` code look similar to the following:

```
using System;
using Microsoft.AspNet.SignalR;
using Microsoft.AspNet.SignalR.Hubs;

[HubName("echo")]
public class EchoHub : Hub
{
    public string Say(string message)
    {
        if (new Random().Next(2) == 0)
            throw new ApplicationException("Doh!");
        return message;
    }
}
```

This version of the `Say()` method just returns the supplied `message` parameter similar to the *Calling a server-side Hub method*, but we have modified it to throw an exception every now and then.

2. We then need to add an HTML page, which we'll call `index.html`.

3. In the body of the page, we put a couple of buttons, some instructions to display, and a `ul` element in order to append messages that we want to show on the screen as shown in the following code:

```html
<button id="connect">Connect</button>
<button id="say" style="visibility: hidden">
    Say hello
</button>
<p>
    Try stopping the web server while clicking buttons...
</p>
<ul id="messages"></ul>
```

4. We move to the `<head>` section and add the usual JavaScript references as follows:

```html
<script src="Scripts/jquery-2.1.0.js"></script>
<script src="Scripts/jquery.signalR-2.0.2.js"></script>
<script src="/signalr/hubs"></script>
```

5. Now, let's proceed step by step with the client-side code. We first add an empty script block as follows:

```html
<script>
...
</script>
```

6. In the block, we add a simple utility function to append text messages inside the `ul` element previously mentioned as shown in the following code:

```javascript
var print = function (message) {
    $('#messages').append($('<li/>').html(message));
};
```

7. Then as usual, we add a jQuery document ready call (using the shorthand version):

```javascript
$(function() {
...
});
```

8. In the document ready call, we first notify that the page is ready and then take a reference to the `hub` object and the `echo` hub, as we already did in the previous recipes. This is shown in the following code:

```javascript
print('Ready');
var hub  = $.connection.hub,
    echo = $.connection.echo;
```

9. Here, let's add our first error handler by calling the `error()` method on the `hub` reference, as shown in the following code:

```
hub.error(function(error) {
    print('An error occurred on the hub connection: ' +
        error);
});
```

The callback that we supplied will be invoked any time an error occurs while SignalR is in a valid state, as explained earlier. This will also receive any error causing SignalR to perform some retry attempts to recover from the problem; the error would be received regardless of the final outcome of the recovery process.

10. We then handle the `click` event on the `connect` button, and in the handler we first print that we are connecting and then we hide the `connect` button itself, as shown in the following code:

```
$('#connect').click(function () {
    print('Connecting...');
    $('#connect').css('visibility', 'hidden');


    ...
});
```

11. We are ready to connect using the following line of code:

```
var started = hub.start();
```

The `start()` call returns a JavaScript `promise` object that we'll use to set up both a function to be called back when the connection is ready (`done()`), and another function to be triggered when an error occurs (`fail()`).

12. Let's fill the `done()` callback that we mentioned in the previous step. First we print a message saying that we are connected, then we show the button to invoke the `Say()` method, and finally we prepare an event handler for the `click` event. The following code depicts this:

```
started.done(function() {
    print('Connected!');
    $('#say').css('visibility', 'visible');
    $('#say').click(function () {
        print('Saying...');
        ...
    });
});
```

13. We complete the body of the `click` handler that we just introduced with a call to the `Say()` method on the `echo` proxy. We know that such a method returns a `promise` object, where we handle the possible outcomes using both `done()` and `fail()`; because we want to stay on the safe side for any other client-side unhandled error, we surround everything with a `try...catch` block as shown in the following code:

```
try {
    var call = echo.server.say("hello!");

    call.done(function(message) {
        print('Said: ' + message);
    });
    call.fail(function(error) {
        print('An error has occurred during the method
            call: ' + error);
    });
} catch (error) {
    print('An general SignalR error has occurred somewhere
        between client and server: ' + error);
};
```

The content of the `catch` block is trivial, while the body of the `try` block is very similar to what we already did previously in this chapter, with only the addition of the fail handler to intercept the errors that occur during the remote method invocation. Here, the roles are well defined: the `fail()` callback will intercept any asynchronous error that occurs during the remote invocation, while the `catch` block will intercept any synchronous error that occurs on the client. In particular, a synchronous failure can occur if we try to invoke a remote method while the connection is in an invalid state.

14. We're almost done. Only a fail handler for the connection promise is missing, which we add after the `started.done()` call:

```
started.fail(function (error) {
    print('An error has occurred connecting: ' + error);
    $('#connect').css('visibility', 'visible');
});
```

Here, we just print the reason for the error and display the `connect` button to allow the user to attempt again.

The best way to understand what's going on here is to load the `index.html` page and try it. You will first connect and then you'll be allowed to say hello, which sometimes will fail because of the random exception thrown on the server side.

I also recommend that you try performing the same operations while randomly disrupting the connection, which you can easily achieve by stopping and restarting the hosting web server (by default, it would be an instance of IIS Express). If you do this after loading the page but before connecting or after connecting but before calling the `Say()` method, you will see different error messages. If you keep trying to trigger remote calls, you will clearly notice that the error messages change depending on whether a connection time out has expired already or not (more about this in *Chapter 6, Handling Connections*).

How it works...

The internals of these mechanisms are pretty complex and are also influenced by the actual transport strategy used by SignalR. For the goal of this book, it should be enough to say that each of these strategies applies all the necessary checks, maintains the needed state, performs the required retries to keep things working, and, if it's the case, raises useful exceptions that highlight what went wrong.

There's more...

We've been digging quite deep into how errors are handled in such an asynchronous context, but in the following chapters we'll see even more tools that SignalR provides, in order to enhance how server-side errors are sent to clients and control the various possible states that a connection can go through. All of them are very useful to build complex applications where a high degree of fault tolerance is a requirement.

4
Using the .NET Hubs Client API

In this chapter, we will cover:

- ▶ Starting a Hub connection
- ▶ Setting up connection transport strategies
- ▶ Calling a server-side Hub method
- ▶ Adding a client-side method on the proxy and calling it from the server
- ▶ Managing errors across a complex asynchronous workflow

Introduction

In this chapter, we will take a deeper look at the .NET client library on the Hubs API. From a functional perspective, this API does not differ from the JavaScript one; in fact, it basically offers the same features, the only difference being the platform it operates on. Hence, in this chapter, we'll keep the same outline that we used in *Chapter 3, Using the JavaScript Hubs Client API*, with recipes that are similar to the ones in that chapter.

This chapter will concentrate exclusively on the .NET client's code that we'll be writing; however, as usual, we will need a counterpart for the server Hub. In order to avoid repetition and complexity, we will use the same servers that we used in *Chapter 3, Using the JavaScript Hubs Client API*, and we'll connect the new clients to those servers to perform the operations. Clients will perform mostly the same actions as the corresponding ones from there. In this way, you will have a chance to easily compare the two APIs in action, discovering similarities and differences. We can say that for a full comprehension of the current chapter, the previous one is a prerequisite.

The first thing worth noticing here is the fact that the .NET client does not bring any dynamic proxy feature. Everything is based on what is exposed by a specific type called `HubConnection`. Whether we need to perform calls on a remote Hub or we want to supply some function to be called back on, we'll have to use a couple of generic methods on `HubConnection` to achieve our goal, and use a string to specify the method names. We'll cover this in detail later in this chapter.

Dynamic programming shows up again here with method arguments. As long as they are serializable, we can use any type of argument, no matter whether we're calling a Hub's method remotely or we're triggering a client-side callback. The receiving part has to just declare that it's expecting a dynamic value, and SignalR will do the rest to make the supplied values available, without any need of sharing common assemblies in order to distribute the type definitions to be shared between the server and client sides.

The other interesting aspect that we'll be digging into is how the asynchronous nature of SignalR is expressed by the .NET client API. The **Task Parallel Library** (**TPL**) is at the core of this client; in our samples, we'll be showing how that neatly integrates with the **async/await** support introduced in C# 5.0. That said, the goal of this book is not to teach how async/await works; that alone can be the topic for an entire book. For this reason, we'll be writing code that might look naïve and may not fully exploit the power of async/await, but it will be hopefully easy to follow and understand. At the same time, there will be enough details to proof the points that we will be making in our recipes.

For the following recipes, we will always start with console application projects and all our code will be contained in the default `Program` class. For each recipe, we will need to go to NuGet, and from there add the **Microsoft ASP.NET SignalR .NET Client** client library, which is the actual full name of the .NET client library we are dissecting here. This is shown in the following screenshot:

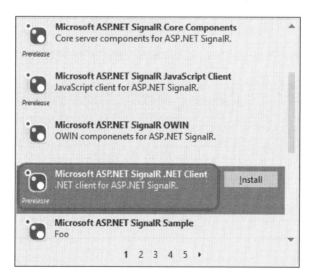

That's it; now we are ready to start.

Starting a Hub connection

In the first recipe of this chapter, like we did in the first one in *Chapter 3, Using the JavaScript Hubs Client API*, we'll start describing the very first operation that is necessary in every SignalR client: connecting to a server.

Getting ready

For this recipe, we will connect to the Hub exposed in the *Starting a Hub connection* recipe from *Chapter 3, Using the JavaScript Hubs Client API*. So please make sure that you've already started that application before testing the following code.

How to do it...

After creating our console application as described in the *Introduction* section, and naming it `Recipe20`, we just need to edit its code by performing the following steps:

1. We first add the necessary `using` directives as follows:

   ```
   using System;
   using System.Threading.Tasks;
   using Microsoft.AspNet.SignalR.Client;
   ```

2. Then we drop the current empty `Main()` method entry and replace it with the following code:

   ```
   static void Main(string[] args)
   {
       Do().Wait();
   }
   static async Task Do()
   {
       ...
   }
   ```

   Why this? This is a trick that we need to put in place in order to be allowed to write the async/await code in the context of the `Main()` method of a console application. The problem is that the `await` keyword is allowed only inside methods marked with the `async` directive, but `Main()` cannot be marked like this. With this workaround, we write our client code inside the `Do()` method, which is marked with `async`, and therefore can host `await` statements. Then we wait for its completion using the `Wait()` call. We'll be using this strategy through all the recipes of this chapter.

   These kind of matters are actually out of the scope of this book. If you want to dig deeper, you will find a lot of related material available on the Web and you can refer to *Appendix B, Insights*, for a few references about it.

3. Let's move on and prepare the connection using the following lines of code:

```
const string url = "http://localhost:36982";
var connection = new HubConnection(url);
```

Here, we first prepare the URL of the server that we want to contact, and then pass it into the constructor of the `HubConnection` type we are building. `HubConnection` is the type that we need to connect to a remote Hub. Please note that the port number we specify (`36982`) must match the port number used in the server project that we are using here. You should check which one is the actual number, and adapt the one used here in case it's different.

4. We are ready to connect to our Hub using the following code:

```
await connection.Start();
```

The method we use to perform the connection is called `Start()`, which is the equivalent of the one that we find inside the JavaScript client library. This method is asynchronous and it's actually awaitable (it returns a `Task` result). Therefore, we can prefix the call with the `await` keyword. By doing this, any code after the line with the keyword `await` is only executed after `Start()` has actually been completed. This is a very neat way to write code that would normally lead to (maybe deeply nested) callbacks. In complex scenarios, such code could easily become hardly readable; however, using `await`, we can greatly improve this aspect. For more information about async/await, refer to *Appendix B*, *Insights*.

5. When the connection is available, we just output a message as shown in the following code:

```
Console.WriteLine("Connected, transport is: {0}",
    connection.Transport.Name);
Console.ReadLine();
```

Here, we use the `Transport` member of our connection to print the strategy that has been chosen by SignalR to establish the communication channel, and then we wait for the user to press *Enter* before exiting the application.

When launching the application, your client will connect asynchronously, the code will wait for the connection to be available, and then it will print the transport that has been used to establish it.

You could also conduct an interesting experiment by removing the `await` keyword before the `Start()` call; you will most likely see the `WriteLine()` call write an empty string instead of a proper transport name. That's because the code does not wait for the asynchronous call to be completed, it instead continues immediately after exiting from `Start()` and tries to print the transport name, which is not yet available. Remember, the `Start()` method exits immediately, but this does not mean that the actual connection is ready yet!

Earlier, we said "most likely" because, theoretically, from the time `Start()` exits to the instant when `WriteLine()` is called, the asynchronous call will actually have enough time to be completed. In practice, this is very unlikely, because the network will always be slower than a couple of CPU cycles.

How it works...

Behind the scenes, during the `Start()` call, the client and server negotiate the best transport strategy to use. This phase occurs on the network, and as already mentioned in the past, anything requiring remote communication happens asynchronously. That's why an asynchronous method is used to expose this specific characteristic in a neat and idiomatic way. The async/await support does the rest to make the code easily readable. It really looks like sequential code, but in fact it's not. We could write the same code using the C# 4.0 syntax, and it would be something like the following code:

```
static Task Do()
{
    const string url = "http://localhost:36982";
    var connection = new HubConnection(url);

    return connection.Start().ContinueWith(_ =>
    {
        Console.WriteLine("Connected, transport is: {0}",
            connection.Transport.Name);
        Console.ReadLine();
    });
}
```

This is functionally equivalent to the previous version, but more verbose for sure and less readable. We had to remove the `async` keyword from the `Do()` method definition, and then we returned the `Task` result from the `ContinueWith()` method call performed on the result of the `Start()` method. This is a native way of declaring a continuation on a `Task` object, and it's (well, more or less) what the C# compiler is doing behind the scenes when translating the `await` syntactic sugar into actual API calls. You can easily imagine how much more cumbersome the code would become in case of many nested callbacks. On the other hand, please remember that writing asynchronous code is complex by nature, and the async/await support does not make the problem simpler; it's just giving us a cleaner syntax, but the complexity is still there!

Setting up connection transport strategies

When a connection is performed, a transport strategy must be put in place in order to properly move bits back and forth between the client and server. Let's recap them quickly:

- **WebSocket**: This is an HTML5-related protocol that provides full duplex communication channels over a single TCP connection, and is available in modern web browsers and web servers

- **Server-Sent Events**: This is a strategy based on the EventSource HTML5 support, which allows a server to stream messages to the connected clients

- **Long Polling**: This is quite a basic technique, which involves opening a connection and keeping it artificially alive to create the illusion of a persistent connection

You might have noticed that **Forever Frame**, which was available with the JavaScript client library, is not there. That's because this is a purely browser-dependent strategy, and it does not apply in this case. For some more detail about transport options, please have a look at *Appendix B, Insights*.

Let's see how we can specify the load sequence for the remaining strategies when writing a .NET client.

Getting ready

For this recipe, we will use the server that we used in the *Setting up connection transport strategies* recipe from *Chapter 3, Using the JavaScript Hubs Client API*, so please make sure you have already launched that server before testing the following code.

How to do it...

After creating a new console application, which we will name `Recipe21`, following the process described in the *Introduction* section, we will just need to edit its code by performing the following steps:

1. We first add the necessary `using` directives as follows:

```
using System;
using System.Threading.Tasks;
using Microsoft.AspNet.SignalR.Client;
using Microsoft.AspNet.SignalR.Client.Http;
using Microsoft.AspNet.SignalR.Client.Transports;
```

2. Then, we drop the current empty `Main()` method entry and apply the trick that we already described in the previous recipe to allow us to use the `async/await` syntax, as shown in the following code:

```
static void Main(string[] args)
{
    Do().Wait();
}
static async Task Do()
{
    ...
}
```

3. Let's move on and prepare the connection with the following code snippet:

    ```
    const string url = "http://localhost:39944";
    var connection = new HubConnection(url);
    ```

    Please check whether the port number (39944) matches the one used by the server project we are connecting to here.

4. We are ready to connect to our Hub. The following code is used for that purpose:

    ```
    await connection.Start(
        new AutoTransport(
            new DefaultHttpClient(), new IClientTransport[]
            {
                new WebSocketTransport(),
                new ServerSentEventsTransport(),
                new LongPollingTransport(),
            }));
    ```

    As we did in the previous recipe, we call the Start() method exposed by the connection object to negotiate and establish the communication channel. However, in this case, we use a more verbose overload to specify which transport strategies we want to try, and in which sequence. The verbosity is increased by the fact that this overload involves a few extra types (AutoTransport, DefaultHttpClient, and IClientTransport); so, if compared with the JavaScript version, it is definitely longer. But, at the end it brings the same functionality.

5. When the connection is available, we just want to output a message as shown in the following code:

    ```
    Console.WriteLine("Connected, transport is: {0}",
        connection.Transport.Name);
    Console.ReadLine();
    ```

    Here, we use the Transport member of our connection to print the strategy that has been chosen by SignalR to establish the communication channel, and then we wait for the user to press *Enter* before exiting the application.

When launching the application, the client will connect asynchronously. It will wait for the connection to be available, and then it will print the transport that it used to establish it. Apart from the transport negotiation bits, everything else is equivalent to what we saw in the previous recipe. Therefore, please refer to it if you want some more details about what's going on.

Calling a server-side Hub method

After learning how to perform a connection and customize the transport strategy, let's move to the natural next step: calling a server-side Hub method. We are going along the same path as the one we took in *Chapter 3*, *Using the JavaScript Hubs Client API*; therefore, this recipe will match what we did in the *Calling a server-side Hub method* recipe in that chapter. When we compare both the recipes, we can see one big difference between them: the .NET Hubs API does *not* have a concept of dynamic proxy. We'll see how we can call a remote Hub using a more general-purpose API than the magical one that we saw for the JavaScript client. Such a type of generic proxy indeed exists in the context of the JavaScript client, too; we will see that in detail later in the book.

Getting ready

For this recipe, we will use `EchoHub` exposed in the *Calling a server-side Hub method* recipe from *Chapter 3*, *Using the JavaScript Hubs Client API*, which must therefore be started before testing the code from this recipe.

How to do it...

Let's create a console application project as described in the *Introduction* section, and let's name it `Recipe22`. Then, let's modify the code of the `Program.cs` file by performing the following steps:

1. We first prepare the basis for our code as follows:

```
using System;
using System.Threading.Tasks;
using Microsoft.AspNet.SignalR.Client;

static void Main(string[] args)
{
    Do().Wait();
}
static async Task Do()
{
    const string url = "http://localhost:39492";
```

```
var connection = new HubConnection(url);


    . . .
}
```

Please make sure the port number (39492) matches the one used by the server project that we are using. For more detail about what's going on here, please check the previous recipes of this chapter.

2. Now, we need to create a proxy for the remote hub with the following code:

```
var echo = connection.CreateHubProxy("echo");
```

The CreateHubProxy() method creates a proxy object (echo) referencing the remote Hub whose name has been passed as the argument of the call. This reference will allow us to perform remote calls and, as we'll see in future recipes, to specify the functions to be called back from the server-side code.

3. We are ready to connect to our Hub using the following line of code:

```
await connection.Start();
```

This code is asynchronously initiating the connection and, as we already saw in earlier recipes, we then wait for its completion thanks to the await keyword.

4. When the connection is ready, we can call any method exposed by the remote Hub with the following code:

```
var response = await echo.Invoke<string>("Say", "hello!");
```

We use the echo reference that we took earlier to call the Invoke() method on it. The Invoke() method receives as its first argument the name of the remote method to call (Say), followed by a *params array* containing the arguments required by the method itself (in this case, the message to echo). Invoke() is a generic method whose type argument is the type of the expected return value. Of course, Invoke() is also an asynchronous method, so we can await it when calling it, and the response will be available asynchronously.

5. We eventually print the response and wait for the user to press *Enter* before exiting the application. The following code facilitates this action:

```
Console.WriteLine(response);
Console.ReadLine();
```

When running this code, the client will connect asynchronously to EchoHub. It will wait for the connection to be available and then perform a remote call. It will then wait for the response to be available and print it.

How it works...

The remote invocation is based on dynamic information and it's resolved at runtime. We specify the method to be called by its name, and we have no specific type representing the actual Hub that we are contacting; hence, there's no way to check whether our call is correct at compile time. We have to make sure everything matches the definition of the method on the Hub (name, number and type of the arguments, and type of the return value) while writing the code, and then let SignalR resolve it at runtime. If that's the case the call will succeed and we will receive the corresponding return value asynchronously, as usual with SignalR.

Adding a client-side method on the proxy and calling it from the server

In our journey through the recipes from *Chapter 3, Using the JavaScript Hubs Client API* and their adaptation to the .NET client Hubs library, we have just arrived at the point where we have to modify the recipe that has a similar name, in which we saw how we can define a client-side method to be called directly from inside a remote Hub. The server that we built there is already calling back its caller; therefore, in this recipe, we'll just need to connect to it, call the Say() method, and wait for the callback to happen.

Getting ready

The following code will connect to the EchoHub exposed in the *Adding a client-side method on the proxy and calling it from the server* recipe from *Chapter 3, Using the JavaScript Hubs Client API*, which we have to run before testing this Recipe.

How to do it...

Let's create a console application project as described in the introduction, and let's name it Recipe23. The source code of the Program class must be modified using the following steps:

1. Let's write the skeleton of our client code as follows:

```
using System;
using System.Threading.Tasks;
using Microsoft.AspNet.SignalR.Client;

static void Main(string[] args)
{
    Do().Wait();
```

```
}
static async Task Do()
{
    const string url = "http://localhost:42171";
    var connection = new HubConnection(url);

    var echo = connection.CreateHubProxy("echo");

    ...
}
```

The port number we specify (`42171`) must match the port number used in the server project that we are connecting to. Please verify if that's the case. More details about this code can be found in the previous recipes in this chapter.

2. On the proxy reference that we just retrieved, we can define any callback we might need. In this case, we proceed using the following code:

```
echo.On("Greetings", message =>
    Console.WriteLine(message));
```

The `On()` method allows us to define a callback method, giving it a name and defining its arguments and body, which in this case is an instance of an `Action` delegate receiving a string and printing it on the standard output window. It's like subscribing to an event, although the syntax is not the classic one for event handlers. When a server Hub pushes a method call on any of the available sets of connected clients (in the case of the server we are connecting to here, `Clients.Caller`), the request for that call is transferred onto the client and SignalR triggers the corresponding handler that we just registered over there using `On()`. The resolution, as usual, is performed at runtime.

As for the JavaScript client, the declaration of these event handlers must be done before connecting to the server.

3. Now we are ready to connect to our Hub using the following line of code:

```
await connection.Start();
```

This code is asynchronously initiating the connection and, as we already saw in earlier recipes, we are waiting for its completion thanks to the `await` keyword.

4. When the connection is ready, we can call the `Say()` method exposed by the remote Hub with the following code:

```
await echo.Invoke<string>("Say", "hello!");
```

The call will be executed asynchronously, and again we wait for its completion.

5. We eventually make our code wait for the user to press *Enter* before exiting the application. The following code depicts this:

```
Console.WriteLine("Press Enter to exit");
Console.ReadLine();
```

This code follows an awaited statement, therefore it will be executed only when the asynchronous call to `Invoke()` will be completed.

Launching the code, we will see how the `hello!` message pushed by the server towards the caller is eventually printed on the console.

How it works...

What happens when we execute this code? The `Invoke()` call will trigger the execution of the `Say()` method on the server-side Hub, which we know will call back the caller trying to invoke a client-side method called `greetings()`, if available. In our case, we have registered one with the `On()` method, which will just print the received `message` parameter on the console.

This sample is already showing how asynchronous code can easily become difficult to grasp. You might have noticed that in steps 3 and 4, we perform two subsequent asynchronous calls using `await`; this means that the first call will be awaited, and when completed, the second one will be triggered and again awaited before calling `Console.ReadLine()`. We can really appreciate the advantages of the async/await syntax here, because without it we would have two nested callbacks, and code would be harder to read and understand.

On the other hand, we could easily play with this code and observe subtly different behaviors. Pay attention to the sequence of messages on the screen. You will see that the `hello!` messages are always printed before the `Press Enter to exit` one. The .NET client is, in some way, making the remote asynchronous call run synchronously with respect to the client-side `Invoke()` call. It's as if the `On()` handler became part of the body of the `Invoke()` call.

Because of what we just said, if we now try to remove the `await` keyword in front of the `Invoke()` call and then launch the application again, everything would work as before, except that the two messages on the screen would appear in reverse order! Why? The `On()` handler is executed as it was part of the call that triggered it (the `Invoke()` call), but the `Invoke()` call is not awaited now. Hence, the asynchronous execution of the whole block consisting of the `Invoke()` and `On()` calls is completed after the `Console.WriteLine()` line, because writing a message on the console is for sure much faster than any operation involving network communication. We still have a chance to see the `hello!` message on screen because the `ReadLine()` call is making the process wait for interaction, and this gives time for the asynchronous invocation to be completed. However, the flow is totally different. If in this case, we remove the `ReadLine()` call, we will not see the `hello!` message printed at all.

Hopefully, this short digression around asynchronous code has been interesting; however, a good understanding of such concepts is important to write better SignalR code for sure, especially when using the .NET client library.

Managing errors across a complex asynchronous workflow

In the last recipe of the chapter, as we did in *Chapter 3, Using the JavaScript Hubs Client API*, we'll learn how to handle errors occurring during all the possible SignalR operational steps and connection states.

The `HubConnection` class from the .NET client offers a specific `Error` event, which is useful to manage most of the exceptions raised by SignalR itself, whereas any server-side exception occurring during a Hub method invocation can be trapped simply by surrounding the client-side invocation in a `try...catch` block. We'll talk a little bit more about the latter case while commenting on the code of this recipe.

Getting ready

Before proceeding with this recipe, please remember to start the server application that we used in the homonymous recipe called *Managing errors across a complex asynchronous workflow* from *Chapter 3, Using the JavaScript Hubs Client API*. This is because our code will connect to its Hub, whose method is already randomly throwing exceptions that we'll take advantage of in order to test our error-handling strategy.

How to do it...

We first create a console application project, named `Recipe24`, as described in the *Introduction* section, and then we'll work on the source code of the `Program` class, applying the following steps:

1. We first introduce the basic stuff using the following code:

    ```
    using System;
    using System.Threading.Tasks;
    using Microsoft.AspNet.SignalR.Client;

    static void Main(string[] args)
    {
        Do().Wait();
    }
    static async Task Do()
    {
        const string url = "http://localhost:42477";
        var connection = new HubConnection(url);
        var echo = connection.CreateHubProxy("echo");


        ...
    }
    ```

As usual, the port number we specify (42477) must match the one used in the server project that we are connecting to.

2. We add a helper method to the `Program` class, which we'll use to print out colorful messages easily on the standard output window:

```
public static void AsColorFor(this ConsoleColor color,
    Action action)
{
    Console.ForegroundColor = color;
    action();
    Console.ResetColor();
}
```

3. We go back to the `Main()` method, where we now define our `Error` event handler as shown in the following code:

```
connection.Error += error =>
    ConsoleColor.Red.AsColorFor(() =>
        Console.WriteLine("Error from connection: {0}",
            error));
```

The event's goal is straightforward: any error happening on the connection will trigger it. Its signature is simple. We just need to define an argument to receive the trapped exception, which we'll then print in red using our helper method.

4. We are ready to start writing our specific workflow to simulate different error conditions. In *Chapter 3, Using the JavaScript Hubs Client API*, we used a pretty interactive way to simulate and handle errors from a web page. Now, we'll use a simplified strategy where a set of operations is continuously repeated inside an infinite loop. The reason for this choice is the fact that this is a book about SignalR and not about asynchronous programming in general. In order to have an exhaustive sample working properly, we would have to go through a lot of off-topic code just to correctly handle a set of tricky issues originated by the usage of nested asynchronous calls from a command-line interactive process. It's better to keep it simple and concentrate on SignalR's features. Let's go back to the `Do()` method and complete it with the following code:

```
do
{
    . . .

    await Task.Delay(3000);
} while (true);
```

This simple code is just looping indefinitely, and at every iteration, it waits for three seconds before moving forward.

The code we are going to write inside the loop is simple. Basically, it will check if we are connected to the hub, and if we're not, it will establish a connection. Then, it will check again if the connection is valid and, if that's the case, it will try to call the Hub method exposed by the server that we are using. While doing these operations, it will constantly print out messages describing how things are going. A bunch of try... `catch` blocks will trap errors and print them.

5. We first print out the current state of the connection with the following code:

```
Console.WriteLine("State: {0}", connection.State);
```

6. After that, we test if we are currently disconnected, and if that's the case, we call `Start()` using the `await` prefix to wait for its completion. The connection attempt is done inside a `try...catch` block to trap networking issues; for example, in case the remote host is unreachable. The following code depicts this:

```
if (connection.State == ConnectionState.Disconnected)
{
    try
    {
        await connection.Start();
        Console.WriteLine("Connected!");
    }
    catch (Exception ex)
    {
        ConsoleColor.Yellow.AsColorFor(() =>
            Console.WriteLine("Error connecting: {0}", ex));
    }
}
```

7. Then, we adopt a similar strategy when calling the remote method; we first check if we are connected, and if that's the case, we call `Invoke()` to trigger the remote invocation. A `try...catch` block is there to protect us from errors occurring during the remote invocation (server-side errors trigger `InvalidOperationException` errors on the client). Again, we're using `await` to handle the asynchronous call and wait for its completion, as shown in the following code snippet:

```
if (connection.State == ConnectionState.Connected)
{
    try
    {
        var response = await echo.Invoke<string>("Say",
            "hello!");
        ConsoleColor.Green.AsColorFor(() =>
            Console.WriteLine("Said: {0}", response));
    }
    catch (InvalidOperationException ex)
    {
        ConsoleColor.Blue.AsColorFor(() =>
```

```
                    Console.WriteLine("Error during Say: {0}", ex));
            }
        }
```

We are ready to launch the application and observe the messages printed on the screen. While the client is running, we can try to stop and restart the server to see how both the error-handling logic that we put in place and the SignalR connection-handling strategies work together.

How it works...

The code that we used is pretty simple. It applies a simple pattern where operations are performed inside a `try...catch` block, and then a success message is printed. The message would, of course, be skipped in case an exception is triggered, and the corresponding `catch` handler would print out the details about the error that occurred. The whole loop is repeated every three seconds, which allows us to manipulate the availability of the server while the client runs. In this way, we can observe how the client reacts to different anomalous conditions we are creating. The `try...catch` blocks work well along with the `await` keyword, making asynchronous exceptions flow into the `catch` blocks as if they were happening synchronously.

In order to understand better what is going on here, let's see a list of possible abnormal conditions that we can simulate:

- **Launch the application before starting the server**: The process will continuously try to connect and fail until the server becomes available, printing out yellow messages from the `catch` handler that matches the `Start()` invocation. If we turn on the server while the client is still running, at some point the connection will succeed and the **Connected!** message will be displayed.

- **Server-side errors**: When connected, the `Invoke()` method calls will reach the server-side Hub method, which will randomly fail because of the way it's implemented. If successful, the client will receive a `hello` string, and it will display it in green, whereas, in case of a remote failure, the corresponding `catch` block will kick in and display a blue message about the remote problem.

- **Server becomes unavailable after connection**: If we now stop the server, at some point the SignalR connection will enter an invalid state (normally, `Reconnecting`). Therefore, none of our `if` statements will pass and at each iteration, nothing will happen. Behind the scenes, SignalR will be trying to reconnect, but it will fail because the server is unavailable. This kind of error is trapped by the Error handler on the connection, and it will be displayed in red. If the server does not become available before a specified time, (in which case, SignalR would successfully reconnect and things would go back to normality), SignalR will decide to stop trying to reconnect and move to the `Disconnected` state. In this situation, our first `if` block will be executed and the related connection attempts will fail, displaying yellow error messages. If we turn on the server at this point, the connection will be established successfully, and we'll go back to normality.

The actual internals of these mechanisms are complex and influenced by the actual transport strategy used by SignalR. As we already said while illustrating the corresponding recipe from the previous chapter, going too deep into technical detail about how things are handled behind the scenes would be out of the scope of this book. SignalR is simply smart enough to perform all the necessary checks and handshake tasks to supply both a natural error handling and an integrated connection lifecycle handling.

5
Using a Persistent Connection

In this chapter, we will cover the following recipes:

- ▶ Adding and registering a persistent connection
- ▶ Sending messages from the server
- ▶ Sending messages to the server
- ▶ Exchanging messages between a server and a JavaScript client
- ▶ Exchanging messages between a server and a .NET client

Introduction

In our journey through all the features exposed by SignalR, so far we have been analyzing and dissecting how we can use the Hubs API to deliver real-time, bidirectional messaging inside our applications. The Hubs API offers a high-level abstraction over the underlying connection, effectively introducing a **Remote Procedure Call** (**RPC**) model on top it. SignalR is also offering a low-level API, which is the foundation Hubs is built on top of. However, it's also available to be used directly from inside our applications and it's called the **Persistent Connection API**.

A Persistent Connection API is a more basic representation of what the concrete network connection really is, and exposes a simpler and rawer API to interact with. We hook into this API by inheriting from a base class (`PersistentConnection`) in order to add our own custom Persistent Connection manager. It is the same approach we have been using when defining our custom Hubs by deriving from the `Hub` class. Through a registration step, we'll then let SignalR know about our custom type in order to expose it to our clients.

The `PersistentConnection` type exposes a few properties supplying entry points from where we send messages to the connected clients, and a set of overridable methods we can use to hook into the connection and messaging pipeline in order to handle the incoming traffic. This chapter will be an introduction to the Persistent Connection API, hence we'll be looking at just a portion of it in order to deliver some basic functionalities. We will also try to highlight what the peculiar attributes of this API are, which characterize it as a low-level one—still delivering powerful features, but without some of the nice mechanisms we have for free when using the Hubs API.

For the next four recipes, we will always start with **empty web application** projects, and we'll use simple HTML pages for the client portions. However, for the last one, we'll be building a **console application**. As usual, if you want more information on these steps, you can refer to *Appendix A, Creating Web Projects*, at the end of the book.

Adding and registering a persistent connection

In this first recipe of the chapter, we'll introduce the `PersistentConnection` type, and we'll go into the details about how it works, how to use it, and how to register it into SignalR to expose it to the connected clients. Our goal for the sample code is to trace any attempt of connection from a client towards the exposed endpoint. We will also write a minimal JavaScript client in order to actually test its behavior.

Getting ready

Before writing the code of this recipe, we need to create a new empty web application that we'll call `Recipe25`.

How to do it...

Let's run through the steps necessary to accomplish our goal:

1. We first need to add a new class derived from `PersistentConnection`. We can navigate to **Add | New Item...** in the context menu of the project from the **Solution Explorer** window, and from there look for the **SignalR Persistent Connection Class (v2)** template and use it to create our custom type, which we'll name `EchoConnection`. Visual Studio will create the related file for us, adding some plumbing code in it. For our recipe, we want to keep it simple and see how things work step by step, so we'll remove both methods added by the wizard and leave the code as follows:

```
using Microsoft.AspNet.SignalR;
namespace Recipe25
{
    public class EchoConnection : PersistentConnection
    {
    }
}
```

We could reach the same result manually, but in that case we would have to take care to add the necessary package references from NuGet first. The simplest way in this case would be to reference the Microsoft ASP.NET SignalR package, which will then bring down any other related and necessary module. The process of doing that has already been described earlier, and it should already be well known. With that reference in place, we could then add our class, starting with a simple empty file, with no need for any wizard.

2. We then need to add an OWIN Startup class and set it up so that the `Configuration()` method calls `app.MapSignalR<...>(...);` in order to properly initiate the persistent connection class we just added. We should end up with a `Startup.cs` file that looks like the following code:

```
using Microsoft.Owin;
using Owin;
[assembly: OwinStartup(typeof(Recipe25.Startup))]
namespace Recipe25
{
    public class Startup
    {
        public void Configuration(IAppBuilder app)
        {
            app.MapSignalR<EchoConnection>("/echo");
        }
    }
}
```

We already described the usage of the `OwinStartup` attribute at the beginning of the book; therefore, we'll skip any details about that. The usual `Configuration()` method calls `MapSignalR()`, but this time it uses a different overload, supplying `EchoConnection` as the type of our connection class and `/echo` as the name of the related endpoint. Behind the scenes, what `MapSignalR()` does is quite similar to what was happening when we were using the Hubs API; however, in this case, there is a little bit less magic because we have to explicitly specify both the type of the connection class and the URL from where it will be exposed. If we had more than one connection class to expose, we would have to call the `MapSignalR()` method once for each of them, and we would have to specify different URL addresses each time. It's worth noting that the endpoint name *must* begin with a `/` character. If we omit it, SignalR will raise an exception.

3. Let's go back to our `EchoConnection` class and write some code to be executed when a new connection is performed. In order to achieve that, we have to override the `OnConnected()` method from `PersistentConnection` as shown in the following code:

```
protected override Task OnConnected(IRequest request,
    string connectionId)
{
    System.Diagnostics.Trace.WriteLine("Connected");
    return null;
}
```

`OnConnected()` is one of the overridable methods mentioned in the *Introduction* section of the chapter, and its role is to give us a point from where we can handle every incoming connection.

The first argument of the method is an instance of an object implementing the `IRequest` interface, which is a SignalR interface whose role is to describe the HTTP incoming request. It's similar to the very well-known ASP.NET `Request` object, but this version is much lighter and focused on what's needed in the context of SignalR, without exposing anything that could harm its efficiency, such as the (somewhat infamous) `Session` object or a read-write `Cookies` collection.

The second argument is of type `string` and contains the connection identifier generated during the handshaking steps performed while setting up the connection.

`OnConnected()` returns a `Task` instance, and in this way it's declaring its asynchronous nature. But, in our case, we do not really have anything special to send back to its caller, so finalizing the code of the method with `return null;` will be just fine.

The only relevant line of code in our method is simply sending a diagnostic message to any Trace listener available.

We are done, and it's been pretty straightforward. Now any client hitting the /echo endpoint will be handled by this class, and at every *new connection*, the OnConnect() method will be called. When we say new connection, we actually mean whenever SignalR performs a full handshaking cycle, selecting and applying a connection strategy as we already saw earlier in the book. If a specific client (for example, a browser window) loses its connection and is able to reconnect just after the reconnection retry timeout has expired, a new full-blown connection will be built, a new connectionId value will be assigned to it and OnConnect() will be called again.

We need a client to test if everything is working properly. To achieve this goal, let's add an HTML page called index.html, which we'll use to build our client. In this page, we'll link all the necessary JavaScript files that have already been added to the project when the Microsoft ASP.NET SignalR package has been referenced. Let's proceed.

4. We first reference jQuery using the following code:

```
<script src="Scripts/jquery-2.1.0.js"></script>
```

5. Then we need to link the SignalR JavaScript library with the following line of code:

```
<script src="Scripts/jquery.signalR-2.0.2.js"></script>
```

At this point, we used to add a reference to the dynamic hubs endpoint in the previous recipes, but this is not the case here. We do not need it because we are not using the Hubs API, and therefore we don't need dynamic proxies that are typical of that way of using SignalR. The SignalR JavaScript library that we just added contains all that's necessary to use the Persistent Connection API.

6. We finally add a simple script to connect to the server as follows:

```
<script>

    $(function() {
        var c = $.connection('echo');
        c.start()
          .done(function(x) {
             console.log(c);
             console.log(x);       //x and c are the same!
          });
    });

</script>
```

Here we first interact with the `$.connection` member we already saw when describing the Hubs API, but in this case we do not use it to access the `hubs` property. Instead, we use it as a function to ask SignalR to create a `connection` object pointing at the endpoint we specify as its only argument (echo). The returned object has a similar role to the one the `hubs` member has; in fact, we can call `start()` on it to launch the actual connection process, and the returned value is again a JavaScript promise object whose completion we can wait for, thanks to the `done()` method, in order to ensure that a connection has been fully established. Our simple code prints out both the `connection` object we obtained (the c variable) and the argument supplied to the `done()` callback (the x variable) just to show that they are actually the same object, and we are free to pick any of them when a connection reference is needed.

To test what we did, we just need to run the project from Visual Studio and open the `index.html` page using the **Developer Tools** of the browser of choice to check the messages printed on the **browser console**.

How it works...

The SignalR `$.connection` object exposes the low-level connection object, which is the real subject of this chapter. Its server-side counterpart can be any type derived from `PersistentConnection` that has been previously registered under the same endpoint address targeted when calling the `$.connection()` function. Any major event happening on the connection is then exposed on the server by events that can be intercepted by overriding a bunch of protected methods. In this recipe, we saw how we can be notified about new connections just by overriding the `OnConnected()` method. We'll see a few more of those in future recipes.

The rest of the client-side code is very simple, and it's very similar to what we have been doing when starting connections with the Hubs API; the only big difference so far is the fact that we do not use the dynamically generated `hubs` member anymore.

Sending messages from the server

Now that we have a good idea about how `PersistentConnection` can be registered and then used in our applications, let's go deeper and start sending some data with it. As usual, in SignalR, we need a client and a server to establish a connection, and both parts can send and receive data. Here we'll see how a server can push messages to any connected client, and we'll analyze what a message looks like.

We already mentioned the fact that any communication from client to server could, of course, be performed using plain old HTTP, but pushing information from a server to any connected client without any specific client request for that data is not normally possible, and that's where SignalR really helps.

We'll also start appreciating the fact that this API stands at a lower level when compared to the Hubs API because its features are more basic, but at the same time we'll see that it's still a very useful, powerful, and easy-to-use API.

Getting ready

Before writing the code for this recipe, we need to create a new empty web application, which we'll call `Recipe26`.

How to do it...

The following are the steps to build the server part:

1. We first need to add a new class derived from `PersistentConnection`, which we'll name `EchoConnection`. We can go back to the previous recipe to see the options we have to accomplish that, always paying attention to every detail in order to have the right package references in place. We want to end up with an `EchoConnection.cs` file containing an empty class having the following code:

```
using Microsoft.AspNet.SignalR;
namespace Recipe26
{
    public class EchoConnection : PersistentConnection
    {
    }
}
```

2. We then need to add the usual OWIN Startup class and set it up so that the `Configuration()` method calls `app.MapSignalR<EchoConnection>("/echo");` in order to properly wire the persistent connection class we just added to our project. This is actually the same step we took in the previous recipe, and we will be doing the same through the remainder of this chapter. The final code will look like the following:

```
using Microsoft.Owin;
using Owin;
[assembly: OwinStartup(typeof(Recipe26.Startup))]
namespace Recipe26
{
    public class Startup
    {
        public void Configuration(IAppBuilder app)
        {
            app.MapSignalR<EchoConnection>("/echo");
        }
    }
}
```

3. Back to our `EchoConnection` class, we want to redefine the `OnConnected()` overridable method, whose function we already described earlier, and from there send a message to the client that just connected. This is as simple as coding the following:

```
protected override Task OnConnected(IRequest request,
    string connectionId)
{
    return Connection.Send(connectionId, "Welcome!");
}
```

The `PersistentConnection` class exposes several useful members, and one of the most important is for sure the `Connection` property, of type `IConnection`, which returns an object that allows us to communicate with the connected clients. A bunch of methods on the `IConnection` interface let us send data to specific sets of connections (`Send()`), or target all the connected clients at the same time (`Broadcast()`). In our example, we use the simplest overload of `Send()` to push a string payload down to the client that just connected. Both `Send()` and `Broadcast()` run asynchronously and return a `Task` instance, which we can directly use as the return value of the `OnConnect()` method.

Another relevant member inherited from `PersistentConnection` is the `Groups` member, which exposes a couple of `Send()` overloads to push messages down to connections belonging to a specific group. `Groups` also exposes a set of capabilities to manage the members of specific groups the same way the Hubs API does. The concept of groups is very powerful and has already been well illustrated in *Chapter 2, Using Hubs*. There is no conceptual difference here with what we explained earlier, therefore we'll skip any further explanation about it.

All the methods we just mentioned expect a last parameter of type object, which is the actual payload of the call. This value is automatically serialized before going on the wire to reach the clients. When there, the involved client library will deserialize it, giving it back its original shape using the best data type available according to the actual client library used (JavaScript or .NET). In our example, we used a simple `string` type, but any serializable type would do, even an anonymous type.

Back to this sample, any client connecting to the `/echo` endpoint will be handled by the `OnConnect()` method exposed by `EchoConnection`, whose body will send back the message `Welcome!` using the `Send()` call.

Let's build an HTML page called `index.html` to host our client code. In this page, we'll link all the necessary JavaScript files as we already did in the previous recipe, and then we'll add a few lines of code to enable the client to receive and log whatever the server sends.

1. We first reference jQuery and SignalR with the following code:

```
<script src="Scripts/jquery-2.1.0.js"></script>
<script src="Scripts/jquery.signalR-2.0.2.js"></script>
```

2. We then add the following simple piece of script:

```
<script>

    $(function () {
        var c = $.connection('echo');
        c.received(function(message) {
            console.log(message);
        })
        .start();
    });

</script>
```

Here, we first interact with the `$.connection` member in the same way we did in the previous recipe, in order to create a `connection` object towards the endpoint we specify as its argument (echo). We can then call `start()` on the returned object to perform the actual connection, and again the returned value is a JavaScript `promise` object whose completion we could wait for in order to ensure that a connection has been fully established. Before starting up the connection, we use the `received()` method to set up a callback that SignalR will trigger whenever a message will be pushed from the type derived from `PersistentConnection` down to this client, regardless of the actual method used on the server side (`Send()` or `Broadcast()`). Our sample code will just log the received string onto the console. We'll dig more into the `received()` method later in this chapter.

We can test our code by running the project from Visual Studio and opening the `index.html` page using the Developer Tools of the browser to see the received message printed onto the console.

How it works...

Any type derived from `PersistentConnection` that has been correctly registered behind an endpoint can be used to send and receive messages. The underlying established connection is used to move bits back and forth, leveraging a low-level and **highly optimized application protocol** used by SignalR to correctly represent every call, regardless of the underlying **networking protocol**. As usual, everything happens in an asynchronous manner.

We have been mentioning the fact that this is a low-level API compared to Hubs; the reason is that we don't have a concept of methods that we can call on both sides. In fact, what we are allowed to exchange are just data structures; we can do that using a pair of general-purpose methods to send and receive them. We are missing a higher abstraction that will allow us to give more **semantic meaning** to what we exchange, and we have to add that ourselves in order to coordinate any complex custom workflow we want to implement across the involved parts. Nevertheless, this is the only big difference between the two APIs, and almost every other characteristic or capability is exposed by both of them, apart from a couple of shortcomings when dealing with serialization, which we'll illustrate later in this chapter.

You might think that there is no real need to use the Persistent Connection API because Hubs is more powerful and expressive, but that's not always true. For example, you might imagine a scenario where you want your clients to be in charge of dynamically deciding which Hubs to load among a set of available ones, and for that they might need to contact the server anyway to get some relevant information. Hubs are loaded all at once when calling `start()`, so you would not be able to use a Hub to do the first handshaking. But a persistent connection would be just perfect for the job, along with some other advanced feature we'll see in *Chapter 7, Analyzing Advanced Scenarios*, because that can be made available and used before starting any hub.

Sending messages to the server

After looking at how to send messages from the server to the connected clients, let's swap sides and check how to perform the same operation, but in the opposite direction. We'll illustrate this scenario by building a simple JavaScript client that will send a message to the server as soon as the connection will be available.

This specific case is not really useful if taken alone, because any communication from client to server could be easily done by using plain old HTTP. However, when combined with the reception counterpart, it enables the construction of complex, real-time client-server workflows.

Getting ready

Before writing the code of this recipe, we need to create a new empty web application, which we'll call `Recipe27`.

How to do it...

Let's first check how to build the server portion using the following steps:

1. We first add a new class named `EchoConnection` that is derived from `PersistentConnection`, as we already did in the previous recipes of this chapter, and we will clean up the content generated by Visual Studio in order to have an empty class body, as follows:

```
using Microsoft.AspNet.SignalR;
namespace Recipe27
{
    public class EchoConnection : PersistentConnection
    {
    }
}
```

2. As usual, we then add the OWIN Startup class with a `Configuration()` method calling `app.MapSignalR<EchoConnection>("/echo");` to map our Remove class derived from `PersistentConnection`, as shown in the following code:

```
using Microsoft.Owin;
using Owin;
[assembly: OwinStartup(typeof(Recipe27.Startup))]
namespace Recipe27
{
    public class Startup
    {
        public void Configuration(IAppBuilder app)
        {
            app.MapSignalR<EchoConnection>("/echo");
        }
    }
}
```

3. In our `EchoConnection` class, we can handle any incoming message in one place by simply overriding the `OnReceived()` method exposed by `PersistentConnection` as follows:

```
protected override Task OnReceived(IRequest request,
    string connectionId, string data)
{
    ...
}
```

This method will be called every time a client will use the available API method to send messages, and it will be supplied the following:

- An instance of `IRequest` that contains some context information related to the current HTTP request
- The identifier of the calling connection
- A string payload containing the body of the request

It's very basic and straightforward, but simple to use. One important detail we can appreciate here is the fact that the data payload is of type `string`, while the counterpart server-side `Send()` method we saw in the previous recipe was accepting any `object` and taking care of its serialization on the wire. In the case of `OnReceived()`, we stay at a lower level because the API does not offer any way to specify how the payload should be deserialized; therefore, the most sensible representation for the message is a string, which is the simplest way to represent the most common case of simple textual messages. This does not prevent us from sending more complex objects on the wire, but the deserialization task is not automatic, and we have to take care of it by ourselves.

4. Let's complete the body of our `OnReceived()` method with a simple call to send what we just received to any Trace listener available, and then by returning a `null` value, as follows:

```
System.Diagnostics.Trace.WriteLine(
    string.Format("Received: {0}", data));
return null;
```

Let's now build a corresponding client. As we always did through this chapter so far, we will use an HTML page called `index.html`. As usual, we'll need to reference the JavaScript files we already used in the previous recipes first, and then we'll add a couple of lines of code to send a message to the server as soon as the connection will be available.

1. We first reference jQuery and SignalR using the following code:

```
<script src="Scripts/jquery-2.1.0.js"></script>
<script src="Scripts/jquery.signalR-2.0.2.js"></script>
```

2. We then add our piece of script as follows:

```
<script>

    $(function () {
        var c = $.connection('echo');
        c.start()
          .done(function() {
            c.send('hello');
        });
    });

</script>
```

How it works...

Through the $.connection member, we first create a connection object pointing to the /echo endpoint, then we can call start() on it to perform the actual connection, and eventually we use the done() method to declare the function callback to be asynchronously invoked when the connection will be ready. Inside the callback, we can safely call the send() method on the connection object, passing on whatever value we want (in this case, a hello string). SignalR will take care of building a proper representation of it, serializing it as a string, and using JSON if necessary. As we already said earlier, the payload will be received by the server as a plain string anyway, so this feature is clearly handy on the client side but has to be handled with care because it forces us to perform an explicit deserialization step on the server.

We are done. Let's open the index.html page and check the **Output** window in Visual Studio to see the **hello** string printed out.

Exchanging messages between a server and a JavaScript client

Let's move on and put things together in order to build a simple test application where both the server and client will be sending and receiving payloads. To make things more interesting, we'll stop using simple strings, and we'll be illustrating how to handle serialization and deserialization of complex objects. In order to do that inside our type derived from PersistentConnection, we'll be using the **JSON.Net** library from **Newtonsoft**, which has been chosen as the default JSON handling library by the ASP.NET team, and it's already referenced any time you add SignalR on your server-side projects.

Getting ready

Before writing the code of this recipe, we need to create a new empty web application, which we'll call Recipe28.

How to do it...

As usual, we start with the server-side portion of the application using the following steps:

1. We add a new class named EchoConnection that is derived from PersistentConnection, cleaning up the content generated by Visual Studio in order to have an empty class body:

    ```
    using Microsoft.AspNet.SignalR;
    namespace Recipe28
    {
        public class EchoConnection : PersistentConnection
    ```

```
        {
        }
    }
```

2. Let's then add the OWIN Startup class with a `Configuration()` method calling
    `app.MapSignalR<EchoConnection>( "/echo");` to map the class derived
    from `PersistentConnection` as follows:

```
using Microsoft.Owin;
using Owin;
[assembly: OwinStartup(typeof(Recipe28.Startup))]
namespace Recipe28
{
    public class Startup
    {
        public void Configuration(IAppBuilder app)
        {
            app.MapSignalR<EchoConnection>("/echo");
        }
    }
}
```

3. Back to our `EchoConnection` class, we can handle any incoming message by
    overriding the `OnReceived()` method exposed by `PersistentConnection`.
    That's where we will handle any incoming payload, analyze them, and build the
    corresponding response messages. In this example, we'll be using the `Broadcast()`
    method to distribute them to all the connected clients, as shown in the following code:

```
protected override Task OnReceived(IRequest request,
    string connectionId, string data)
{
    var payload = Newtonsoft.Json.JsonConvert
        .DeserializeAnonymousType(
            data,
            new { body = "" });
    var body = string.Format("You said: {0}",
        payload.body);
    return Connection.Broadcast(new { body = body });
}
```

We first make use of the `JsonConvert` helper class from JSON.Net to access the `DeserializeAnonymousType()` method that allows us to map a JSON string onto an anonymous type defined on the fly by passing an empty instance of it as the second argument of the call. Anonymous types are very handy when we need to define local data structures with no special behavior and without the burden of a full-blown class definition. Different anonymous type instances are matched across the code scope, and if they contain the same members (of the same type and in the same order), they end up being of the same type. `DeserializeAnonymousType()` returns a value of type `T`, where `T` is the same as the type of the template anonymous type instance we passed to it, which in this case is this `new { body = "" }` instance. The payload variable will therefore be of the same type, and this means that we are in fact defining the shape of the content we expect to find in the received data string. At this point, we can easily read inside the payload in a strongly typed manner and use its content to build a new object with the same shape but different content (`new { body = body }`), and use it to broadcast our response to all the connected clients.

The approach we used when dealing with the serialization is just an example illustrating one option, and we could have taken several other approaches, but it should illustrate the kind of problems you might have to face when using the Persistent Connection API, and which direction to take when trying to solve them.

Let's now build a JavaScript client exchanging messages with the same shape as the ones we just defined.

1. We first reference jQuery and SignalR using the following code:

```
<script src="Scripts/jquery-2.1.0.js"></script>
<script src="Scripts/jquery.signalR-2.0.2.js"></script>
```

2. We then define our client logic with the following code:

```
<script>

    $(function () {
        var c = $.connection('echo');
        c.received(function(message) {
            console.log('Received: ' + message.body);
        })
        .start()
        .done(function () {
            c.send({ body: 'hello' });
        });
    });

</script>
```

This code is pretty simple. It's just using both the `send()` and `received()` methods we saw in the previous recipes of the chapter, making sure that `received()` is called before starting the connection and `send()` is used when the connection is ready.

We are ready to test our code by launching the project from Visual Studio and navigating to the `index.html` page, while opening the Developer Tools of the browser we are using to check the shape of the received message. If we open multiple tabs pointing at the same page, we'll see how the messages are broadcasted to all the already available clients as soon as they connect for the first time.

How it works...

What's more interesting is how we deal with the exchanged payloads, which are JavaScript objects with the same shape of the anonymous types inside the server-side `OnReceived()` method. We send an object like `{ body: 'hello' }` and we expect to receive messages with the same shape. SignalR is smart enough to match these equivalent definitions when going from the server to the client, whereas it needs some help from us when going the other way round, as we saw when describing what we have to do to interpret the incoming payload in the `OnReceived()` method.

Exchanging messages between a server and a .NET client

SignalR's natural environment is the Web, that's why we tend to prefer the JavaScript client for our examples that illustrate its features. Nevertheless, the .NET client is as important and relevant as the JavaScript one, and it definitely deserves to be analyzed too. This last recipe of the chapter will be a translation of what we did in the previous recipe, but here the JavaScript client code will be replaced by C# code hosted in a console application. The server-side portion of this example will be the same as the one we wrote in the previous recipe, hence we'll avoid repeating the same code here and we'll be connecting to that application instead, using the same approach we had been applying throughout *Chapter 4, Using the .NET Hubs Client API*.

Getting ready

As already mentioned, we'll be connecting to the server we wrote in the previous recipe, so make sure you have that code ready and running before proceeding. Let's then create a console application project, naming it `Recipe29`, and then let's add to it the **Microsoft ASP. NET SignalR .NET Client** package from NuGet, as already explained in *Chapter 4, Using the .NET Hubs Client API*.

How to do it...

The Program class source code must be modified in the following manner:

1. We first add the necessary using directives as follows:

   ```
   using System;
   using System.Threading.Tasks;
   using Microsoft.AspNet.SignalR.Client;
   ```

2. We then apply the strategy we already described in *Chapter 4, Using the .NET Hubs Client API*, in order to be able to use the async/await syntax for our asynchronous calls as follows:

   ```
   static void Main(string[] args)
   {
       Do().Wait();
   }
   static async Task Do()
   {
       ...
   }
   ```

3. Let's start writing the actual implementation of the Do() method by preparing the connection as follows:

   ```
   const string url = "http://localhost:14622/echo";
   var connection = new Connection(url);
   ```

   The SignalR client library exposes a Connection type, which is the equivalent of the $.connection object we used with the JavaScript client. This type plays the same role as the HubConnection type we saw in *Chapter 4, Using the .NET Hubs Client API*, but it works on the lower-level Persistent Connection API. It has to be configured with an endpoint to target, represented by the URL we are passing as its only argument. The port number we specify (14622) must match the port number used to expose EchoConnection in the previous recipe. Please verify and fix it if it does not.

4. We can now attach event handlers on the `Received` event member exposed by `connection`. In our case, we define just one handler in order to send to the standard output the message we will receive in response to our outgoing call:

```
connection.Received += message =>
    Console.WriteLine("Received: {0}", message);
```

`Received` differs from the equivalent `On()` method from `HubConnection` because in this case we deal with a classic .NET event handler, while `On()` has the goal of registering a callback function to be called by name directly from the server. The more general-purpose approach of the Persistent Connection API fits nicely with the idiom exposed by a plain old .NET event handler.

As for the JavaScript client, the declaration of these event handlers must be done before connecting to the server.

5. Now we are ready to connect to our Hub using the following code:

```
await connection.Start();
```

This code is asynchronously initiating the connection and, as we already saw in the earlier recipes, we are waiting for its completion thanks to the `await` keyword.

6. When the connection is ready, we can call the `Send()` method exposed by the `Connection` type and supply our payload to it as follows:

```
connection.Send(new { body = "Hello" });
```

The `Send()` method is very straightforward, and it's basically the same as the one we saw when discussing the JavaScript client. The supplied payload is an instance of an anonymous type, whose shape must match the one we are expecting to receive on the server side of the previous recipe, and you can easily verify that it does. In this way, we'll ensure that the server will be able to correctly understand what we are sending to it.

7. We eventually make our code wait for the user to press *Enter* before exiting the application as follows:

```
Console.WriteLine("Sending...");
Console.ReadLine();
```

There is something worth noting about the `Received` member: it does not conform to the traditional signature of an event handler. Usually, two arguments are expected as follows:

▸ The sender of the event

▸ A type derived from `EventArgs` that passes any context information

In the case of `Received`, the sender is not provided, and the context is in the form of a simple string containing the received payload. Should the server send a complex object, the `Received` event would be supplied with its JSON representation.

We are ready to test our code by launching the project from Visual Studio and observing the output displayed on the console window.

How it works...

What goes on behind the scenes is no different from what we have been describing earlier in this chapter, but there is something interesting to highlight about the way we called `Send()`. In fact, even if it's an asynchronous method and could therefore be awaited, in our code we are not waiting for its completion as we have normally been doing earlier in the book. Because of that, the final effect is something like what's shown in the following screenshot:

You can see that the **Sending...** message is printed out before the received payload, and that's because we did not wait for `Send()` to complete. We can modify our call on the `Send()` method to be like the following code:

```
await connection.Send(new { body = "Hello" });
```

In this case, the output will change, reflecting the fact that we used `await` to wait for the call to complete, and the two messages would be swapped.

It's also worth noting that the server payload is received as a string, whose content represents the JSON serialization of the object prepared on the server side. This illustrates the fact that, even if the type used to exchange messages is a simple string, a complex object is able to go through anyway, and it can be received and then properly deserialized if enough knowledge about its shape is available to the client.

6

Handling Connections

In this chapter, we will cover the following recipes:

- ▶ Controlling the lifetime of a connection
- ▶ Handling a connection transient state
- ▶ Establishing a cross-domain connection

Introduction

After having analyzed most of the features SignalR exposes to enable us to add real-time messaging features to our applications, we move into a different set of useful characteristics we can exploit to control our application. In particular, we'll have a deeper look at a bunch of APIs we can leverage to control different aspects concerning the connections we establish across clients and servers. In fact, SignalR works across networks, which we all know we cannot fully trust, and over HTTP, which imposes certain rules when dealing with things such as server origin and connection lifetime or state.

Controlling the lifetime of a connection

SignalR lets us control several aspects of the **connection lifetime** on both the server and the client side. SignalR has the goal of delivering a simple experience based on the idea of a persistent connection, but we cannot really rely on the assumption that it will always be available, because too many factors may interfere with it. While it's true that SignalR does its best to isolate us from these kind of problems, thanks to smart connection strategies and recovery procedures, on the other hand we might need to have finer control over what's happening behind the scenes, and we might want to handle the anomalies and the reconnection procedures ourselves.

In this first recipe of the chapter, we'll use a Hub to illustrate how we can monitor when the connection state changes over time. Later, we will also write a simple JavaScript client in order to show how we can perform the same kind of checks on the client side.

Getting ready

Before writing the code of this recipe, we need to create a new **empty web application** project, which we'll call `Recipe30`.

How to do it...

Let's build our project, concentrating first on the server-side code, using the following steps:

1. We first add a new empty Hub by navigating to **Add | New Item...** on the context menu of the project in the **Solution Explorer** window, and from there looking for the **SignalR Hub Class (v2)** template to create our `EchoHub` class. We just want to monitor the connection status and therefore will not need any specific method on our Hub. Let's make it look like the following code:

```
using System.Diagnostics;
using System.Threading.Tasks;
using Microsoft.AspNet.SignalR;
using Microsoft.AspNet.SignalR.Hubs;

namespace Recipe30
{
    [HubName("echo")]
    public class EchoHub : Hub
    {
    }
}
```

2. We then need, as usual, a `Startup` class, which we will create in the same way we did so far for most of the recipes. However, this time, we will specify a set of useful parameters inside the `Configuration()` method, as shown in the following code:

```
public class Startup
{
    public void Configuration(IAppBuilder app)
    {
        GlobalHost.Configuration.DisconnectTimeout =
            TimeSpan.FromSeconds(30);
        GlobalHost.Configuration.ConnectionTimeout =
            TimeSpan.FromSeconds(110);
        GlobalHost.Configuration.KeepAlive =
            TimeSpan.FromSeconds(10);

        app.MapSignalR();
    }
}
```

The `GlobalHost` object exposes a `Configuration` member, through which we can change some default settings that influence how the connection handling is performed (the values in the sample code are the current defaults defined by SignalR). The values are described as follows:

- `DisconnectTimeout`: This asks SignalR to wait a maximum number of seconds after a transport connection is lost before raising a `Disconnected` event, and terminating the failed logical connection

- `ConnectionTimeout`: In case **long polling** is used, transport connections will be kept around for a maximum number of seconds waiting for a response; when that timeout expires with no activity, the client will be forced to open a new connection

- `KeepAlive`: For transports other than long polling, this regulates how often a keepalive packet is sent to avoid the underlying connection being dropped because of inactivity; this value must be no more than one-third of the `DisconnectTimeout` value, and SignalR automatically adjusts this value accordingly to this rule if `DisconnectTimeout` is specified without setting `KeepAlive` explicitly afterwards

3. Let's go back to our `EchoHub` class to override a set of methods exposed by any Hub-derived type. Those methods will notify us about specific logical events happening on the connection. When we say *logical event*, we are talking in the context of the level of abstraction defined by SignalR on top of the actual events occurring at the transport or physical level on the network. Let's look at the following code:

```
public override Task OnConnected()
{
    Trace.WriteLine(string.Format("Connected: {0}",
        Context.ConnectionId));
    return base.OnConnected();
}
public override Task OnDisconnected()
{
    Trace.WriteLine(string.Format("Disconnected: {0}",
        Context.ConnectionId));
    return base.OnDisconnected();
}
public override Task OnReconnected()
{
    Trace.WriteLine(string.Format("Reconnected: {0}",
        Context.ConnectionId));
    return base.OnReconnected();
}
```

As we can see, there are three methods that can be overriddenRedundant:

- ❑ `OnConnected()`: This is triggered *only the first time a connection is established*, and a new connection ID is assigned to the calling client

- ❑ `OnReconnected()`: This can be triggered several times, *once each time a connection is reestablished* by SignalR *after a lower-level network disconnection*, and this happens every time SignalR is able to rebuild the same logical connection on top of a potentially new underlying one; in this case, *the connection ID does not change*

- ❑ `OnDisconnected()`: This is triggered when a *low-level disconnection* occurs and *SignalR is not able to establish it again* before the `DisconnectTimeout` interval has expired; the logical connection is dropped, and in order to contact the server again, the *client will have to start a new connection*, thus *receiving a new connection ID*

Inside our method implementations, we just trace the name of the event and the connection identifier involved, and then call the base implementation.

Let's now build a client we will use to test our code. Both the JavaScript (the one we are going to use) and the .NET client libraries have similar connection control features. In our code, we will use them to perform the same kind of checks we've been performing on the server side.

4. We add an HTML page called `index.html`, which we'll use to build our client, and where we'll reference the usual JavaScript files that have already been added to the project when the Microsoft ASP.NET SignalR package has been referenced by adding `EchoHub`. Somewhere in the page body, we'll also add a button that we'll use to toggle a connection to the server and test our control code, as shown in the following code:

```
<script src="Scripts/jquery-2.1.0.js"></script>
<script src="Scripts/jquery.signalR-2.0.2.js"></script>
<script src="/signalr/hubs"></script>
. . .
<button id="toggle" disabled="true">
    Toggle connection</button>
```

5. We are ready to write our client code inside a script block, initializing a couple of useful reference variables as follows:

```
<script>
    $(function() {

        var hub - $.connection.hub,
            echo = $.connection.echo;

        . . .

    });
</script>
```

6. On the `hub` variable, we can supply a set of callback functions to be called when specific connection events happen:

```
hub.starting(function () {
    console.log('starting'); //no hub.id yet!
});
hub.reconnecting(function () {
    console.log('reconnecting: ' + hub.id);
});
hub.reconnected(function () {
    console.log('reconnected: ' + hub.id);
});
hub.disconnected(function () {
    console.log('disconnected: ' + hub.id);
});


. . .
```

The names and their corresponding meanings are straightforward. Because a connection is always initiated by the client, we have a `starting` event and a `reconnecting` event available, which are client-only events with no matching counterpart on the server side.

7. We can also supply a callback to be called whenever a change in the connection state happens, as depicted in the following code:

```
hub.stateChanged(function (state) {
    console.log('stateChanged: ' + hub.id);
    console.log(state);
    $("#toggle").attr('disabled',
        state.newState !=
            $.signalR.connectionState.connected &&
        state.newState !=
            $.signalR.connectionState.disconnected);
});


. . .
```

In the callback supplied to the `stateChanged()` method, we can output the current state whenever it changes, and we enable or disable the `toggle` button accordingly. The possible connection states are defined as properties exposed by the `$.signalR.connectionState` member declared inside the referenced `jQuery.signalR-(version).js` file.

8. Now we do quite a curious thing. Have a look at the following code:

```
echo.client.dummy = function() { };
```

. . .

Why this? In this example, we are using the Hubs API with dynamic proxies because it's the most common, simple, and straightforward way to use SignalR. However, as of today, the previously mentioned server-side events are not generated if there are no client-side callbacks available. We need to have at least one of them in place, even if we will never call it; that's why we added the dummy one. It's worth making clear that, although it's something that we do on the client side, this is not necessary to make the *client-side* events work. It's there to make the *server-side* ones work, and there's no need to call that method from the server at all. Of course, if you already have proper client-side callbacks to be invoked from the server side, those will be just fine with no need for a dummy one, and the client-side events will work just fine. It's a curious and quite strange thing to do, but that's how it currently works and it might be improved in future versions.

9. Let's finalize our client-side portion with the following code, which will toggle the connection on or off each time a button called **toggle** is clicked on:

```
var starter = function() {
    return hub
    .start()
    .done(function () {
        console.log('connected: ' +
        hub.id);
    });
};

$("#toggle").click(function () {
    $("#toggle").attr('disabled', true);
    if ($.signalR.connectionState.disconnected ==
        echo.connection.state)
        starter();
    else if ($.signalR.connectionState.connected ==
        echo.connection.state)
        hub.stop();
});

starter();
```

It's interesting to observe the usage of the `stop()` member exposed by `hub` to explicitly and gracefully end a connection. We never explicitly mentioned it before because it's quite a rare thing to do, but it's good to know that it's possible in case you need it.

We are ready to test the code that we just wrote by launching the application and navigating to the `index.html` page. Each time we'll click on the **toggle** connection button, we'll alternatively turn the connection on and off, and these actions will trigger the client- and server-side events that we hooked into with our code. It will be interesting for you to try breaking the network connection between the browser and the web server in any way you may want too, and observe the reconnection events happening automatically according to the timeout values we have set earlier.

How it works...

What happens under the hood is pretty smart and complex, and the details are out of the scope of this book. That said, it's important to understand that each time a persistent connection is created, SignalR tries its best to keep it alive despite any possible lower-level network disruption, hiding these kind of problems from us. Whenever these attempts fail and SignalR decides that the connection is lost, it will not try to fix it anymore; the only way for the client to connect again will be to perform a full connection restart, hence generating a new connection ID. This is one of the reasons why the action of associating any state information to a connection identifier, which is one of the most common needs, it's definitely possible but should be done in full awareness of these implications. You will have to write defensive code that is aware of the fact that the connection ID might go away anytime.

Handling a connection transient state

In the previous recipe, we talked about how a persistent connection can experience problems that SignalR tries to fix automatically. We also saw that such a logical connection is represented by a unique identifier, which is lost when SignalR is not able to recover from underlying failures anymore. As long as the persistent connection is alive, SignalR offers a simple way to associate some transient state to it in the form of a **property bag** that can be read and written on both the client and server side. For simple scenarios, where we want to maintain some information associated with each connection and use it on both sides to adjust the behavior of available methods/callbacks, this API can be quite useful. The usual scenarios could be related to classical cross-cutting concerns (authorization and logging), but it could be used for anything.

In this recipe, we'll build a simple case where we maintain a transient property called `name`, and we manipulate it on both sides to show how SignalR keeps it in sync transparently whenever a call is performed from one side to the other. Keep in mind that no state synchronization is performed unless a call is triggered; that's when the state is transported and eventually aligned on the other end.

We make the sample a little bit more interesting by adding some client-side logic to store such a transient property in a **persistent cookie** whenever it's modified, and then retrieve it back from there when we refresh the page. This way, this transient state will actually become locally persistent, supplying a simple mechanism to make such a state resilient to connection failures. The cookie is just used on the client for the goal we just mentioned, and it's never used on the server. That comes at a cost, of course, because our code will need to write the cookie each time we modify the state, as we'll see soon.

Getting ready

Before writing the code of this recipe, we need to create a new empty web application, which we'll call `Recipe31`.

How to do it...

The structure of this project is pretty standard, with the usual suspects in place. We will perform the following steps:

1. We need a `Startup` class, which we will create as we did so far for most of the recipes. The following code is added to it:

```
public class Startup
{
    public void Configuration(IAppBuilder app)
    {
        app.MapSignalR();
    }
}
```

2. Then we need a Hub, and we use the **SignalR Hub Class (v2)** template to create it and name it `EchoHub`. The details (`using` directives, name) are the same we saw in most of the previous recipes, so we'll skip them. We will need just one method, which will conveniently return a simple string, but we'll also use the transient state API to make a simple value go back and forth between the server and the client, as follows:

```
public string SayHello()
{
    Clients.Caller.name = Clients.Caller.name ?? "(no name)";
    return "Hello!";
}
```

The highlighted line of code accesses the `Caller` member from the `Clients` property that we inherited from the base class `Hub`, and from there it first reads a property called `name`, which then is assigned a default value `"(no name)"`; if it happens to be empty. This `name` property does not exist out of the box; we just defined it dynamically. We already saw in the previous recipes that `Caller` is a dynamic property, and this characteristic is leveraged to allow developers to add properties on it as they are needed. Such properties are automatically kept in sync on both the server and the client when any remote call happens. This code is pretty simple. If `name` has a value, that value is kept; if not, it's set to a fixed value. The only possible way to have `name` different from `null` before this line is to have it assigned by the client.

Let's move to the client side, where we'll access the same `name` property, using a cookie to persist its value across different connections.

1. We add an HTML page called `index.html`, linking the usual JavaScript files that have been added to the project when the Microsoft ASP.NET SignalR package has been referenced by adding our server-side bits. At some point in the page body, we'll also add a textbox to edit the `name` property, and a button to call our server-side Hub method, as shown in the following code:

    ```
    <script src="Scripts/jquery-2.1.0.js"></script>
    <script src="Scripts/jquery.signalR-2.0.2.js"></script>
    <script src="/signalr/hubs"></script>
    . . .
    Name: <input id="name" type="text"/>
    <button id="sayHello">Say Hello!</button>
    ```

2. Let's then add a script block and start writing our code by adding a couple of utility functions to read and write the persistent cookies as follows:

    ```
    <script>

        function setCookie(name, value, expirationDays) {
            var d = new Date();
            d.setTime(d.getTime() +
                (expirationDays * 24 * 60 * 60 * 1000));
            var expires = "expires=" + d.toGMTString();
            document.cookie =
                name + "=" + value + "; " + expires;
        }
        function getCookie(name) {
            var start = name + "=";
            var items = document.cookie.split(';');
            for (var i = 0; i < items.length; i++) {
                var c = items[i].trim();
                if (c.indexOf(start) == 0)
    ```

```
                            return c.substring(start.length,
                                c.length);
                    }
                    return "";
            }

            . . .


    </script>
```

This code is pretty simple, and it's not directly related to SignalR, so we'll skip any comment about it.

3. We then move on to write our actual logic inside of the usual jQuery callback that is triggered when the page document is ready. Refer to the following code:

```
    $(function () {

            var cookieName = 'name',
                hub = $.connection.hub,
                echo = $.connection.echo;

            $("#name").val(getCookie(cookieName));

            . . .

    });
```

We start by defining a few handy variables, and then we assign a `name` textbox with the value read from a cookie called `name`, if that exists. If it does not, an empty value is put in the textbox.

4. We declare a new function, `sayHello()`, whose goal is to handle the transient state and sync it with both the persistent cookie and the textbox, as follows:

```
    var sayHello = function() {
            echo.state.name = $("#name").val();
            setCookie(cookieName, echo.state.name, 7);
            echo.server
                .sayHello()
                .done(function () {
                    console.log(echo.state.name);
                });
    };

    . . .
```

The `echo` variable that references the dynamic proxy contains a member called `state`, which is the property bag where the transient state is maintained. It plays the same role as the `Caller` member we saw on the server side, and the property values set there are kept in sync between the client and server each time a message goes in one direction or the other. The code is quite simple. We assign the value of the textbox to the transient state, then we save it in the cookie, and finally we call the `sayHello()` method exposed by `EchoHub`, which in theory has nothing to do with the state itself, but in practice makes it travel towards the server transparently, as mentioned while introducing this recipe.

5. We finalize our code by starting the connection, and when the connection is ready we execute the previously defined `sayHello()` method. Finally, we bind the same `sayHello()` function to the `click` event of the button on the page as follows, to allow us to call it again whenever we want:

    ```
    hub
        .start()
        .done(sayHello);

    $("#sayHello").click(sayHello);
    ```

We can test our code by launching the project and navigating to `index.html`. The very first time the persistent cookie will be empty, and it will then be filled with the value in the textbox each time we click on the button on the page. Every following time we load the page, the textbox and the transient state property called `name` will be set with the value read from the cookie. Each value put in the property bag will travel to the server side at each button click because of the call towards the Hub method, and this transparently pushes the state bag to the server. The same happens the other way round, when we modify the state bag on the server that's propagated to the client when the server-side method returns, or in case any client callback execution is triggered by the Hub.

Establishing a cross-domain connection

So far across this book, we've mostly been looking at *web* scenarios, where web browsers connect to web servers. Moreover, we saw that .NET clients are also used, thanks to the SignalR .NET client library, and we have shown how to perform self-hosting of a SignalR server inside a .NET process. In all these cases, we've always been working in scenarios where the channel between the client and server was established in optimal conditions. On one hand, a .NET client does not have any particular problem in connecting to any type of server, whereas all our examples using web browsers as clients have always been written as simple and self-contained web applications, implying that the asynchronous requests performed by the client code were always going towards the same endpoint from where the client itself was downloaded. This is the most common *same-origin* scenario, but there might be other scenarios where the client code does not come from the same origin it tries to connect to. We call such a case a **cross-origin** scenario, where the client code is hosted on a different domain from the one hosting the SignalR endpoint we want to connect to.

This scenario is quite common in cases where a service is intended to be consumed by third-party applications, usually developed and hosted independently from the service itself. In such cases, the JavaScript code consuming the service would most likely come from a different origin than the one exposing it. This is a more delicate situation because it can introduce security issues. Therefore, such kinds of communication is normally forbidden, and that's a relevant problem for the SignalR JavaScript client library.

If we assume that we are using a modern browser (IE greater than 9, and any other recent browser), we can leverage the fact that they all implement the **Cross-Origin Resource Sharing** (**CORS**) specification. As usual, we will not go too much into the details because it is beyond the scope of this book. What we need to know is that the CORS specification allows a web server to list specific client origins to which access should be granted. You can easily check the CORS specification details on the Web, for example, starting with Wikipedia: `http://en.wikipedia.org/wiki/Cross-origin_resource_sharing`.

We do not treat the legacy browser scenario, but it's also supported. It involves enabling **JSONP support** (`http://en.wikipedia.org/wiki/JSONP`), and it's described in SignalR's official documentation.

Getting ready

Before writing the code of this recipe, we need to create a new empty web application, which we'll call `Recipe32`, and we'll use it as the application delivering the client portion of our solution. We will need a server portion from a different application, and for that we'll use the one we built in the previous recipe. In this way, we avoid wasting too much time building things we already know and that are not the actual point of this recipe. For this reason, please make sure that the code for `Recipe31` is ready and working before proceeding.

How to do it...

Let's start with the client code in `Recipe32`, because it's the simplest part of the solution. We'll be using Hubs through the SignalR dynamic proxies feature. We will perform the following steps:

1. Because we are not building a server portion in this project, we'll just need to reference the **Microsoft.AspNet.SignalR.JS** NuGet package using either the **Manage NugGet Packages...** project context menu or the **Package Manager Console**.

2. We then add an HTML page called `index.html`, linking the usual JavaScript files that have been added to the project with the previous step, as shown in the following code:

```html
<script src="Scripts/jquery-2.1.0.js"></script>
<script src="Scripts/jquery.signalR-2.0.2.js"></script>
```

3. We can now add a reference to the Hub endpoint, but with an important difference as compared to any other previous recipe. This is done using the following code:

```
<script src="http://localhost:42613/signalr/hubs">
</script>
```

The difference here is that we specified an *absolute* address for the dynamic endpoint, which of course makes sense because that's what we want to achieve. The address is pointing to the server exposed by `Recipe31`. In case the port number (42613) is different in your code, please fix it accordingly.

4. Let's then add our script block, which in this case is pretty simple. Therefore, we'll show it all at once, as follows:

```
<script>
    $(function () {
        var echo = $.connection.echo;

        $.connection.hub.url =
            "http://localhost:42613/signalr";

        echo.client.greetings = function (message) {
            console.log(message);
        };

        $.connection.hub
            .start()
            .done(function () {
                echo.server.sayHello()
                    .done(function (message) {
                        console.log(message);
                    });
            });
    });
</script>
```

Most of the code is not really new here. It's just doing the things that we already did several times earlier. The only relevant code here is the highlighted line, where we specify where our hub proxy has to point when contacting the server, and again we use an absolute address pointing to the server exposed by `Recipe31`. We never had to do that previously because the default address for that property matches the one from where the running code has been downloaded, which is just fine for same-origin scenarios.

What we did so far does not illustrate anything special. This is plain, simple SignalR client code, where the only different thing is the usage of absolute addresses pointing to an origin that is different from the one hosting the page. But, as we briefly explained earlier, this code would not work unless we do not enable cross-origin requests on the server we are trying to contact. What is more specific to the CORS support happens on the server, therefore the rest of the recipe will be about how to modify the code we wrote for `Recipe31` in order to add the CORS support we need.

1. On the `Recipe31` project, we need to add a specific NuGet package called **Microsoft.Owin.Cors**, which will contain what we need to enable the CORS support.

2. We open the `Startup.cs` file and modify its content to make it look like the following code:

```
using Microsoft.Owin;
using Microsoft.Owin.Cors;
using Owin;

[assembly: OwinStartup(typeof(Recipe31.Startup))]

namespace Recipe31
{
    public class Startup
    {
        public void Configuration(IAppBuilder app)
        {
            app.Map("/signalr", map =>
            {
                map.UseCors(CorsOptions.AllowAll);

                map.RunSignalR();
            });
        }
    }
}
```

We added the `using Microsoft.Owin.Cors;` directive and then changed the contents of the `Configuration()` method to use the more low-level `Map()` method instead of the simpler and normally used `MapSignalR()` method. Here, we first define the route behind which the SignalR endpoint will be exposed (`"/signalr"`), then we specify that such mapping must use CORS support (`map.UseCors(CorsOptions.AllowAll)`), and finally we start the route. The stock `CorsOptions.AllowAll` option opens the access to any client origin.

We can now run both `Recipe31` and `Recipe32`, and we'll see how the `index.html` page will log a `hello` message onto the console, demonstrating that we've been able to connect to a server living on a different origin from the one where the client code is hosted!

There's more...

The code we wrote is still pretty naïve, because we went from a scenario where no cross origin client was allowed to a new one where *every* cross-origin request is happily processed. This might be too relaxed, and we might want to be able to decide a specific set of origins we want to enable while leaving out everybody else. That's, of course, possible. Instead of using the ready-made `CorsOptions.AllowAll` option, we can build a new one from scratch, specifying a custom value to use for the `PolicyProvider` member. This will look like the following code:

```
var corsPolicy = new CorsPolicy
{
    AllowAnyHeader = true,
    AllowAnyMethod = true
};
corsPolicy.Origins.Add("http://localhost:10457");

map.UseCors(
    new CorsOptions
    {
        PolicyProvider = new CorsPolicyProvider
        {
            PolicyResolver =
                r => Task.FromResult(corsPolicy)
        }
    });
```

We first build a custom `CorsPolicy` instance, saying we allow all headers and all methods, and then supply a single address to the `Origins` collection. The address we specify is intended to be the one where `Recipe32` is hosted. Please check that `10457` is the right port number in your case. Then we make a call to the `UseCors()` method, supplying an instance of `CorsOptions` whose `PolicyProvider` member has been assigned to a custom `CorsPolicyProvider` instance, which specifies a `PolicyResolver` lambda returning the `CorsPolicy` instance we just built. The code is pretty simple and should be a good starting point for you to implement more sophisticated requirements, such as reading the origins to be enabled from a configuration file.

7
Analyzing Advanced Scenarios

In this chapter, we will cover:

- ▶ Generating static files for JavaScript proxies
- ▶ Authorizing requests on a Hub
- ▶ Authorizing requests on a persistent connection
- ▶ Authorizing requests in a self-hosting context
- ▶ Scaling up
- ▶ Scaling out with Azure
- ▶ Scaling out with Redis
- ▶ Scaling out with SQL Server
- ▶ Establishing proxy-less connections
- ▶ Introducing dependency injection (simple approach)
- ▶ Introducing dependency injection (advanced approach)
- ▶ Using dependency injection to replace a default behavior
- ▶ Extending the Hub pipeline
- ▶ Handling errors

Introduction

So far, we have been making our way through most of the available features that can be leveraged to exchange real-time client/server messages, and at the same time we've been analyzing what SignalR delivers in order to monitor our connections and keep them under control. In this chapter, we'll be putting messaging features aside and concentrating on what we can do to solve common but orthogonal problems, which are key when moving from playground projects to real-world applications that have to deliver value in an efficient manner. Among other things, we'll see more about error management, talk about authentication and authorization, go through the different mechanisms available to scale and optimize our applications, and finally hook into SignalR's available extensibility points to show how to solve interesting and relevant infrastructural issues.

Generating static files for JavaScript proxies

One of the most fascinating things about SignalR is its ability to generate JavaScript dynamic proxies on the fly for any server-side Hub. These proxies make writing client-side code very easy and natural, but there's a price to pay, because the dynamic endpoint has to generate all the necessary plumbing code on the fly when requested. Although SignalR optimizes this process with caching strategies, this approach cannot be as efficient as a static and cacheable file. For this reason, SignalR's team decided to provide a way to distribute JavaScript dynamic proxies through a *statically generated script*.

In this recipe, we'll write a very basic application using dynamic proxies, and then we'll rework it to replace the dynamic endpoint with an equivalent static file.

Getting ready

Before writing the code of this recipe, we need to create a new empty web application, which we'll call `Recipe33`.

How to do it...

Let's quickly build our sample project using the following steps:

1. We first add a new empty Hub, which we'll call `EchoHub`, using the **SignalR Hub Class (v2)** template, as we have already done many times earlier. It will contain a simple method to return a hardcoded message, as shown in the following code:

    ```
    using Microsoft.AspNet.SignalR;
    using Microsoft.AspNet.SignalR.Hubs;

    namespace Recipe33
    {
        [HubName("echo")]
    ```

```
public class EchoHub : Hub
{
    public string SayHello()
    {
        return "Hello";
    }
}
```

2. We then create the `Startup` class with the appropriate template, containing a basic bootstrap sequence, as follows:

```
using Microsoft.Owin;
using Owin;
using Recipe33;

[assembly: OwinStartup(typeof(Startup))]

namespace Recipe33
{
    public class Startup
    {
        public void Configuration(IAppBuilder app)
        {
            app.MapSignalR();
        }
    }
}
```

3. We finally add an HTML client page called `index.html`. The code to be added to this page is as follows:

```
<script src="Scripts/jquery-2.1.0.js"></script>
<script src="Scripts/jquery.signalR-2.0.2.js"></script>
<script src="/signalr/hubs"></script>
<script>
    $(function() {
        var hub = $.connection.hub,
            echo = $.connection.echo;

        hub.start().done(function() {
            echo.server.sayHello()
                .done(function(message) {
                    console.log(message);
                });
        });
    });
</script>
```

In its head section, we'll reference the required JavaScript libraries as usual, and then the dynamic endpoint. We'll also add some trivial code to just prove that the connection is actually working. At this stage, there should not be any need to go through this code in detail, so we'll just list it and move on.

We can test the code we just wrote by launching the application and navigating to the `index.html` page. The page will just emit a message onto the browser console, displaying what's received from the server-side Hub.

This was simple so far, and as usual we used the `/signalr/hubs` endpoint, but that's the piece that has to be generated every time the application starts up, with some (although limited) waste of resources and some difficulties to face when dealing with caching. These issues can be easily solved using a utility distributed with SignalR called `signalr.exe`.

The `signalr.exe` utility is a simple command-line application that can be used for a few support tasks. It can be used to manage custom **performance counters**, and it is able to generate a static version of a dynamic endpoint. This is the functionality we're after in this recipe, therefore let's see how and where we can get this utility, and later on how to use it. We will perform the following steps:

1. We first need to reference a NuGet package called `Microsoft.AspNet.SignalR.Utils`, which does not actually add any assembly to the project; instead, it downloads the `signalr.exe` utility we mentioned earlier.

2. In order to find the utility, we have to open the `packages` folder for our solution on disk; from there, we navigate into the folder named after the package name (at the time of writing, it was `Microsoft.AspNet.SignalR.Utils.2.0.2`) and then we move inside the `tools` folder, where eventually we find it. Let's annotate the full path of this folder and move on.

3. Let's now open a console window and set our current directory to the `bin` folder, where the application assembly can be found, inside the project's directory, and from there let's launch the following command:

   `[path to signalr utility]\signalr ghp`

   This command scans the current folder looking for all the assemblies containing hubs. It processes them, accessing their internals to generate the JavaScript dynamic proxies code, and eventually saves them in a static file conventionally called `server.js` and positioned in the current folder.

4. The last step is pretty simple: we take the `server.js` file and copy it into the `scripts` folder of our application, maybe renaming it with a more meaningful name. In this case, we'll name it `EchoHub.js`. At this point, the only thing to do is to change the dynamic endpoint reference in `index.html` from `/signalr/hubs` to `Scripts/EchoHub.js`.

We are done. We can retest the application and verify that we still get the message on the browser console. We are avoiding a dynamic step and we can more easily work on caching the static file the way we think it's more appropriate. The online documentation of this utility can be found at `http://www.asp.net/signalr/overview/signalr-20/hubs-api/hubs-api-guide-JavaScript-client`.

Authorizing requests on a Hub

In real-world applications, one of the most common concerns we have to deal with is recognizing our users and granting or denying rights to perform actions. The first part is normally called the **Authentication** process, and it has to do with the steps necessary to ensure the identity of a user. SignalR does not offer any feature for that because it delegates the task to the hosting environment, whether that is ASP.NET or a self-host application. The second component of our concern is the **Authorization** process, which assumes the user has already been authenticated and uses his/her identity to decide what the user can or cannot do. In this case, SignalR offers a couple of mechanisms to deal with it: one specific to Hubs and another one for persistent connections in general. We'll see both of these in this and the next recipe, in the context of ASP.NET web applications, while the following one will illustrate the necessary basic steps to enable the authentication support in a self-hosting environment through the features provided by the infrastructure.

In this recipe, we'll write a very basic ASP.NET web application using Hubs, which we'll later adjust to take care of authorization. For the authentication part, we'll take advantage of the automatic features available with ASP.NET, and we'll build our example on the **Windows Authentication** host mechanism exposed by **IIS** and **IIS Express**.

Getting ready

Before writing the code of this recipe, we need to create a new empty web application, which we'll call `Recipe34`.

How to do it...

We'll proceed by writing the basic sample code with neither authentication nor authorization in place. We will be adding those later. After creating the empty web application, we add functionalities through the following steps:

1. We first add a new Hub, called `EchoHub`, using the **SignalR Hub Class (v2)** template as usual. We'll make its code look like as follows:

    ```
    using Microsoft.AspNet.SignalR;
    using Microsoft.AspNet.SignalR.Hubs;

    namespace Recipe34
    {
        [HubName("echo")]
        public class EchoHub : Hub
        {
    ```

```csharp
        public string Hello()
        {
            return "Hello!";
        }
    }
}
```

2. We then add the `Startup` class, which will just contain a basic initialization sequence, as follows:

```csharp
using Microsoft.Owin;
using Owin;

[assembly: OwinStartup(typeof(Recipe34.Startup))]

namespace Recipe34
{
    public class Startup
    {
        public void Configuration(IAppBuilder app)
        {
            app.MapSignalR();
        }
    }
}
```

3. The server-side portion is ready. Let's quickly add an `index.html` page and add the client code to it. All the necessary references are already in place because they have been automatically added when we created our Hub. Add the following code to the `index.html` page:

```html
<script src= "Scripts/jquery- 2.1.0.js" ></script>
<script src="Scripts/jquery.signalR-2.0.2.js" ></script>
<script src= "/signalr/hubs"></script>
<script>
    $(function () {
        var echo = $.connection.echo;
        $.connection.hub
            .start()
            .done(function() {
                echo.server.hello()
                    .done(function(message) {
                        console.log(message);
                    });
            });
    });
</script>
```

We can test what we wrote so far by navigating to `index.html` and observing the **Hello!** message printed on the browser console.

Now we know that our code is functional, hence let's add what's needed to add authorization rules to our Hub. As already mentioned, we need the hosting infrastructure to perform the authentication steps first. In the case of an ASP.NET application, we have several options, and discussing them is out of scope here. For our goal, it is enough to know that all of them are integrated and capable of providing the necessary information to perform the following authorization tasks. Let's move on to the following authorization steps:

1. For our example, we'll leverage the Windows Authentication mechanism, which is the default one for ASP.NET and can be easily enabled in IIS or IIS Express. Our examples are based on the latter, and switching from the default Anonymous Authentication to Windows Authentication can be easily done through the **Properties** window of the project inside Visual Studio, as shown in the following screenshot:

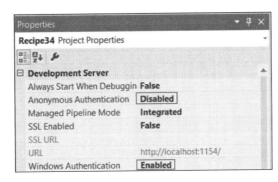

    With those settings in place, the Windows identity of the current user will be transmitted in the context of each request towards the server.

    The authorization process available for Hubs is based on an attribute called `AuthorizeAttribute`, and it clearly resembles the features available in other frameworks, such as Web API or MVC identity associated to the current request. This attribute can be used to mark either single methods or an entire Hub. The attribute can accept values for two properties, `Users` and `Roles`, to which we can provide a list of users or roles that are authorized to execute the annotated method or Hub. Those properties will be checked against the identity associated to the current request.

2. Let's modify our Hub to authorize a specific user to remotely call any contained method using the following code:

    ```
    [HubName("echo")]
    [Authorize(Users = "DOMAIN\user")]
    public class EchoHub : Hub
    {
    ...
    }
    ```

We just added `AuthorizeAttribute` on the definition of the `EchoHub` class and specified a sample name for the user to authorize. You will have to adapt the actual content of the string to some meaningful identity, or maybe switch to the `Roles` property if that better suits your case.

With this simple addition, we can test our application again and check whether we receive the **Hello!** string or not, based on the actual parameters supplied to the attribute. In particular, you can try with different fake identities first and then with the user identity you are currently using to spot the difference in the actual behavior.

There's more...

We've been illustrating authorization in the context of Windows Authentication, for which we did not provide deep details, but those are easily available on the Web. The same can be said for all the remaining authentication mechanisms available for ASP.NET. You can easily use any of them, and they will nicely fit with the authorization infrastructure.

The other thing to highlight is the fact that the `AuthorizeAttribute` type can be used to mark either a type, as we showed, or a method declaration. This provides us with a flexible mechanism that we can use to apply fine-grained authorization strategies, where we can take different decisions on a method-by-method basis if necessary, or more simply, apply a global decision for a whole Hub.

Authorizing requests on a persistent connection

Hubs is generally an easier API to use as compared to Persistent Connection, and that's the case for the authorization process too. With this recipe, we'll see how to provide the same behavior for a persistent connection.

We'll be writing a simple ASP.NET application first, and then we'll add the necessary authorization features to reach the same goal. For the authorization, we'll be using Windows Authentication again, and we'll configure IIS Express accordingly.

Getting ready

Before writing the code of this recipe, we need to create a new empty web application, which we'll call `Recipe35`.

How to do it...

We first create an empty web application, and we'll make it functional without any authorization bits, which we'll be adding afterwards. We'll perform the following steps:

1. We start by adding a class named `EchoConnection` that is derived from `PersistentConnection`. To do that, we can navigate to **Add | New Item...** from the context menu of the project entry inside the **Solution Explorer** window, and from there look for **SignalR Persistent Connection Class (v2)**. We'll add a simple method to broadcast back whatever data is received from the connected client. The code is as follows:

```
using System.Threading.Tasks;
using Microsoft.AspNet.SignalR;

namespace Recipe35
{
    public class EchoConnection : PersistentConnection
    {
        protected override Task OnReceived(
            IRequest request,
            string connectionId,
            string data)
        {
            return Connection.Broadcast(data);
        }

        . . .

    }
}
```

The dots are there to mark where we'll be adding the authorization bits.

2. As usual, we need to add the `Startup` class. In this case, we are using a persistent connection; therefore, we'll have to use the corresponding mapping extension method, as shown in the following code:

```
using Microsoft.Owin;
using Owin;
using Recipe35;

[assembly: OwinStartup(typeof(Startup))]

namespace Recipe35
{
    public class Startup
    {
```

```
public void Configuration(IAppBuilder app)
{
    app.MapSignalR<EchoConnection>("/echo");
}
}
}
```

The only relevant portion is the line where `MapSignalR()` is called to wire our `EchoConnection` type to the `/echo` endpoint.

3. Let's move to the client side by creating an `index.html` page and adding some simple testing code to it, as follows:

```
<script src="Scripts/jquery-2.1.0.js"></script>
<script src="Scripts/jquery.signalR-2.0.2.js"></script>
<script>
    $(function() {
        var c = $.connection('echo');
        c.received(function(data) {
            console.log(data);
        });
        c.start()
          .done(function () {
              c.send('hello');
          });
    });
</script>
```

This kind of code has already been illustrated in *Chapter 5, Using a Persistent Connection*, so we'll skip any further comments.

Testing this application is very simple. We browse to the `index.html` page and look at the browser's console to see a **hello** string popping up. After verifying that it works, we can move on and add the authentication and authorization bits. For any general discussion about those topics, you can refer to the *Authorizing requests on a Hub* recipe. Let's proceed with the following steps:

1. We first need to take care of the authentication, and we'll do it by moving from the default Anonymous Authentication to the Windows Authentication mechanism using the **Properties** window of the project inside Visual Studio, as shown in the following screenshot:

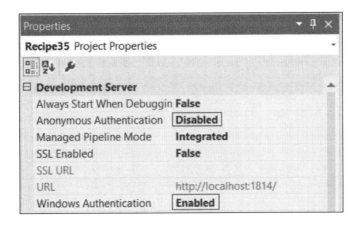

2. As usual, persistent connection exposes a more low-level API for everything, and authorization is no exception. In order to check if the connecting user can be authorized to perform the incoming call, we have to override the `AuthorizeRequest()` method, and from there do all the necessary checks to decide whether to accept or reject the request, as shown in the following code:

```
protected override bool AuthorizeRequest(
    IRequest request)
{
    return request.User.Identity.Name ==
        @ "DOMAIN\user" ;
}
```

The `AuthorizeRequest()` method is automatically called every time a remote request is performed, and it's supplied with a reference to the current request. The authorization step has already taken place, therefore the `request` argument contains all the information necessary to apply our authorization process. The method has to return a Boolean value, which will either be true to authorize the call or false to deny access, and that's it. In our example, we simply get access to the current principal token and check whether the name of the user matches a specific one, but of course in real-world applications we would perform a more meaningful authorization process.

We are now ready to test the application again by changing the string we verify the identity against, as we did in the previous recipe. We'll observe that the **hello** string will be printed only if the authorization process will pass. Using breakpoints in Visual Studio, we can verify that each request is actually passing through the `AuthorizeRequest()` method, and that its output is governing the actual execution of the request.

Authorizing requests in a self-hosting context

Earlier in this book, we've been illustrating how SignalR can be hosted in a traditional Windows process, thanks to the self-hosting support provided. While this opens up several new and interesting scenarios, on the other end this is a much more basic infrastructure, and we might therefore lose useful or necessary features exposed by the ASP.NET environment. In some cases, we might even need to learn about some manual steps that we have to perform in order to gain access to equivalent functionalities.

This is the case for the authentication process, which needs different additional steps according to the specific authentication scheme used. Our goal is to illustrate the point, and therefore we'll stick with the simplest case, represented again by Windows Authentication. The key part here is that it is definitely possible to support several other authentication mechanisms; although, for those, we might need to get our hands dirty by digging into the **Owin hosting infrastructure** (http://owin.org/), which is actually taking care of these details.

For this, we'll build the server-side portion from scratch, while for the client side we'll reuse what we wrote for the *Authorizing requests on a Hub* recipe with a couple of small modifications, so please make sure you have already read that recipe and have the related code ready and working.

Getting ready

To build a self-hosting application, we start by creating a **console application** and then perform the following steps:

1. Navigate to **File | New Project** from the menu items.
2. Navigate to **Installed | Visual C#** in the dialog box and select the **Windows** folder.
3. On the central panel of the dialog box, select **Console Application**, give it a name (`Recipe36` in this case), and click on **OK**. Visual Studio will add a `Program.cs` file containing the startup code for our application, which at first will look like the following code:

```
namespace Recipe36
{
    class Program
    {
        static void Main(string[] args)
        {
        }
    }
}
```

How to do it...

This is not a web application, therefore we need to add the SignalR packages manually, as already explained in *Chapter 1, Understanding the Basics*. We'll need to install the **Microsoft ASP.NET SignalR Self Host** package using either the **Package Manager Console** window or the **Manage NuGet Packages...** dialog box. Having done that, we proceed using the following steps:

1. We first add a plain old class called `EchoHub`, and we modify it to make it derive from `Hub` as usual. We'll then add the necessary plumbing code and a simple test method as follows:

```
using Microsoft.AspNet.SignalR;
using Microsoft.AspNet.SignalR.Hubs;

namespace Recipe36
{
    [HubName("echo")]
    [Authorize(Users = @"DOMAIN\user")]
    public class EchoHub : Hub
    {
        public string Hello()
        {
            return "Hello!";
        }
    }
}
```

   Pretty simple. The only thing to highlight is the addition of the `AuthorizeAttribute` to establish an authorization rule, as we already saw in the *Authorizing requests on a Hub* recipe for the Hubs API.

2. We then move on to add the usual `Startup` class, which we can create from scratch, and make it look like the following code:

```
using System.Net;
using Microsoft.Owin;
using Owin;

[assembly: OwinStartup(typeof(Recipe36.Startup))]

namespace Recipe36
{
    public class Startup
    {
```

```
public void Configuration(IAppBuilder app)
{
    ...

    app.MapSignalR();
}
}
}
```

It's mostly standard code. We just marked with dots the place where we'll have to add some code to take care of a couple of issues that must be solved to have our authorization process in place. These issues are as follows:

- Allowing **cross-origin** requests, which is needed because we'll be using a browser as the client, and the pages will be hosted by a different application
- Wiring the Windows Authentication pipeline to pull the appropriate *credentials* into the process

3. The first bits to add are related to the **Cross-Origin Resource Sharing** (**CORS**) support, which we've been illustrating in the *Establishing a cross domain connection* recipe from the previous chapter. For that, we need to add the `Microsoft.Owin.Cors` NuGet package first, then add a `using Microsoft.Owin.Cors;` directive, and finally perform the actual call to enable CORS support, as follows:

```
app.UseCors(CorsOptions.AllowAll);
```

4. The second task is related to Windows Authentication support. Unless we do not change what's configured by default, the self-hosting infrastructure is based on the `HttpListener` type, which is provided by a specific NuGet package called **Microsoft.Owin.Host.HttpListener**, and is already available here because it is automatically added by **Microsoft.AspNet.SignalR.SelfHost**. In an Owin application, the `IAppBuilder` interface exposes a `Properties` member giving access to the available modules. We can use it to access the `HttpListener` instance to tweak its configuration, as follows:

```
var listener = (HttpListener)
    app.Properties["System.Net.HttpListener"];
listener.AuthenticationSchemes =
    AuthenticationSchemes.IntegratedWindowsAuthentication;
```

We first extract the `HttpListener` module from the `Properties` collection, and then configure its `AuthenticationSchemes` member to support Windows Authentication. That's what we need, and that's enough to hook the authentication process in our application.

5. We need one last step, which is the actual hosting of the application behind a specific endpoint. For that, we need to go back to the `Program` class we introduced at the beginning of the recipe and fill its `Main()` method with the following code:

```
using (WebApp.Start<Startup>("http://localhost:9191/"))
{
    Console.WriteLine(
        "Server running at http://localhost:9191/");
    Console.ReadLine();
}
```

In the *Adding a Hub to a self-hosting application* recipe of *Chapter 1*, *Understanding the Basics*, we already illustrated this step in detail. Briefly, what we are doing here is launching our application using the `Startup` class written earlier and exposing it on port `9191` of the `http://localhost` address.

We're done with the server. Now, we just need a client to test if everything works. We'll simplify this task by using the application we built for the *Authorizing requests on a Hub* recipe, which, by the way, is already configured to support the Windows Authentication process. We just need to slightly modify the `index.html` client page so that it will point to the server from this current recipe. That's pretty simple—we just need to adjust a couple of lines, as follows:

```
<script src="http://localhost:9191/signalr/hubs"></script>
<script>
    $(function () {

        $.connection.hub.url =
        'http://localhost:9191/signalr';

        . . .

    });
</script>
```

We modified the address of the dynamic endpoint, and we did the same for the actual address where the hub we are contacting must reside. Both are now pointing to port `9191`, where our server is exposed.

We are ready for testing: we first launch the console application and wait for it to be running; then we move to the project from the *Authorizing requests on a Hub* recipe and navigate to its `index.html` page. The output console of the browser will show the **Hello**! message received from our self-hosted Hub only if the authorized username matches the one of the user currently connecting.

Scaling up

This chapter is dedicated to more advanced scenarios, and strategies to guarantee high performance to our applications are a very good fit for this section of the book. We already talked about how optimized the overall design of SignalR is, and how well performing its runtime behavior is, but this does not mean that we will never face scalability issues. There are ways to scale the performance of SignalR vertically on a single box—for example, adding more memory (**scaling up**)—and it's also possible to scale SignalR horizontally by adding more servers (**scaling out**) and making them exchange messages so that broadcasting is correctly replicated. Clients must be able to keep on working as usual, regardless of the actual physical endpoint they connect to and unaware of the changes in the infrastructure.

In this first recipe dedicated to scaling strategies, we'll discuss the first kind of optimization: scaling up. The format will slightly deviate from the usual one because there is no easy way to verify the benefits of our actions; therefore, we'll just list the available options and describe the advantages they bring.

How to do it...

Let's start with what we can do at the coding level using the following features:

1. When we have methods on a Hub that exchange instances of complex types, sometimes we might realize that there is too much information going on the wire, and that we could actually save bandwidth and therefore performance by compacting what we transmit somehow. The goal can be achieved by shortening the names of the properties contained in the exchanged types, or even by completely removing some members if they are not needed on the other end of the connection. This could of course be done manually, but we can make use of some interesting serialization attributes exposed by **Json.Net**, which is the default serialization library used by ASP. NET since Version 4.0.

    For example, we could do something like the following:

    ```
    public class Payload
    {
        [JsonProperty("s")]
        public string Salutation { get; set; }

        [JsonIgnore]
        public string DummyStuff { get; set; }
    }
    ```

    The first member, `Salutation`, is marked with the `JsonProperty` attribute, whose role is to specify an alternate name to use when serializing on the server. In the example, we change the name of the property from `Salutation` to `s`, but this just happens when sending to the client, hence we do not have to give up on more descriptive names in the rest of our server-side code.

The second member is annotated with the `JsonIgnore` attribute, which is used to completely remove the related value from the stream of bytes sent to the client. This can be useful when our types might contain information that is relevant on the server but not on the client.

In both cases, we have to realize that the client will have to deal with the shape of the data as it is after the transformation, that is, with shortened names and missing fields.

2. Another trick we can use to improve the performance is to apply some form of data compression. In order to work properly, SignalR must fully control what goes on the wire; therefore, it's not easily possible to hook any sort of transparent and low-level compression strategy. That said, there might be scenarios where SignalR is used to provide more general-purpose infrastructure services where performance is really an issue. In such cases, we might want to give up on business methods and data structures and move to more general-purpose methods that exchange streams of bytes, whose content is a compressed version of the actual information. Clients and servers will have to agree on a compression strategy, and that's easier when the client is a .NET application too because that would help in sharing the compression components. In general, the resulting code will be more complex, but the gain in performance might well be worth the effort.

3. Among the configuration parameters exposed by SignalR, there is one we can tweak to improve the performance profile. The `DefaultMessageBufferSize` value can be modified in the following manner:

```
GlobalHost.Configuration.DefaultMessageBufferSize = 500;
```

By default, SignalR keeps the last 1000 messages in memory, but if their payload is large, this might have a negative impact on the memory footprint. Therefore, decreasing such a number might be a good countermeasure to take. This code should be placed inside the `Configuration()` method of the `Startup` class, just before initializing SignalR.

We have a few more options thanks to a few parameters exposed by specific hosting platforms. Please be aware that these settings will affect every other application hosted by the same environment. They are as follows:

1. When we use IIS as our hosting platform, we can regulate the maximum number of concurrent requests per application. The default value here is 5000, but it can be increased by running a specific command-line application from an elevated session as follows:

```
cd %windir%\System32\inetsrv\

appcmd.exe set config /section:system.webserver/serverRuntime
/appConcurrentRequestLimit:10000
```

2. When ASP.NET is used as the hosting platform, there are a couple more parameters that we can fine-tune, as follows:

   ❑ `maxConcurrentRequestsPerCPU`: With this parameter, we can increase the maximum number of concurrent requests per CPU that ASP.NET can process. This setting can be found inside the `aspnet.config` file, whose locations usually are:

```
%windir%\Microsoft.NET\Framework\v4.0.30319\aspnet.config
%windir%\Microsoft.NET\Framework64\v4.0.30319\aspnet.config
```

   The mentioned key must be located inside the `configuration/system.web/applicationPool` node of the file.

   ❑ `requestQueueLimit`: When the previous limit is exceeded, ASP.NET starts using a queuing mechanism, and the size of the queue is regulated by this parameter, which can be found inside the `processModel` node of the `machine.config` file.

There's more...

Tweaking parameters like the ones we just described in a proper way is not a trivial task. They affect the behavior of the whole server, and therefore they might have an impact on other non-SignalR applications. For these reasons, it's not easy to give a general guidance about them. For example, factors like the availability of WebSocket as a connection strategy can greatly influence the way you might want to fine-tune these values. In an environment where WebSocket connections are many more than traditional HTTP connections, you might want to try to set the previous numbers in the order of hundreds of thousands, while such values would probably be too high if the ratio between the two types of connections is reversed.

For more information about these options, and about scaling up SignalR in general, you can start by checking the official documentation at `http://www.asp.net/signalr/overview/signalr-20/performance-and-scaling/signalr-performance`.

Scaling out with Azure

Scaling up a single machine can help just up to a certain limit, beyond which we have no other option but trying to add more servers. Of course, this poses different issues; the most relevant being, how we can keep the redundant infrastructure transparent to users. This principle is the base of a solution that can scale at will and according to usage. The overall idea here is to have a load-balancing infrastructure that can transparently route the clients to different servers.

The problem is that this way we lose any guarantee about which of our servers will satisfy a request; therefore, those would need a system to exchange messages and information in order to provide a seamless and fully functional experience to users, especially when performing broadcasts towards all the open connections, which are likely to be scattered across the whole web farm.

Such systems exist, and are called **backplanes**. At the time of this writing, SignalR provided three official backplanes, which will be illustrated here—each one with different characteristics and performance profiles. They are based on the following technologies:

▸ **Windows Azure Service Bus**

▸ **Redis**

▸ **SQL Server**

While analyzing them, we should always be aware of the general problems backplanes are trying to solve, and we have to understand that a backplane is a mechanism based on a *continuous replication* of messages across servers. This can help when the goal is to increase the amount of connections we can handle, but the natural drawback is an impact on the messaging throughput. Applications performing high-frequency broadcasting (think about real-time games performing several refreshes per second) might suffer from it, and some ad hoc alleviating strategies might be needed.

For reasons of simplicity, our recipes will not involve any load-balancing system; that's an infrastructural concern, and it's out of scope here. Nevertheless, we will be able to demonstrate our point by instantiating different servers and showing how they support broadcasting towards all the connected clients regardless of the actual endpoint they're attached to, which is the necessary requirement to support true load-balancing strategies.

In this recipe, we'll describe the first of the three available backplanes: the **Windows Azure Service Bus** backplane.

Getting started

In order to illustrate our point, we'll first build a basic sample web application and make it work in the simplest scenario possible, where just one server is available. We'll then make use of a Windows Azure Service Bus instance for the backplane, and we'll demonstrate how that helps.

We'll finalize the example by deploying the application on Azure. This is not strictly necessary, but it is an interesting option to illustrate here. For that, we'll need to build a **Windows Azure Cloud Service** project, whose template is added by installing the free Windows Azure SDK, available at `http://www.windowsazure.com/en-us/downloads/`.

Before proceeding, please make sure Windows Azure SDK is installed and the mentioned project template is available in Visual Studio.

For this recipe, we'll also assume some basic knowledge about what Windows Azure is and how it works, and we will take for granted that you already have an account on Azure, which you will use to deploy this solution. Azure offers trial subscriptions and very convenient plans for MSDN subscribers, so it should not be a problem for you to get ready with these requirements and follow the rest of this recipe.

How to do it...

Let's quickly build the sample project using the following steps:

1. We first add a new empty Hub called EchoHub using the **SignalR Hub Class (v2)** template as usual. Its implementation will be as simple as the following one:

```
using Microsoft.AspNet.SignalR;
using Microsoft.AspNet.SignalR.Hubs;

namespace Recipe38
{
    [HubName("echo")]
    public class EchoHub : Hub
    {
        public void SayHello()
        {
            Clients.Others.greetings("Hello!");
        }
    }
}
```

We're just exposing a simple Hub with a single method that will broadcast a message to every other connected client each time it will be called.

2. Let's prepare the following code for our Startup class, created as usual using the corresponding template:

```
using Microsoft.Owin;
using Owin;

[assembly: OwinStartup(typeof(Recipe38.Startup))]

namespace Recipe38
{
    public class Startup
    {
        public void Configuration(IAppBuilder app)
        {
            ...

            app.MapSignalR();
        }
    }
}
```

The code is pretty much the same as we have seen many times, but we already left some space, marked with dots, for a couple of lines that we'll need later on.

3. We finally prepare the code for our client page, called `index.html` as usual, which will contain a button to call a method on the server and an unordered list to display the received messages, as follows:

    ```
    <button id="sayHello">Say hello!</button>
    <ul id="messages"></ul>
    ```

4. The JavaScript code is pretty straightforward too, as follows:

    ```
    <script src="Scripts/jquery-2.1.0.js"></script>
    <script src="Scripts/jquery.signalR-2.0.2.js"></script>
    <script src="/signalr/hubs"></script>
    <script>

        $(function() {
            var echo = $.connection.echo;

            echo.client.greetings = function(message) {
                var $li = $('<li/>')
                    .html(message);
                $('#messages').append($li);
            };

            $.connection.hub
                .start()
                .done(function() {
                    $('#sayHello').click(function() {
                        echo.server.sayHello();
                    });
                });
        });

    </script>
    ```

It prepares a callback to be invoked by the server when a broadcast is performed by the `Clients.Others.greetings("Hello!");` call and binds a call towards the server on the `click` event from to the button on the page.

We can test what we did so far by opening the `index.html` page in multiple browser windows and clicking on the button on each of them. We'll observe how the messages are broadcasted to the various clients. Once we are sure that everything works as expected, we can move on and see how to hook a Windows Azure Service Bus backplane into the application by performing the following steps.

1. We log in to the Windows Azure Management Console using our account, then we move to the **SERVICE BUS** section on the sidebar to the left, and we click on the **CREATE** button to add a **namespace**. A Service Bus namespace is used by the backplane to send and receive the messages in a *publish/subscribe* fashion. In the creation window displayed, we have to specify a name for the namespace; for example, `SignalRCookbookNS`.

2. When the namespace will be ready, we'll select it and then open the **CONNECTION INFORMATION** window; there, we'll find an **Access Connection String** (**ACS**) entry we need to write down because we'll need it soon.

3. We move back to the `Recipe38` application in Visual Studio to add the `Microsoft.AspNet.SignalR.ServiceBus` NuGet package, which will enable support for the Windows Azure Service Bus backplane.

4. We then move to the `Startup` file, where we add the following code just before the call to the `MapSignalR()` method along with a `using Microsoft.AspNet.SignalR;` directive:

   ```
   var connectionString =
       "namespace connection string";
   GlobalHost.DependencyResolver.UseServiceBus(
       connectionString, "Recipe38");
   ```

   We use the `UseServiceBus()` method to start up the related support. The value of the supplied connection string is the one we just copied from the management console, while the `"Recipe38"` string is a *topic* name that Azure will use to group together the messages for this application.

If we now repeat the same test we performed earlier, we should see the same expected behavior happening; however, we might have to retry a few times at the beginning because the Service Bus might need a few seconds to warm up.

At this point, we can be pretty sure that our application is relying on the Service Bus instance we just created, but to double check it, we can perform a further step and try to do a full deploy of the web application onto Azure. This way, we should be able to run the sample both locally and from the cloud at the same time, and have both instances exchanging messages thanks to the backplane. Let's see how to deploy the application using the following steps:

1. We start by opening the **Add New Project** dialog box by navigating to **File | New Project...**, and there we look for the **Cloud templates** folder in the **C#** section, from where we pick the **Windows Azure Cloud Service** template to create our project named `Recipe38.Azure`, as shown in the following screenshot:

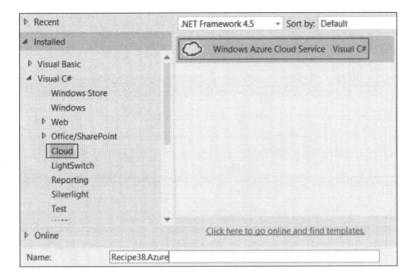

2. The following step of the creation wizard will show a window from where we can pick several types of roles that we want to add to the project; however, in our case, we'll be attaching to the `Recipe38` web application we already created, so at this stage we simply click on the **OK** button without selecting any role type, leaving the right-hand side of the screen empty, as shown in the following screenshot:

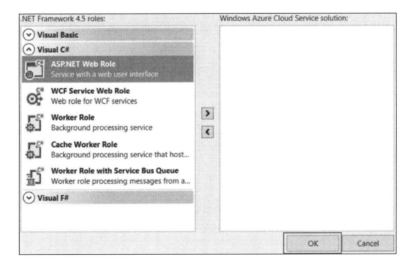

The final effect will be the creation of the project.

3. Let's now look for the `Recipe38.Azure` project inside the **Solution Explorer** window and expand it. We'll see a bunch of nodes there, but we're just interested in the **Roles** one, on which we'll right-click to open its context menu, as shown in the following screenshot:

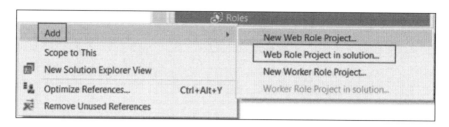

Our goal is to generate a role from the web application we built earlier; therefore, we select the **Add...** item and then the **Web Role Project in solution...** item. This will present a list of projects from where we'll pick **Recipe38**. This will add a new entry under the **Roles** node for our project.

We might also want to redefine the number of instances of our application we want Azure to start. We achieve that by double clicking on the **Recipe38** node we just mentioned to open its **Configuration** window, where we can tweak the **Instance count** parameter, as shown in the following screenshot:

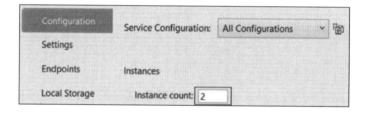

After building it, our Cloud Service hosting the application will be ready to be deployed; therefore, we have to perform the necessary steps to publish it on Azure as follows:

1. We log in again into the Windows Azure Management Console using our account, and then we prepare a new Cloud Service instance by opening the **NEW** wizard and clicking sequentially on **COMPUTE**, **CLOUD SERVICE**, and **QUICK CREATE**. We'll give the instance a name, for example, `SignalRCookbookRecipe38`; we'll select a deploy region and a subscription plan; and we'll confirm the creation. It's recommended to deploy it in the same region we choose for the Cloud Service.

2. Similarly, we'll create a new storage account by opening the **NEW** wizard and clicking sequentially on **DATA SERVICES**, **STORAGE**, and **QUICK CREATE**. We'll give the instance a name, for example, `signalrcookbookstorage`; we'll select a deploy region, a subscription plan, and a replication strategy; and we'll trigger the creation.

3. We are done with the preparatory work we needed on the Windows Azure Management Console. Now, we can go back to Visual Studio to finalize the publication. We just need to build our solution and deploy the Cloud Service using the **Publish** menu item available on the project context menu. We'll be asked to authenticate on Azure with our credentials, and then we'll be presented a wizard window from where to configure the final settings of our setup. They should be pretty straightforward; most of them will correspond to items we created during the previous steps. When asked which environment to use, let's select **Staging** because that's the most appropriate for a test application like this one.

The publication step can take a few minutes, and we can monitor its progress from both Visual Studio and the Windows Azure Management Console. When finished, we can select our **SignalRCookbookRecipe38** Cloud Service from the Management Console; then open the corresponding dashboard for the Staging environment and, on the right-hand side bar, look for the **SITE URL** link, which we can then use to finally see our sample application in action. Let's open a few new browser instances pointing to that address, along with the ones we previously pointed at the application running locally, and let's observe how the triggered messages flow across all of them, local and remote, thanks to the backplane infrastructure we just prepared.

How it works...

This backplane is based on the topics feature exposed by the Service Bus, which delivers a publish/subscribe model where publishers are able to queue messages, and multiple subscribers can read them concurrently. Each message is read by all the subscribers, and this is exactly what SignalR needs in order to replicate every message across all the available nodes.

Most of the details about how SignalR actually implements the backplane are out of the scope of this book. The only interesting thing we'd like to discuss here is that all the backplanes are written the same way, leveraging an extensibility point provided by SignalR. SignalR exposes an interface called `IMessageBus`, and it needs an instance of a type implementing that interface to work properly. Every single incoming or outgoing message goes through this service, regardless of the presence of any external backplane. If we do not inject a different implementation, SignalR creates an instance of a default and embedded type implementing `IMessageBus` which handles messages in memory, and sets it as the current backplane.

This is how SignalR makes a standalone setup work, therefore we might say that every SignalR application is actually working through a backplane, where the default one works in memory. This smart strategy makes it easy to inject a different strategy to tackle specific scalability issues when they show up, and it allows anybody to create a custom backplane if none of the existing ones is satisfactory.

Scaling out with Redis

The Windows Azure Service Bus backplane is very interesting, but it's also based on an external infrastructure, which might not always be a viable option. Also, the resilience characteristics of the Windows Azure Service Bus are great for guaranteed delivery, but they have some impact in terms of messaging throughput. Therefore, the SignalR team provided a high-performance alternative with a backplane based on **Redis**.

Redis is an in-memory key-value store, with a persistence strategy to make data durable, but its main focus is speed, which it achieves through its in-memory model. It has a publish/subscribe structure whose characteristics are ideal to be used as the foundation for a SignalR backplane.

In this recipe, we'll describe how to set up a Redis instance on a Windows machine, and how to configure the Redis backplane on a sample application.

Getting started

In order to keep the discussion focused on the actual topic, we'll reuse the code we wrote in the previous recipe and just highlight the differences we'll need to introduce for the Redis backplane. We'll need a new empty web application, which we'll name `Recipe39`.

We, of course, need a Redis instance as the backend of our backplane. Redis is a Linux-based system, but an unsupported version working on Windows, managed by a team at Microsoft, is available. This version is in general a little bit behind the official one, and it's probably not recommended in a production environment. But, it's just fine for our demonstration purposes, so we'll use it here. We have two ways to get the binaries, which are as follows:

> ▶ Get the C++ source code from GitHub at the following address and compile it with Visual Studio:
>
> `https://github.com/MSOpenTech/redis`

> ▶ Download the readymade binaries from the following site:
>
> `https://github.com/mythz/redis-windows`

Both ways work fine and are pretty simple, even if you are not an experienced C++ developer. When you have it ready, you can open a command-line window, set the current directory to the folder where you have placed the binaries, and launch Redis using the following command:

```
msvs\x64\Release\redis-server.exe redis.conf
```

The previous command line is based on the folder structure that is created when downloading and compiling the source code directly. You might have to adapt it if you download the binaries directly. In any case, what you need to do is locate `redis-server.exe` and launch it by supplying the path of the `redis.conf` configuration file. You might also want to open the configuration file, look for the `requirepass` setting, and use it to specify a connection password to be used later when configuring the backplane (you might have to uncomment the corresponding configuration line).

How to do it...

As already mentioned, we'll base our discussion on the code we wrote for `Recipe38`, therefore here we'll just quickly mention the necessary steps:

1. We first add a Hub class called `EchoHub` and a test page called `index.html`. Please check the previous recipe for more details about the code to put in there.

2. Let's then prepare the following code for our `Startup` class, created, as usual, using the corresponding template:

```
using Microsoft.Owin;
using Owin;

[assembly: OwinStartup(typeof(Recipe39.Startup))]

namespace Recipe39
{
    public class Startup
    {
        public void Configuration(IAppBuilder app)
        {
            ...

            app.MapSignalR();
        }
    }
}
```

We added some dots to mark the place where we'll later be adding a couple of lines initiating the Redis backplane.

Before proceeding, we should test what we did so far and observe that everything is working as expected. We can proceed by opening the `index.html` page in multiple browser windows, and by clicking on the displayed button to observe how the messages are broadcasted to the various clients. We can now continue by adding the Redis backplane using the following steps:

1. We first need to add the `Microsoft.AspNet.SignalR.Redis` NuGet package to enable support for the Redis backplane.

2. We then go back to the `Startup` class, where we add the following code just before the call to the `MapSignalR()` method (we need to add a `using Microsoft.AspNet.SignalR;` directive to make it compile):

   ```
   GlobalHost.DependencyResolver.UseRedis(
           "localhost", 6379, "pwd", "Recipe39");
   ```

   We use the `UseRedis()` method to start up the related support, and we need to provide the following parameters:

   - The network address where to find the Redis instance we want to use
   - The port on which Redis is listening (the default value is `6379`)
   - The password we configured in the `redis.conf` file
   - A name for a topic, which is used to group together all the related messages; in this case, we use the name of the recipe

We are ready to test the application again, and we should not notice any disruption, with all the messages correctly broadcasted across all the open browser instances. We can also observe the messages flow using the `redis-cli.exe` utility in the following manner:

```
msvs\x64\Release\redis-cli.exe –a the_password
redis 127.0.0.1> subscribe Recipe39
```

With this utility, we connect to the same instance we use from inside our application, using the `-a` option to specify the password we set up in `redis.conf` earlier. When connected, we subscribe to the same topic used by our application by entering the `subscribe Recipe39` command. At this point, whenever we'll click on a button in our application page, a message will be printed in this console window.

We can perform a further test to confirm how the backplane is able to work across multiple servers. We open a new command-line window and launch an instance of IIS Express pointing to our application as follows:

```
"%programfiles%\IIS Express\iisexpress.exe" /path:[path]
        /port:[port]
```

The [path] argument must be the absolute path of the folder containing the source code of our application, while the [port] value must be different from the one configured in Visual Studio, and in general must be a free IP port. When the new IIS Express instance is ready, we can open a new browser window pointing at the port we just specified. As a result, we'll see a new copy of our test page, but, regardless of being on a different web server instance, any message sent from here will reach the other windows we opened earlier, and the other way round will work too, all thanks to the Redis backplane.

Scaling out with SQL Server

The SignalR team provides a third backplane option, based on **Microsoft SQL Server**. This one could be a good fit if both Windows Azure and Redis are not an option for you. It has good resilience characteristics, although it's not the best option in terms of performance.

In this recipe, we'll assume you have a SQL Server instance available, and we'll see how to plug the SQL Server backplane into a simple application inspired by the previous scale-out recipes.

Getting started

As we did previously, we'll reuse the code we wrote in the recipe about the Windows Azure Service Bus backplane, and we'll just show what's to be different when we add the SQL Server backplane. We'll perform our demonstration using a new empty web application named Recipe40.

In order to correctly support the backplane, we need to perform the following actions:

1. We need to create an empty database. It does not need to have any special name, and the necessary tables will be created by the backplane itself the first time it's activated.

2. Our application will run under a specific process account, maybe through impersonation; therefore, we'll have to determine the actual identity that will connect to the SQL Server instance and give it the necessary permissions to log in and create tables. The same idea applies if we opt for a SQL Authentication identity. This is necessary just for the first time the backplane connects to the database to create the tables it needs. After that, we could downgrade the permissions we granted to a more traditional read/write set of permissions, or switch to a more adequate user.

3. Although we will not proceed with this specific step in our discussion, in a production environment it's highly recommended that you enable the SQL Server **Service Broker**, whose messaging and queuing features greatly enhance the performance of the SQL Server backplane by notifying it directly, in a push fashion, when control messages need to be exchanged. You can check the SQL Server documentation for more details about it, available at http://technet.microsoft.com/en-us/library/bb522893.aspx.

How to do it...

Our sample code will be the same as we wrote for `Recipe38`; let's quickly review it:

1. We first add a Hub class called `EchoHub` and a test page called `index.html`, whose content will be the same as we had prepared for the previous two recipes.

2. We then need a `Startup` class that looks like the following code:

```
using Microsoft.Owin;
using Owin;

[assembly: OwinStartup(typeof(Recipe40.Startup))]

namespace Recipe40
{
    public class Startup
    {
        public void Configuration(IAppBuilder app)
        {
            ...

            app.MapSignalR();
        }
    }
}
```

We'll be adding the missing code later when plugging the SQL Server backplane.

We can proceed with a first test pass by opening the `index.html` page in multiple browser windows and by clicking on the button on each of them to verify that messages are broadcasted across clients. When done, we can proceed by adding the SQL Server backplane using the following steps:

1. We first need to add the `Microsoft.AspNet.SignalR.SqlServer` NuGet package to enable support for the SQL Server backplane.

2. We then go back to the `Startup` class code, where we first add a `using Microsoft.AspNet.SignalR;` directive and then the following call just before invoking the `MapSignalR()` method:

```
string connectionString = "[connection string]";
GlobalHost.DependencyResolver
            .UseSqlServerSqlServer(connectionString);
```

This code is pretty simple: the `UseSqlServerSqlServer()` method starts the backplane, and we just have to provide the necessary connection string to have access to the database we created earlier.

We are ready to perform a new test on the application by launching it again from Visual Studio in multiple browser windows, and we should not notice any difference from the behavior we observed earlier, with the messages correctly broadcasted across all the clients. You can double-check that the backplane is effectively in place by inspecting the content of the tables in its database.

We can then perform a further test to clearly observe how the backplane works across multiple servers. We open a new command-line window, and from there we launch an instance of `IIS Express` pointing at our application:

```
"%programfiles%\IIS Express\iisexpress.exe" /path:[path]
    /port:[port]
```

As we did in the previous recipe, we are starting a new web server instance that will publish our application: the `[path]` argument must be the absolute path to the folder of our application, and the `[port]` value must be a free IP port. When the new `IIS Express` instance is started, we can open a new browser window pointing at the port we just specified, and a new copy of our test page will be loaded. Regardless of being on a different web server instance, any message sent from here will reach the other windows we opened earlier, and vice versa, thanks to the SQL Server backplane.

Establishing proxy-less connections

One of the biggest differences that we might have observed when comparing the .NET client library against the JavaScript one, is the presence of the dynamic proxies on the latter. SignalR takes advantage of the dynamic nature of the JavaScript language to generate proxies on the fly. Proxies greatly simplify both the calls towards the server-side Hub and the declaration of the callbacks that will be invoked from within any server-side Hub context, but the .NET client does not have this luxury. We have to resort to a calling strategy based on strings used to refer to the actual method names exposed by the Hub.

On the other hand, we have already highlighted during the *Generating static files for JavaScript proxies* recipe that the generation of dynamic proxies has its drawbacks, which we then solved by using the `signalr.exe` utility to create the proxies statically and persist them in a file to be referenced in our client pages. In this recipe, we illustrate a different option we have, which consists of avoiding JavaScript proxies completely. The **proxy-less** approach provides the JavaScript client with the same client model we have with the .NET client, where generic calls allow us to invoke Hub methods and declare callbacks by name. In this recipe, we'll analyze this API in detail.

Getting ready

Before writing the code of this recipe, we need to create a new empty web application, which we'll call `Recipe41`. We'll illustrate how to use proxy-less connections to call a Hub method from the client and how to define a callback to be invoked from the server.

How to do it...

After creating our sample empty web application, we will add the necessary pieces, as follows:

1. We add a new Hub called `EchoHub` using the **SignalR Hub Class (v2)** template as usual. The following is the code we need:

```
using Microsoft.AspNet.SignalR;
using Microsoft.AspNet.SignalR.Hubs;

namespace Recipe41
{
    [HubName("echo")]
    public class EchoHub : Hub
    {
        public void SayHello()
        {
            Clients.Caller.greetings("Hello!");
        }
    }
}
```

This method is simply invoking a callback named `greetings` on the caller.

2. We add the `Startup` class with a simple standard initialization sequence, as follows:

```
using Microsoft.Owin;
using Owin;
using Recipe41;

[assembly: OwinStartup(typeof(Startup))]

namespace Recipe41
{
    public class Startup
    {
        public void Configuration(IAppBuilder app)
        {
            app.MapSignalR();
        }
    }
}
```

3. Let's switch to the client code, which we place inside our usual `index.html` page, and let's proceed step by step to analyze the specific details of the proxy-less strategy. All the necessary files to reference have already been added during the creation of the `EchoHub` class earlier. We just need to add them to the page as follows:

```
<script src="Scripts/jquery-2.1.0.js"></script>
<script src="Scripts/jquery.signalR-2.0.2.js"></script>
```

Here, we notice the first difference: there's no reference either to the dynamic proxies endpoint or to any file containing the statically generated code for the proxies.

4. We now open a script block where we put our code and begin by creating a `connection` object as follows:

```
<script>
    $(function() {
        var connection = $.hubConnection();


        . . .
    });
</script>
```

The proxy-less API is made available by invoking the `$.hubConnection()` function, whose return value will be used to create any generic proxy on demand. Apart from this additional feature, this `connection` object will play the same role we usually observed on the `$.connection.hub` member, which is not available if we avoid the dynamic proxy endpoint.

5. Let's use the `connection` object to create a generic proxy to access the server-side `EchoHub` class using the following code:

```
var echo = connection.createHubProxy('echo');
    . . .
```

Here, we are using the general-purpose `createHubProxy()` method, which requires the name of the Hub and returns a proxy we can use to refer to it. This proxy has the same role as that of a dynamically generated one, but because we have no code in place to project the shape of the server-side Hub on top of it, it will just expose a few general-purpose methods to interact with it.

6. Our sample will need a `greetings()` callback matching the dynamic call occurring inside `EchoHub`. The following is its definition:

```
echo.on('greetings', function (message) {
    console.log(message);
});
    . . .
```

The `on()` method is the one we need in order to attach the function we want to be triggered when a callback invocation is triggered by the server-side portion of our application, as it's the case for the `greetings()` method. It's a generic method that requires the name of the callback and the corresponding function to call. It's probably less appealing than the dynamic version, but it's functionally equivalent.

7. Now, we just need to start up the connection and perform a simple call towards the server Hub as follows:

```
connection
    .start()
    .done(function () {
        echo.invoke('sayHello');
    });
```

The `connection` object is used to start the connection in the same way as we've been doing so far with `$.connection.hub`, by calling the `start()` method. After that, we define what to do when the connection is ready by specifying a callback through the `done()` method exposed by the promise returned by `start()`. That callback triggers the `sayHello()` server-side method using the `invoke()` generic method exposed by the generic proxy we obtained earlier. Again, we perform an invocation using a string to represent the name of the method, but apart from that this strategy is totally equivalent to the one with dynamic proxies. If the server-side method requires arguments, they can be passed after the method name, and the promise methods like `done()` or `fail()` are available as usual.

We can test what we wrote so far by navigating to `index.html` and observing the console printing the **Hello!** string.

How it works...

It's worth mentioning that the dynamic proxy strategy works on top of the proxy-less one. The actual core of the SignalR JavaScript client is, in fact, the proxy-less API, while the dynamic proxies are just sugar on top of it to make it more palatable and easier to use. Behind the scenes, every dynamic proxy uses the proxy-less API to make things happen.

Although the dynamic proxy strategy might make the proxy-less one look not so interesting, you might find scenarios where you have no option than using it. For example, sometimes you might not be able to determine in advance what dynamic proxy endpoint to load, or from where. In such cases, you might have to recur to the proxy-less strategy, so it's a good idea to know about it and understand how to use it.

Introducing dependency injection (simple approach)

Let's now enter a different territory, where we'll learn how to fully integrate our code with the internal behaviors of SignalR. SignalR offers a powerful way to extend its functionalities through a **dependency injection** API and strategy. Thanks to that, we can easily hook into the Hub creation process, and consequently we have a way to inject other objects into it and make them available to its methods.

In this recipe, we'll illustrate how we can transparently inject a specific reusable logic inside a Hub when it's created. The Hub will expose a simple method receiving a string and returning a corresponding translation obtained from a translator service injected at its creation.

Getting ready

For this recipe, we'll use a new empty web application, which we'll call `Recipe42`.

How to do it...

After creating our empty web application, we will add all the parts we need using the following steps:

1. We start with a new Hub called `EchoHub`, created by using the **SignalR Hub Class (v2)** template. The following code, which is used for this first iteration, will just return the received message *as it is* back to the caller:

```
using Microsoft.AspNet.SignalR;
using Microsoft.AspNet.SignalR.Hubs;

namespace Recipe42
{
    [HubName("echo")]
    public class EchoHub : Hub
    {
        public string SayAnything(string message)
        {
            return message;
        }
    }
}
```

2. We then add the `Startup` class with the standard initialization sequence as follows:

```
using Microsoft.AspNet.SignalR;
using Microsoft.Owin;
using Owin;
using Recipe42;

[assembly: OwinStartup(typeof(Startup))]

namespace Recipe42
{
```

```
public class Startup
{
    public void Configuration(IAppBuilder app)
    {
        app.MapSignalR();
    }
}
```

3. Our client page will connect to `EchoHub` to send a text to translate from English to Italian, looking forward to receiving the translation in order to display it on the page, as follows:

```
<script src="Scripts/jquery-2.1.0.js"></script>
<script src="Scripts/jquery.signalR-2.0.2.js"></script>
<script src="/signalr/hubs"></script>
<script>

    $(function () {
        var hub = $.connection.hub,
            echo = $.connection.echo;

        hub.start().done(function () {
            $("#translate").click(function () {
                echo.server.sayAnything(
                    $("#text").val())
                    .done(function (message) {
                        $("#translated").text(message);
                    });
            });
        });

    });

</script>
```

The `sayAnything()` method is called on the server, and its answer will be received by the callback specified using the `done` member, and from there displayed on the page.

4. Finally, the following is the simple HTML body code we need to collect the input and display the translated message once received:

```
Text: <input type="text" id="text"/>
<button id="translate">Translate</button>
<p id="translated"></p>
```

If we test what we wrote so far, we'll see the input text comes back untouched to the client because our `EchoHub` is not able to translate it yet. Let's therefore introduce our fancy translation infrastructure.

1. Inside the same file where the `EchoHub` is defined, we add the `ITranslator` interface, defining a contract that any translator will have to implement, as follows:

```
public interface ITranslator
{
    Task<string> Translate(string message);
}
```

We clearly state that we expect the translation task to be slow and expensive by declaring its behavior as asynchronous. This is done by specifying `Task<string>` as the return value of the `Translate()` method.

2. We then define an implementation for `ITranslator` and call it `Translator`. The implementation will use the simple and free **MyMemory** translation service, calling it asynchronously, as follows:

```
using System.Net.Http;
using System.Threading.Tasks;
using Newtonsoft.Json;

namespace Recipe42
{
    class Translator : ITranslator
    {
        public async Task<string> Translate(string message)
        {
            using (var w = new HttpClient())
            {
                var url = string.Format(
                    "http://api.mymemory.translated.net" +
                    "/get?q={0}!&langpair=en|it",
                    message);
                var t = await w.GetStringAsync(url);
                var o = JsonConvert
                        .DeserializeObject<dynamic>(t);
                return o.responseData.translatedText;
            }
        }
    }
}
```

The received response is a block of JSON code that we easily parse to extract the translated text before returning it to the caller. The usage of the `async` and `await` keywords makes the structure of our code straightforward.

3. We are now ready to use our brand new translator. We could easily instantiate it directly inside the `EchoHub` and use it, but we would have all the well-known problems generated by hardcoded dependencies. We want to supply any dependency from outside using an appropriate constructor; therefore, our `EchoHub` code must be changed to look like the following:

```
public class EchoHub : Hub
{
    private readonly ITranslator _translator;

    public EchoHub(ITranslator translator)
    {
        _translator = translator;
    }

    public string SayAnything(string message)
    {
        return _translator.Translate(message);
    }
}
```

Now, a translator is supplied to `EchoHub` during its creation, stored in the `_translator` instance field, and then used inside the `SayAnything()` method.

The problem is our hub code would not work anymore because SignalR wouldn't know how to instantiate such a Hub. By default, SignalR creates hubs by invoking their parameter-less constructor, which therefore must exist, but that's not the case for `EchoHub` because of the way we modified it. We need to tell SignalR that each time it's going to create any `EchoHub` instance, it will have to create it the right way. Let's see how.

1. Let's go back to the `Startup` code file, where we can interact with the `DependencyResolver` member exposed by the `GlobalHost` object. `DependencyResolver` exposes an API we can use to tweak the way Hubs and other internal objects are created. In particular, we can declare a **factory function** to be invoked each time a specific type of object is instantiated by SignalR, and this strategy is available for any hub object we define. We just need to register our factory function just before calling `MapSignalR()`, as shown in the following code:

```
GlobalHost.DependencyResolver.Register(
    typeof(EchoHub),
    () => new EchoHub(new Translator()));
```

The code is pretty straightforward. It's basically specifying how a specific type instance (in this case, `EchoHub`) has to be created by the SignalR runtime whenever needed, and the lambda function we define returns an instance of `EchoHub` that is created using the available constructor, supplied with a new instance of the translator type.

Now our application works again, our page is able to translate any input string from English to Italian, and it does it in a clean way with its dependencies correctly handled.

How it works...

The **Inversion of Control (IoC)** principle is at the heart of SignalR runtime, and dependencies can be easily hooked through custom factories. SignalR delivers a simplified dependency injection system exposed by the `DependencyResolver` member of `GlobalHost`, but even that part is easily replaceable with any other custom implementation that we might prefer, and that's exactly what we'll be doing in the next recipe.

You can start reading about the Inversion of Control principle at this link: `http://en.wikipedia.org/wiki/Inversion_of_control`.

Introducing dependency injection (advanced approach)

The previous recipe was interesting and showed good potential, but we might need more. SignalR is a framework that supplies quite a specific set of features, hence it's likely to be used from inside more complex applications, with different modules and components. In such a design, chances are that the host application will already have some other general-purpose dependency injection system in place, probably using one of the many good Inversion of Control container libraries available out there. SignalR does not let us down even in this case, allowing us to inject our preferred IoC container into it.

Here, we'll reproduce the same problem that we solved in the previous one (the translator service), but this time we'll use **Ninject** as a general purpose IoC container in order to register and then inject our dependencies.

Getting ready

For this recipe, we'll use a new empty web application, which we'll call `Recipe43`. We will not reiterate the ideas behind this recipe because those are the same we explained in the previous one. We'll just either replicate or mention some bits of code and refer back to the previous recipe for further explanations.

How to do it...

We start by adding the usual blocks of code using the following steps:

1. We first introduce a new Hub called `EchoHub`, and then the `ITranslator` contractand finally the `Translator` service, all of them the same way as we did in the previous recipe. Because of this, we omit their code here and invite you to grab it from there.

2. We then add the `Startup` class and prepare the initialization sequence as follows:

```
using Microsoft.Owin;
using Owin;
using Recipe43;

[assembly: OwinStartup(typeof(Startup))]

namespace Recipe43
{
    public class Startup
    {
        public void Configuration(IAppBuilder app)
        {
            app.MapSignalR(new HubConfiguration
            {
                Resolver = ...
            });
        }
    }
}
```

We are supplying to the `MapSignalR()` method an instance of `HubConfiguration`, which allows us to define a few specific startup parameters. Our code is left incomplete on purpose, with a few dots where we shall assign an instance of *something* to the `Resolver` member of `HubConfiguration`. That will be used as a replacement for the default dependency resolver. We'll be completing this missing portion of code shortly.

3. Let's now start writing our replacement for the dependency resolver available out of the box. We already mentioned that we want to use `Ninject` as our IoC container; therefore, we need to bring it into the project first. Luckily, it's available on NuGet, so we can easily install it using either the **NuGet Package Manager** or by typing in the following command on the **Package Manager Console**:

```
Install-Package Ninject
```

The same would be possible for many other equivalent and interesting libraries, such as `Moq`, `Unity`, `Castle`, `StructureMap`, `Autofac`, and so on.

4. We now add a new class called `NinjectDependencyResolver` to the project and make it derive from `DefaultDependencyResolver`, a base class provided by SignalR to make this particular task easier. It will have to provide a pair of methods (`GetService()` and `GetServices()`) that SignalR will call when looking for instances of services. Their implementation will just forward the actual resolution to a Ninject `IKernel` instance received and stored by the constructor. Here's the code:

```
using System;
using System.Collections.Generic;
using System.Linq;
using Microsoft.AspNet.SignalR;
using Ninject;

namespace Recipe43
{
    class NinjectDependencyResolver :
        DefaultDependencyResolver
    {
        private readonly IKernel _kernel;

        public NinjectDependencyResolver(IKernel kernel)
        {
            _kernel = kernel;
        }
        public override object GetService(Type serviceType)
        {
            return _kernel.TryGet(serviceType) ??
                base.GetService(serviceType);
        }
        public override IEnumerable<object> GetServices(
            Type serviceType)
        {
            return _kernel.GetAll(serviceType)
                .Concat(base.GetServices(serviceType));
        }
    }
}
```

The code is quite simple, but there is an important thing to highlight here: the `GetService()` implementation is asking the `_kernel` private member to resolve the supplied type, but if no match is found, then we pass the task on to the base class. In this way, we do not have to manually register within Ninject all the internal objects SignalR hooks by default; they'll be retrieved using the base class.

For more details about `IKernel` and Ninject in general, please refer to its documentation at `http://www.ninject.org`.

5. Now, we can go back to the `Startup` class and complete its implementation as follows:

```
var standardKernel = new StandardKernel();

. . .

app.MapSignalR(new HubConfiguration
{
    Resolver = new
        NinjectDependencyResolver(standardKernel)
});
```

This makes it clear how the new dependency resolver is created and supplied to the `HubConfiguration` instance. Of course, we'll have to adjust the `using` directives accordingly.

6. The last step is the registration of the `Translator` service inside our container. We have to do it on the `standardKernel` instance, just before the invocation of the `MapSignalR()` method.

```
standardKernel
    .Bind<ITranslator>()
    .To<Translator>()
    .InSingletonScope();
```

We choose a *singleton* lifestyle for our `Translator` object just to show that's possible, but in this specific case, it does not have to be like this.

Our new dependency resolver is ready. It's relying on a stable and widely-used IoC container, and it's fully integrated with SignalR. We just need to test it, and for that we just have to add a page called `index.html` to the project whose content is exactly the same as we wrote in the previous recipe, hence please go there to grab it and paste it into this new file.

This code will work as expected, and our `EchoHub` is taking its dependencies from outside. We've been able to hook a well-known IoC container, such as Ninject, into SignalR's core with just a couple of simple steps.

Using dependency injection to replace a default behavior

SignalR's dependency injection system has been exploited so far to hook into the factory pipeline implemented to create instances of any Hub-derived type, but what's even more interesting about the whole usage of this system is the fact that most of SignalR's internals are exposed through the same mechanism. This means that you can actually replace entire portions of the SignalR machinery. Maybe you know a better way to perform their task, or maybe you just need to add some more features to a specific part, whatever the reason you can do it as we'll see here.

SignalR is organized in services, and all of them have a default implementation available. Let's list a few of them to just give you an idea:

- ▸ IMessageBus: A service implementing this contract processes every single message, sent or received, with the goal of making them available to every subscriber; we already mentioned this interface when explaining how backplanes are implemented.

- ▸ IJavaScriptProxyGenerator: It defines how a service generating JavaScript proxies for any Hub has to look like.

- ▸ IAssemblyLocator: It is a service contract defining how to locate all the assemblies potentially containing hubs.

There are many more, and you can check the source code on GitHub to discover which they are. In this recipe, we'll concentrate on a specific one called IUserIdProvider, and we'll see how to replace it with our custom implementation. The sample application will allow us to send messages to a specific user, and it will achieve this goal by using a specific SignalR API that makes use of the IUserIdProvider service we'll be replacing.

Getting ready

For this recipe, we'll use a new empty web application, which we'll call Recipe44.

How to do it...

After creating our empty web application, we will proceed as usual using the following steps:

1. We start with a new Hub called EchoHub; you can see its code as follows:

```
using Microsoft.AspNet.SignalR;
using Microsoft.AspNet.SignalR.Hubs;

namespace Recipe44
{
    [HubName("echo")]
    public class EchoHub : Hub
    {
        public void SayHello(string recipient)
        {
            Clients.User(recipient).greetings("Hello");
        }
    }
}
```

The SayHello() method has a single parameter for the name of the user we want to target with a message, and it uses the Clients.User member to get the connection(s) owned by the specified user. On the dynamic object returned, it finally calls the greetings() dynamic method. This mechanism works as for every other member of the Clients object we described in the first part of the book.

The Clients.User resolution process is based on IUserIdProvider, which is used by SignalR to extract useful information related to the identity of the connected user from every single request it performs. Let's see how it works.

2. We need to add our custom implementation of IUserIdProvider to the project. For that, we'll introduce a new class called EchoHubUserProvider with the following code:

```
using Microsoft.AspNet.SignalR;

namespace Recipe44
{
    public class EchoHubUserProvider : IUserIdProvider
    {
        public string GetUserId(IRequest request)
        {
            return request.QueryString["user"];
        }
    }
}
```

The class implements `IUserIdProvider`, which implies providing a method called `GetUserId()`, receiving an `IRequest` instance and returning a string. For every incoming request, SignalR will ask the dependency resolver to provide an instance of a service implementing this contract, in order to extract any useful information to determine an identifier for the connected user. The default implementation embedded in SignalR returns the name extracted from the identity principal attached to the supplied `IRequest` instance. Our sample implementation will get that information from a query string parameter called `user`. This means that we'll need to put this value in place, and we'll take care of this detail on the test page.

It's a basic example, with nothing in place to take care of concerns like authentication or security, but it should be enough to let you imagine more sophisticated user-mapping strategies and handshaking workflows. It also shows how you could design an authentication mechanism based on some sort of client-side-generated token.

3. We then create the `Startup` class by performing the usual `MapSignalR()` call, but not before having registered our custom `IUserIdProvider` as follows:

```
using Microsoft.AspNet.SignalR;
using Microsoft.Owin;
using Owin;
using Recipe44;

[assembly: OwinStartup(typeof(Startup))]

namespace Recipe44
{
    public class Startup
    {
        public void Configuration(IAppBuilder app)
        {
            GlobalHost.DependencyResolver.Register(
                typeof(IUserIdProvider),
                () => new EchoHubUserProvider());

            app.MapSignalR();
        }
    }
}
```

The call is very straightforward, and it's using the `Register()` method from `DependencyResolver` as we did when performing the registration and implementation of the `ITranslator` contract in the *Introducing dependencies injection (simple approach)* recipe. This is good news: the same API we leveraged to register a custom service to be injected in a Hub can be used to replace any SignalR default implementation of an internal service!

4. We're almost done. We just need a client test page, which as usual we'll call `index.html`, from where anybody can type in the name of a target user who will receive a `"Hello"` message. First, we'll need some HTML controls on the page for the login process and to send messages, as shown in the following code:

```
<div id="login-form">
    Your name: <input type="text" id="user" />
    <button id="login">Login</button>
</div>
<div id="message-form" style="display: none">
    Say hello to: <input type="text" id="recipient"
    />
    <button id="send">Send</button>
    <ul id="messages"></ul>
</div>
```

5. We then need some JavaScript code to handle the login phase first, and later on the input of the recipient name and the posting of the message:

```
<script src="Scripts/jquery-2.1.0.js"></script>
<script src="Scripts/jquery.signalR-2.0.2.js"></script>
<script src="/signalr/hubs"></script>
<script>

    $(function () {
        $('#login').click(function() {
            $('#login-form').toggle();
            $('#message-form').toggle();

            var hub  = $.connection.hub,
                echo = $.connection.echo;

            hub.qs = { 'user': $('#user').val() };

            echo.client.greetings = function(message) {
                $('<li/>').html(message)
                    .appendTo('#messages');
            };

            hub.start().done(function () {
                $('#send').click(function () {
                    echo.server.sayHello(
                        $('#recipient').val());
                });
            });
        });
    });

</script>
```

There is an interesting and new SignalR feature we need to illustrate in this code. We do not start SignalR immediately after loading the page; instead, we do that just after receiving the username. This is because we want to use the query string to supply that information to SignalR at every call. The hub object exposes a property called qs, which can be assigned a JavaScript object representing a set of parameters we want to send to the server using the query string. This property has to be set before starting the connection, and cannot be changed afterwards. That's why we need to know what to put in there before connecting. We use this feature to take the username supplied and add it as a query string parameter called user, which matches the one expected by the implementation of IUserIdProvider we saw earlier. SignalR will guarantee that such a value will be provided for every request that comes to the server.

We can test our page by opening it in a couple of browser windows. In each of them, we'll type a different username and log in, and finally we'll be able to send direct messages to specific users identified by the names they used to log in and discriminated on the server by our EchoHubUserProvider service. We could even use the same username in multiple tabs, all of them would receive the same message when their user is the target, thanks to the way Clients.User, and IUserIdProvider work together.

How it works...

If we put a breakpoint on the line of code inside the EchoHubUserProvider, we'll see that line hit on every request going to the server. This means that SignalR resolves the user ID at every request and then keeps it around so that an API like Clients.User is able to find the connection mapped to that user. The value returned by GetUserId() becomes a key through which we can find a set of connections just by knowing an identifier associated to the user owning them.

The details about how IUserIdProvider works are interesting, but those wouldn't have been possible without the DependencyResolver API.

Extending the Hub pipeline

Among all the services that SignalR exposes and lets us customize, there is one that is particularly interesting: IHubPipeline. This service, as its name clearly states, represents the full pipeline that underpins a Hub, and its goal is to collect a set of modules to be executed during the initialization of a Hub. Each module implements IHubPipelineModule, and each method exposed by this contract is executed during the bootstrap phase. The job of those methods is to provide a factory methods that SignalR will then invoke during specific moments in the lifetime of every instance of a Hub. There are factories to build incoming and outgoing Hub invocations; to perform connection, reconnection, and disconnection tasks; to authorize connections; and to handle whether a client can rejoin groups on reconnection.

Thanks to the dependency injection mechanism we've been analyzing earlier, we could replace the `IHubPipeline` service with our custom implementation, but that would be a tough task to do without having a negative impact on SignalR's behavior. There are many things at that level that need to be executed, and we cannot afford forgetting about them while implementing a custom pipeline. That's why in this case it is better to avoid starting from scratch, and the recommended workflow is to use the `HubPipeline` member exposed by `GlobalHost`, and to add our modules there. Instead of implementing `IHubPipelineModule` directly, modules should derive from `HubPipelineModule`, which SignalR makes available to simplify the task of introducing new behaviors while still keeping the overall system functional. It exposes all its factory methods as virtual, allowing us to add our logic while still relying on the base type where necessary.

In this recipe, we will illustrate a couple of methods exposed by `HubPipelineModule`, which allow us to intercept the construction of incoming and outgoing invocations, and we'll use them to introduce a simple discrimination logic which, based on the name of the called method, might decide to skip it entirely. We'll build a simple test application and inject such logic on top of it using the `GlobalHost.HubPipeline` entry point.

Getting ready

For this recipe, we'll use a new empty web application, which we'll call `Recipe45`.

How to do it...

Our application will expose a Hub with three similar methods—all with the same behavior but just different names—and three related callbacks. Our discriminating logic will be based on those names. We will perform the following steps:

1. We start by creating the usual `EchoHub` class using the **SignalR Hub Class (v2)** template. The following is the code we need:

```
using Microsoft.AspNet.SignalR;
using Microsoft.AspNet.SignalR.Hubs;

namespace Recipe45
{
    [HubName("echo")]
    public class EchoHub : Hub
    {
        public void SayHello()
        {
            Clients.All.hello();
        }

        public void SayGoodbye()
        {
```

```
        Clients.All.goodbye();
    }

    public void SayAnything()
    {
        Clients.All.anything();
    }
}
}
```

You can clearly see that the methods are trivial, and they all behave in the same way by broadcasting a callback with a name corresponding in some way to the method that triggered it.

2. The client page we'll need to test this hub is fairly simple too. Let's create our usual `index.html` page and put some HTML controls in it as follows:

```
<button id="sayHello">Say hello!</button>
<button id="sayGoodbye">Say goodbye!</button>
<button id="sayAnything">Say anything!</button>
<ul id="messages"></ul>
```

We need a few buttons, one for each method on the hub, and an unordered list to collect the answers. Let's then add some JavaScript code to bind the buttons to server-side calls, and to define callbacks which will append specific messages to the list:

```
<script src="Scripts/jquery-2.1.0.js"></script>
<script src="Scripts/jquery.signalR-2.0.2.js"></script>
<script src="/signalr/hubs"></script>
<script>

    $(function() {
        var hub = $.connection.hub,
            echo = $.connection.echo,
            message = function(m) {
                $('#messages')
                    .append($('<li/>').text(m));
            };

        echo.client.hello = function() {
            message('Hello!');
        };
        echo.client.goodbye = function () {
            message('Goodbye!');
        };
```

```
        echo.client.anything = function () {
            message('Anything!');
        };

        hub.start().done(function () {
            $('#sayHello').click(function() {
                echo.server.sayHello();
            });
            $('#sayGoodbye').click(function () {
                echo.server.sayGoodbye();
            });
            $('#sayAnything').click(function () {
                echo.server.sayAnything();
            });
        });

    });

    </script>
```

3. We finally add the Startup class performing the bootstrap sequence as follows:

```
using Microsoft.AspNet.SignalR;
using Microsoft.Owin;
using Owin;

[assembly: OwinStartup(typeof(Recipe45.Startup))]

namespace Recipe45
{
    public class Startup
    {
        public void Configuration(IAppBuilder app)
        {
            ...

            app.MapSignalR();
        }
    }
}
```

We just placed a few dots where later on we'll be adding some more code to register our custom implementation of IHubPipelineModule.

Let's do a first test of this page, just to verify that each button actually triggers a server-side call that is then reflected in a corresponding client-side callback being invoked to print out a specific message. When everything is good, we can move on to the next set of steps, which are as follows:

1. Let's add to our project the skeleton of a new class called `EchoHubModule`, and let's specify `HubPipelineModule` as its base class, as follows:

```
using Microsoft.AspNet.SignalR.Hubs;

namespace Recipe45
{
    public class EchoHubModule : HubPipelineModule
    {
        . . .
    }
}
```

2. After that, we override the `BuildIncoming()` and `BuildOutgoing()` methods using the following code:

```
public override
   Func<IHubIncomingInvokerContext, Task<object>>
   BuildIncoming(
      Func<IHubIncomingInvokerContext,
         Task<object>>invoker)
{
   Trace.WriteLine("BuidIncoming");
   return base.BuildIncoming(invoker);
}

public override
   Func<IHubOutgoingInvokerContext, Task>
   BuildOutgoing(
      Func<IHubOutgoingInvokerContext, Task>
         invoker)
{
   Trace.WriteLine("BuildOutgoing");
   return base.BuildOutgoing(invoker);
}
```

`BuildIncoming()` is invoked to return a factory method that will be used each time an invocation towards a Hub's method reaches the server, and it will return the actual server-side call to be performed. `BuildOutgoing()` performs a similar task, but it's invoked whenever an invocation towards a client-side callback is happening on the server. Our overrides are pretty basic. They just call into the base implementation to keep the base behavior, but just before that they send a message containing the name of the method to the Trace device.

3. Let's go back to the `Startup` class to add the module registration code as follows:

```
GlobalHost.HubPipeline.AddModule(new EchoHubModule());
```

If we reload our page and press the buttons, we will experience the same behavior as before, but if we take a look at the Trace console in Visual Studio, we will notice that the two messages, **BuildIncoming** and **BuildOutgoing**, are printed out, once each, when the first page connects and the `EchoHub` instance is initialized by SignalR's runtime for the first time. That confirms the fact that these methods are invoked just once at the start-up of the application.

4. Back to our module, let's make our methods more interesting by replacing their `return` statement with something more useful. We start with `BuildIncoming()` as follows:

```
return base.BuildIncoming(ctx =>
{
    Trace.Write(string.Format("I might call
        {0}...",
        ctx.MethodDescriptor.Name));

    if (ctx.MethodDescriptor.Name ==
        "SayHello")
    {
        Trace.WriteLine(" but I won't :(");
        return null;
    }

    Trace.WriteLine(" and I will!");
    return invoker(ctx);
});
```

This code needs some comments:

- We call the base class method again, but this time we supply a lambda expression whose goal is to decide whether we should actually perform the invocation or not. The signature of the lambda expression must, of course, match the one of the incoming `invoker()` parameter.
- Inside the expression, we first print out the name of the method that is going to be called.
- Then we check the method's name to decide what happens next. If that's equal to `SayHello` we want to block its execution, which is as simple as having our expression returning a `null` value. In any other case, we call the `invoker()` parameter we received and return its exit value, which will be a task representing the actual execution of the Hub's method requested by the client.

☐ In both execution branches, we send a message describing what happened to the Trace device.

5. Let's do something similar with `BuildOutgoing()`, as follows:

```
return base.BuildOutgoing(ctx =>
{
    Trace.Write(string.Format("I might call
    back {0}...",
    ctx.Invocation.Method));

    if (ctx.Invocation.Method == "goodbye")
    {
        Trace.WriteLine(" but I won't :(");
        return null;
    }

    Trace.WriteLine(" and I will!");
    return invoker(ctx);
});
```

What happens here is similar to what we did with `BuildIncoming()`—the differences being the following:

☐ We are checking a remote callback invocation, which would be initiated on the server but executed on the client

☐ The context object (`ctx`) has a slightly different shape, but it's still bringing similar information about the requested invocation

☐ Here we check the method's name against the `goodbye` string, with the goal of blocking any call with that name

Our last test session will eventually show a different outcome. The only button fully working would be the **Say Anything** one, whereas the `SayHello()` method would get completely blocked and the `SayGoodbye()` one would run on the server, but with no client callback being triggered. We have been able to both discriminate the execution of specific methods according to a custom execution workflow and print out diagnostic messages while checking each invocation. All this has been possible without having to add a single line of code inside the methods themselves.

There's more...

This sample showed how SignalR allows us to hook code into its own machinery to customize its behavior or add specific behaviors. These kinds of capabilities are generally used to solve orthogonal infrastructural aspects, such as logging, caching, or authorization, which are usually known as *cross-cutting concerns*. If you are curious about it, you can dig more around the discipline of **Aspect Oriented Programming**, maybe starting with this link: http://en.wikipedia.org/wiki/Aspect-oriented_programming.

Handling errors

In this last recipe of the chapter, we want to achieve a smarter exception-handling strategy, and for that we apply some of the lessons we learned about the extensibility features of SignalR, along with some other features specific of error management.

Getting ready

For this recipe, we'll use a new empty web application, which we'll call `Recipe46`.

How to do it...

Our code will contain a Hub with a couple of methods raising exceptions, and the following steps will illustrate how to work around them in order to collect and manage information about the errors:

1. We create a new Hub called `FailingHub` using the **SignalR Hub Class (v2)** template. The following is what it should look like:

```
using System;
using Microsoft.AspNet.SignalR;
using Microsoft.AspNet.SignalR.Hubs;

namespace Recipe46
{
    [HubName("failing")]
    public class FailingHub : Hub
    {
        public void Basic()
        {
            throw new OutOfMemoryException();
        }
        public void Wrapped()
        {
            try
            {
                throw new OutOfMemoryException();
            }
            catch (Exception e)
            {
                throw new HubException("Wrapped",
                    new
                    {
                        Error = e
                    });
            }
        }
    }
}
```

We have two simple methods, both just failing with an `OutOfMemoryException` exception. The second one is called `Wrapped` because we actually put the execution of the failing method inside a `try...catch` block and rethrow the exception wrapped with a `HubException` instance. We'll be explaining the reason for doing this later on.

2. Let's now leverage what we learned in the previous recipe in order to customize the Hub pipeline. There is an interesting factory method on `HubPipelineModule`, called `OnIncomingError()`, that we can override, as shown in the following code:

```
using System.Diagnostics;
using Microsoft.AspNet.SignalR.Hubs;

namespace Recipe46
{
    public class ErrorHandlingPipelineModule :
        HubPipelineModule
    {
        protected override void OnIncomingError(
            ExceptionContext exceptionContext,
            IHubIncomingInvokerContext invokerContext)
        {
            Trace.WriteLine(string.Format(
                "An error occurred while invoking {0}:
                {1}",
                invokerContext.MethodDescriptor.Name,
                exceptionContext.Error));
            base.OnIncomingError(
                exceptionContext, invokerContext);
        }
    }
}
```

Once we know it's available, `OnIncomingError()` is pretty easy to use. It's automatically called whenever an unhandled exception occurs from inside a Hub's method, and it's supplied information about the error itself, and its execution context.

3. Let's now see how to define the `Startup` class to put things together:

```
using Microsoft.AspNet.SignalR;
using Microsoft.Owin;
using Owin;
using Recipe46;

[assembly: OwinStartup(typeof(Startup))]

namespace Recipe46
{
```

```
public class Startup
{
    public void Configuration(IAppBuilder app)
    {
        GlobalHost.HubPipeline.AddModule(
            new ErrorHandlingPipelineModule());

        app.MapSignalR(
            new HubConfiguration
            {
                EnableDetailedErrors = true
            });
    }
}
```

The first line is simply registering our `ErrorHandlingPipelineModule` in the same way we explained in the previous recipe. The following `MapSignalR()` call is supplied a specific configuration instance, which sets the `EnableDetailedErrors` property to `true`. This property explicitly instructs SignalR to send unhandled exception details down to the client who invoked the method. Without that, and for security reasons, the default behavior would just send a generic message with no detail.

4. It's time to prepare the client page and its code. We add `index.html` to the project, and we need to put a couple of buttons there to trigger the two server-side methods along with some JavaScript code, as follows:

```
<script src="Scripts/jquery-2.1.0.js"></script>
<script src="Scripts/jquery.signalR-2.0.2.js"></script>
<script src="/signalr/hubs"></script>
<script>

    var failing = $.connection.failing;

    $.connection.hub
        .start()
        .done(function() {
            $("#basic").click(function() {
                failing.server.basic()
                    .fail(function(e) {
                        console.log(e);
```

```
                    });
                });
                $("#wrapped").click(function () {
                    failing.server.wrapped()
                        .fail(function (e) {
                            console.log(e);
                        });
                });
            });

    </script>
    <button id="basic">Basic</button>
    <button id="wrapped">Wrapped</button>


    . . .
```

Both invocations towards the server-side Hub are followed by the `fail()` invocations in order to specify followed by a callback to be invoked in case of remote error. The details about the error will be printed to the browser's console.

Now, we are ready to test `index.html`. If we click on the **Basic** button, the console will print a simple object that brings back no more than the exception message, whereas the **Wrapped** button will result in a much more detailed object, with a message and a data object as defined inside the Hub method when the `HubException` exception was thrown. If we now go back to the `Startup` class and revert `EnableDetailedErrors` to `false`, the `Wrapped` method will result in the same type of error message because the explicit act of emitting a `HubException` is a stronger declaration of the wish to have details sent to the client. On the other hand, the **Basic** button will receive a very generic error, with a standard message just saying that the invoked method failed. We can therefore combine `HubException` and `EnableDetailedErrors` the way it best fits our needs.

On the server side, the addition of our custom module has resulted in each exception being sent to the Trace device, as we can easily verify by checking the Visual Studio **Trace** window while running the application and clicking on the buttons. In this sample, we leveraged that information to just print out details about the error to the Trace device, but it's definitely an interesting extension point, from where we could inject more useful error-handling strategies to keep the application healthy.

8
Building Complex Applications

In this chapter, we will cover the following topics:

- ▶ Implementing a room-based chat application
- ▶ Implementing a shared whiteboard
- ▶ Implementing a real-time map of flying airplanes
- ▶ Implementing a "pets finder" application
- ▶ Implementing a custom backplane
- ▶ Implementing a real-time error notification system

Introduction

In this chapter, we'll try to put together most of the concepts and features that we have been analyzing so far in order to build a few full-fledged sample applications. Of course, we will not be able to deliver bulletproof solutions where every single detail is deeply tested, every visual widget properly styled, and every workflow ramification thoroughly conceived, but each of the following recipes will give you an idea about how you could structure a real-world project putting several things together and using SignalR to glue them whenever you need to deliver a real-time experience.

For each recipe, we'll give you a brief description of both its goals and its design. We'll proceed by going through the code and trying to minimize its comments unless it's strictly related to SignalR, but at the same time, listing all the relevant parts so that you can get to the end of the exercise having built something that actually works. We will not indulge too much in describing a task such as selecting the right template; this should be clear from the previous recipes. All our samples will be hosted in web applications.

Implementing a room-based chat application

One of the most common types of real-time application is **messaging systems**, and chat applications are a good example of such a category. In this recipe, we will build a web chat where users will log in using a nickname, and once logged in, they will be able to create and join rooms. After joining a room, they will be able to post messages and see what other users say. The application will, of course, miss many of the functionalities that we usually find in a chat application, but it should be good enough to showcase a concrete usage of several SignalR features, namely the following:

- Calling methods on a hub from the client
- Triggering client-side callbacks from the server
- Using the Groups API

Getting ready

Our application will consist of the following:

- A Hub called `ChatHub`, which will handle things such as the login process, rooms management, and message broadcasting.
- A page for the client part, named `index.html`, that displays the list of available rooms and, for each room that the user has joined, a simple "widget" that displays the messages that were exchanged there.
- A JavaScript file called `app.js`, which contains the client-side logic around the SignalR interactions and the **Document Object Model** (**DOM**) manipulations necessary to drive the rendering of the information on the host page.
- A style sheet called `chat.css`.
- Everything else necessary to have things running, as already illustrated throughout the book (the `Startup` class, proper references, and so on).

Therefore, before writing the code of this recipe, we need to create a new empty web application, which we'll call `Recipe47`.

How to do it...

Let's start by preparing the infrastructure that we need. In this case, it is as simple as adding the `Microsoft.AspNet.SignalR` NuGet package, which will download all the up-to-date references that we need. As previously mentioned, we do this before launching any readymade Visual Studio templates in order to be sure that we are running on the latest version of our packages.

We can now start sketching the layout of our `index.html` page. Perform the following steps to do so:

1. Let's first create it and make it look like the following code:

```
<!DOCTYPE html>
<html xmlns="http://www.w3.org/1999/xhtml">
<head>
    <link href="Styles/chat.css" rel="stylesheet" />
    <script src="Scripts/jquery-2.1.0.js"></script>
    <script src="Scripts/jquery.signalR-2.0.2.js"></script>
    <script src="/signalr/hubs"></script>
    <script src="/Scripts/app.js"></script>
</head>
<body>
    ...
</body>
</html>
```

    The `head` section starts with a reference to the `chat.css` CSS style sheet file that we'll be creating later on. Then, we have the usual references to the JavaScript client libraries that we need. To be sure that you have the right version numbers, you can expand the `Scripts` folder in your project, drag the filename, and drop it onto the `head` section of the page.

    We also put the usual reference to the dynamic hubs endpoint (`/signalr/hubs`) in place, and finally a reference to the `app.js` file that we'll be creating shortly; this will contain our application logic.

2. We now need to build the body of the page. Include the following code in the `body` section:

```
<div id="actions">
    <div id="login-box">
        <span>Name:</span>
        <input type="text" id="name" />
        <button id="login">Login</button>
    </div>
    <div id="logout-box">
        <span id="logged"></span>
        <button id="logout">Logout</button>
    </div>
</div>
<div id="rooms-box">
    <div>
```

```
                    <span>New room:</span>
                    <input type="text" id="room" />
                    <button id="new">New</button>
                </div>
                <ul id="rooms"></ul>
            </div>
            <div id="chats-box">
                <ul id="chats"></ul>
            </div>
```

We defined one panel where the nickname can be supplied and a second panel that can be displayed once logged in, along with a button to log out. It's worth noting that we need not worry about either authentication or authorization for this recipe; every username will be valid, and no password is required. Then, we need an input section to use when we want to create a new room, a list for the active rooms, and finally a list of the rooms that we joined, each containing an input section to type new messages and a list for the received messages. The actual widgets representing the rooms the user joined will be dynamically built by some JavaScript code; at this point we just need a container where we can create them on demand.

3. Now, let's add the `chat.css` file that we mentioned earlier, situated in a folder called `Styles`. Its content will take care to properly place all the panels in a rational way on the page. This is not really needed to have the underlying logic working, but without any visual organization, the result would be very confusing and therefore unusable, so we decided to spend some time to list its content with no further comment:

```css
body {
    font-family: "Helvetica Neue", Helvetica, Arial,
sans-serif;
}
button {
    width: 80px;
}
span {
    width: 100px;
    display: inline-block;
}
#actions {
    position: fixed;
    height: 40px; left: 0; right: 0;
    background-color: lightyellow;
}
#login-box {
    float: left;
}
```

```css
#logout-box {
    float: right; display: none;
}
#rooms-box {
    position: fixed;
    top: 40px; left: 0; width: 400px; bottom: 0;
    background-color: lightgreen;
    display: none;
}
#rooms li {
    cursor: pointer;
}
#chats-box {
    position: fixed; overflow-y: scroll;
    top: 40px; left: 400px; right: 0; bottom: 0;
    background-color: lightpink;
    display: none;
}
#chats-box ul {
    margin: 0; padding: 0;
}
#chats-box > ul > li {
    list-style-type: none;
    height: 200px; width: 100%; border: 1px solid black;
}
#chats h4 {
    height: 25px; margin: 0;
}
div.input {
    height: 25px; width: 100%;
}
div.input input {
    left: 0; width: 580px;
}
div.messages-box {
    top: 80px; left: 0; right: 0; height: 150px;
    overflow-y: scroll;
}
span.sender {
    font-weight: bold;
}
```

We are now ready to move on and bring things to life. Let's start from the server side and perform the following steps:

1. We need to create the `Startup` class using the proper template; its body will just have to do the standard bootstrap call in the `Configuration()` method, shown as follows:

```
public class Startup
{
    public void Configuration(IAppBuilder app)
    {
        app.MapSignalR();
    }
}
```

2. It's time for the hub; we'll call it `ChatHub` and mark it with `HubNameAttribute` to specify `"chat"` as its friendly name, as follows:

```
using System.Collections.Generic;
using System.Linq;
using Microsoft.AspNet.SignalR;
using Microsoft.AspNet.SignalR.Hubs;

namespace Recipe47
{
    [HubName("chat")]
    public class ChatHub : Hub
    {
        ...
    }
}
```

3. Our implementation will be very minimalistic; in fact, we'll be avoiding any logic related to the users, such as password management, checks for duplicate nicknames, and even the maintenance of a simple list of the logged users, because these details are not the actual topic of this recipe. We'll just keep a list of rooms, and we'll make it static in order to be available to all instances of `Hub`, as shown in the following code snippet. We will not worry about protecting the collection of rooms from concurrent access:

```
static readonly HashSet<string> Rooms =
    new HashSet<string>();
```

4. Let's proceed with the first method that a user would need to call, `Login`, and its complementary method, `Logout`:

```
public string Login(string name)
{
    Clients.Caller.rooms(Rooms.ToArray());
    return name;
}

public void Logout(string name)
{
}
```

In the `Login()` method, we just trigger the `rooms` callback on `Clients.Caller` to communicate to the caller a list of the existing rooms, and then we return the nickname used to access the chat system. The `Logout()` method does not do anything at all, and it's just used as a placeholder for any related action that we would add in a fully featured system.

Now, things start getting more interesting. A chat room for us is just a topic, and a portion of users might be interested in anything that occurs in that topic. This is the perfect case for SignalR's groups, so we'll model rooms around it by performing the following steps:

5. Let's start assuming that a few rooms already exist, and we want to join a specific one; we'll use the following code:

```
public void JoinRoom(string name)
{
    if (!Rooms.Contains(name)) return;
    Groups.Add(Context.ConnectionId, name);
    Clients.Caller.join(name);
}
```

The code is very simple; we first check whether the requested room name exists in the `Rooms` set, and we leave it if it's not the case. On being successful, we subscribe the caller to a group named after the room name; this way, we'll be able to easily broadcast the messages to all the users in that room by using that group. Before leaving the method, we perform a callback on `Clients.Caller` to notify the caller that they have actually joined the required room. We'll see how that callback is used on the client later on.

6. We've been assuming that some rooms already exist, but at the startup of the system they do not, so let's see how a user can create one. Consider the following code:

```
public void CreateRoom(string name)
{
    if (Rooms.Contains(name)) return;
    Rooms.Add(name);
    JoinRoom(name);
    Clients.All.rooms(new [] { name });
}
```

We first check if a room with the specified name already exists, and we just exit it if it does. If we pass the check, we add the new room to the `Rooms` set (again, we are not performing any concurrency check here), and we let the creator join it by calling the `JoinRoom()` method that we previously described. At this point, we broadcast to all the users the fact that a new room exists, and to do that, we use the same `rooms` callback that we saw earlier, which expects an array of `string` values. This is why we pass our room name inside an array of just one element.

7. We're almost done, but we're still missing the most important piece of logic: the broadcasting of messages to the right rooms. Consider the following code:

```
public void Send(string room, string message,
    string user)
{
    Clients.Group(room).message(room,
        new { message, sender = user });
}
```

The sender of a message will have to specify the room on which they are writing, the text of the message, and their name. With these details, `ChatHub` will know that it will have to target all the subscribers to a group called after the room's name and trigger a client callback (called `message`) supplied with the same parameters. SignalR's groups allow us to perform such a complex operation with just one line of code!

Out `ChatHub` is ready, and it wasn't difficult. Now let's see, with the following steps, how a client could make use of it:

1. We need to add our `app.js` file inside the `Scripts` folder and initialize it with the following code:

```
$(function () {
    var hub    = $.connection.hub,
        chat   = $.connection.chat,
        server = chat.server,
        client = chat.client,
        loginName;

        ...
});
```

As usual, we write our code inside the `$(...)` jQuery handler for the `document.ready` event. We start by simply taking a few references for useful things, such as the `hub` member and the `chat` pointer to our remote hub.

2. Let's write the code that we need to interact with the hub, starting with the startup sequence, as shown in the following code:

```
. . .
hub.start()
    .done(function () {
        . . .
    });
```

We call the `start()` method as we learned earlier, and we prepare a completion callback, to be filled in the next step, by using the `done()` method.

3. Inside the `done()` callback, we wire things that should be enabled only when connected, that is, the login/logout process and the creation of new rooms, as shown:

```
$('#login').click(function () {
    server.login($('#name').val())
        .done(function (name) {
            loginName = name;
            $('#login-box, #logout-box,
                #rooms-box,
                #chats-box').toggle();
            $('#logged').html(loginName);
        });
});
$('#logout').click(function () {
    server.logout($('#name').val())
        .done(function () {
            $('#login-box, #logout-box,
                #rooms-box,
                #chats-box').toggle();
            $('#rooms, #chats').empty();
        });
});
$('#new').click(function () {
    server.createRoom($('#room').val());
});
```

We first bind the `login` button to a `click` handler that will call the remote `login()` method, passing to it the value of the `name` textbox. When the call is completed, we store the chosen login name in a variable and then display the rest of the page to the user. Something similar happens with the `logout` button just the other way round. Finally, the `new` button is bound to a handler, calling the `createRoom()` method of the remote `ChatHub`, which we already described earlier.

We are still missing all the callbacks `ChatHub` is triggering remotely. Let's add them using the following steps, paying attention to the fact that, as you should already know by now, they must be defined before calling `hub.start()`. So, please position the cursor just above it before proceeding:

4. Let's tackle the callbacks in the same order in which we met them on the server side, the first one being `rooms`:

```
client.rooms = function (rs) {
    $.each(rs, function (i, r) {
        $('#rooms').append($('<li/>')
            .html(r)
            .click(function () {
                server.joinRoom($(this).text());
            }));
    });
};
```

It's pretty simple; this one is called when the user logs in and whenever a new room is created, and is supplied with a list of rooms. Our code takes the list of rooms and uses it to append `li` items to the `rooms` unordered list. Each `li` item is bound to a `click` handler that will call the `joinRoom()` remote method; this way, joining a new room is as easy as clicking its name in the list.

5. The second callback we saw was `join`, which is triggered whenever a user joins a new room, shown as follows:

```
client.join = function (r) {
    var $message = $('<input type="text"/>');
    var $li = $('<li/>')
        .append($('<h4/>').html(r))
        .append($('<div/>')
            .addClass('input')
            .append($message)
            .append($('<button/>')
                .attr('id', 'send')
                .text('Send')
                .click(function() {
                    server.send(r, $message.val(),
                                loginName);
                })
            )
        )
        .append($('<div/>')
            .addClass('messages-box')
            .append($('<ul />')
                .attr('data-room', r)));

    $('#chats').append($li);
};
```

This one is longer, but that's mainly because we need to dynamically create several HTML elements to build our room's box, with a proper input area and its list of messages. The only really interesting line of code is the `click` handler, which is attached to a dynamically created button and calls the `send` message on the hub's proxy.

6. Finally, we need the callback to handle incoming messages, shown as follows:

```
client.message = function (room, message) {
    $('[data-room="' + room + '"]')
        .prepend($('<li/>')
            .append($('<span/>')
                .addClass('sender')
                .html(message.sender))
            .append($('<span/>').html(message.message))
        );
};
```

This one is triggered for each message sent to a chat room. We just need to unpack the parameters, find the right room box where we can display it, and prepend it to the corresponding unordered list. A `data-room` custom attribute is used to find the right room box, taking advantage of the fact that the same attribute was set by the `join` callback when creating the visual elements of the room that was just joined by the current user.

We are done, and it was not difficult! We can easily test the chat room system by launching the application, navigating to the `index.html` page from multiple browser windows, and logging into each of them with a different nickname. The rest of the usage should be straightforward and you should appreciate how much we actually achieved with such a small amount of code.

There's more...

This sample is good enough to illustrate how certain SignalR's features can be put together to easily build a complex application such as a chat room system, but of course, this is far from being a professional one. If you want to see a real-world chat application built on SignalR, you should check **JabbR** (`https://jabbr.net/`) from the SignalR team, which is packed with features that anybody would love to get from such an application. Its open source code can be found at `https://github.com/JabbR/JabbR`.

Implementing a shared whiteboard

Our next example of a real-time application is a **shared whiteboard**. SignalR is definitely a good platform to build real-time collaborative tools, because its ability to push information to the clients makes managing a shared status easy, allowing us to keep it synchronized across several instances of the same gadget. Our whiteboard will allow users to join it and draw simple rectangles, which will be broadcasted live to all users. It will also allow us to store them on the server to keep a live history that will be used to generate the current status of the whiteboard to be pushed to new users when they connect. To build these capabilities, we'll use the following SignalR features:

- ▸ Calling methods on a hub from the client
- ▸ Triggering client-side callbacks from the server
- ▸ Using the Groups API
- ▸ Using the state bag
- ▸ Handling server-side errors

Getting ready

Our application will consist of the following:

- ▸ A `Hub` called `WhiteboardHub`, which will be used to handle the login process, to keep the history of shapes, and to broadcast them.
- ▸ A page for the client part, called `index.html`, with a login box and a couple of `canvas` elements to build our drawing surface.
- ▸ A JavaScript file called `app.js`, which contains the client-side logic around the SignalR interactions and the DOM manipulations to build the whiteboard functionalities.
- ▸ A style sheet called `whiteboard.css`.
- ▸ The usual plumbing tools (the `Startup` class, proper references, and so on).

In order to proceed, you'll have to build a new empty web application and call it `Recipe48`.

How to do it...

As usual, as in the last chapter, we start by adding the `Microsoft.AspNet.SignalR` NuGet package, which will download all the up-to-date references that we need.

Let's prepare the visual part of our whiteboard by creating an `index.html` page by performing the following steps:

1. We first add it to the project and then we make it look like the following code:

```
<!DOCTYPE html>
<html xmlns="http://www.w3.org/1999/xhtml">
<head>
    <title></title>
    <link href="Styles/whiteboard.css" rel="stylesheet" />
    <script src="Scripts/jquery-2.1.0.js"></script>
    <script src="Scripts/jquery.signalR-2.0.2.js"></script>
    <script src="/signalr/hubs"></script>
    <script src="Scripts/whiteboard.js"></script>
</head>
    <body>
        Name: <input type="text" id="name"/>
        <button id="join">Join</button>
        <span id="logged"></span>
        <canvas id="surface" width="800" height="600"
            style="z-index: 0"></canvas>
        <canvas id="temp" width="800" height="600"
            style="z-index: 1;
            background-color: transparent"></canvas>
    </body>
</html>
```

The `head` section contains a reference to the `whiteboard.css` CSS stylesheet file, which we'll be illustrating later on, and the usual and up-to-date JavaScript client libraries we need. After that, we reference the dynamic hubs endpoint (`/signalr/hubs`) and a file named `whiteboard.js` for the code of the application; we'll add this one shortly.

Then, we have the page body with a top section for the login bits and then we have the two `canvas` elements overlapping, the one on top being transparent. We use the two of them to make it easier to show you the shape of our rectangles on the top layer while we're still drawing them, and then remove them from there before drawing the final shape on the bottom and final one.

2. Let's finalize the visuals by adding some styling directives. Let's add a file called `whiteboard.css` inside a folder called `Styles` with just one directive in it, shown as follows:

```
canvas {
    background-color: lightgoldenrodyellow;
    position: absolute;
    width: 800px;
```

```
            height: 600px;
            top: 40px;
            left: 10px;
    }
```

Both `canvas` elements are styled the same way, and the `absolute` positioning makes them overlap exactly .

3. It's time to move to the server side of our application. We'll add the usual `Startup` class in its simplest version, shown as follows:

```
public class Startup
{
    public void Configuration(IAppBuilder app)
    {
        app.MapSignalR();
    }
}
```

4. Then, we add the skeleton of `WhiteboardHub`, marked with `HubNameAttribute` to define its friendly name, which will be "`whiteboard`", shown as follows:

```
using System.Collections.Generic;
using System.Collections.Concurrent;
using System.Drawing;
using System.Linq;
using Microsoft.AspNet.SignalR;
using Microsoft.AspNet.SignalR.Hubs;

namespace Recipe48
{
    [HubName("whiteboard")]
    public class WhiteboardHub : Hub
    {
        . . .
    }
}
```

5. We have to keep track of the shapes that have been drawn by the users; for that, we use a static field called `Shapes` of type `ConcurrentDictionary`, whose keys are the names of the users and the values are lists of `Rectangle` objects, as shown in the following code snippet. The field is static because, as you will remember, hubs are instantiated per call and cannot maintain any state across invocations, therefore. In other recipes, we already illustrated more elegant ways to handle this problem, but for this recipe, we'll stick to this simple strategy:

```
private static readonly IDictionary<string,
    IList<Rectangle>> Shapes =
        new ConcurrentDictionary<string,
            IList<Rectangle>>();
```

6. Let's introduce the method used to join the application whose body we'll complete in the following steps:

```
public void Join(string name)
{
    . . .
}
```

7. At the beginning, we deal with the static store for the shapes:

```
if (Shapes.ContainsKey(name))
    throw new HubException(
        "Nickname already taken");

Shapes.Add(name, new List<Rectangle>());
Clients.Caller.name = name;
```

We use the `Shapes` field to check whether the name supplied by the user is already taken. If that's the case, we throw `HubException`, which we know from earlier will be received by the client with all its details; this way, we'll be able to show a proper error message to the user. If we pass the check, we prepare a new store for that user and then add its name to the state bag; later, this will be useful on both sides of the application.

8. Then, we use a little trick, shown as follows, to solve a potential issue in our design:

```
Groups.Add(Context.ConnectionId, "Shapes");
```

Each time a new shape will be drawn, the hub will have to broadcast it to every other user *that joined the whiteboard*, but the `Clients` members that we have out-of-the-box would not allow us to exclude all the users who might have loaded the application and connected to the hub without actually joining the whiteboard. This is why we use a specific group named `"Shapes"` to identify who's actually joined. We put users in it when they join, and we then use this group to broadcast new shapes; this way, we avoid targeting those who had not joined yet.

9. Now, we just need to send the current status of the whiteboard to the user, shown as follows:

```
Clients.Caller.draw(
    from u in Shapes.Keys
    from s in Shapes[u]
    select new
    {
        @from = u,
        x = s.Left,
        y = s.Top,
        width = s.Width,
        height = s.Height
    });
```

This is pretty straightforward; we just put in evidence that the `draw` callback that we are going to call is expected to receive an array of named shapes represented by an anonymous type that contains its coordinates and the name of the user who drew it. The support for transparently transferring complex types is clearly very useful here.

10. We are now ready to show you how the server-side `Draw()` method is implemented. Consider the following code:

```
public void Draw(int x, int y,
    int width, int height)
{
    Shapes[(string)Clients.Caller.name]
        .Add(new Rectangle(x, y, width, height));

    Clients.Group("Shapes", Context.ConnectionId)
        .draw(new []
    {
        new
        {
            from = Clients.Caller.name,
            x, y, width, height
        }
    });
}
```

This is simpler and we can illustrate it in just one pass. Each time a client will have a new shape ready, it will call `Draw` on `WhiteboardHub` to notify its parameters. The method will first store the shape details in the `Shapes` store for the caller, whose name will be available from the state bag, and then, it will notify back the position and size to all the connections that belong to the "`Shapes`" group. This group is made of users who joined the group, but we explicitly exclude the connection of the caller who will not need to know anything about a shape they just created. The notification uses the same `draw` callback that we described earlier, which expects an array of shapes. This is why we take our only rectangle here and enclose it in an array before sending it out.

Writing the server-side part of our whiteboard wasn't difficult, we had to deal with a couple of specific issues, but after all, everything has been done with a couple of simple methods. Let's finalize our application with the code of the client page. We already defined its layout, and we've been quickly describing the logic behind the two overlapping layers; let's make them come alive using the following steps:

1. As usual, everything will be set up in a jQuery `$(document).ready(...)` event handler, written in its shorthand version, shown as follows:

```
$(function() {

    var startPoint    = null,
        currentPoint  = null,
        surfaceLayer  = $("#surface")[0],
        surfaceCtx    = surfaceLayer.getContext("2d"),
        tempLayer     = $("#temp")[0],
        tempCtx       = tempLayer.getContext("2d"),

        hub           = $.connection.hub,
        whiteboard    = $.connection.whiteboard;


    ...


});
```

We start our code by storing a few useful references in some variables. You will recognize the ones related to SignalR, but we also have a few more references to the drawing context of our two overlapping `canvas` elements.

2. Then, we set up a few initial attributes:

```
surfaceCtx.font      = "16px Arial";
surfaceCtx.fillStyle = "#0F0";
tempCtx.fillStyle    = "#AAA";
```

We first define a font family for any text that we'll draw; in fact, we'll be printing the name of the user above the shape he/she just drew on the screen. Then, we set up the color for any final shape (green) and for any transient one (gray) drawn on the temporary layer by dragging the mouse while keeping the left mouse button pressed.

3. The next step is the definition of the `draw` callback, shown as follows:

```
whiteboard.client.draw = function (shapes) {
    var prev = surfaceCtx.fillStyle;
    $.each(shapes, function(i, s) {
        surfaceCtx.fillStyle = "#F00";
        surfaceCtx.fillRect(
            s.x, s.y, s.width, s.height);
        surfaceCtx.fillStyle = "#000";
        surfaceCtx.fillText(s.from, s.x, s.y);
    });
    surfaceCtx.fillStyle = prev;
};
```

As we said earlier, while setting the expectations on this callback, the function is supplied with an array of shapes, which it enumerates and draws on the final surface on the page. These are shapes that come from other users than the connected ones, so we draw them in a different color (red) and with the name of the user who drew them above.

4. The next block of code is the one that handles the actual drawing interaction on the temporary surface. The principle is quite simple and is as follows:

    ❑   When the mouse button is *pushed down*, we store the coordinates of the current point.

    ❑   When the mouse is *moved while the button is still down*, we continuously erase the temporary shape drawn at the previous movement and draw a new one.

    ❑   When the mouse button is *released*, we erase the last transient shape from the temporary surface and we draw a final one on the actual whiteboard, just before notifying its details to the server-side hub.

The following is what it should look like:

```
$('#temp')
    .on('mousedown', function (e) {
        if (!whiteboard.state.name) return;

        startPoint = {
            X: e.offsetX,
            Y: e.offsetY
        };
    })
    .on('mousemove', function (e) {
        if (!whiteboard.state.name) return;

        if (startPoint) {
            if (currentPoint) {
                tempCtx.clearRect(
                    startPoint.X,
                    startPoint.Y,
                    currentPoint.X - startPoint.X,
                    currentPoint.Y - startPoint.Y);
            }
            currentPoint = {
                X: e.offsetX,
                Y: e.offsetY
            };
```

```
            tempCtx.fillRect(
                startPoint.X,
                startPoint.Y,
                currentPoint.X - startPoint.X,
                currentPoint.Y - startPoint.Y);
        }
    })
    .on('mouseup', function () {
        if (!whiteboard.state.name) return;

        if (startPoint) {
            var width = currentPoint.X - startPoint.X,
                height = currentPoint.Y - startPoint.Y;

            tempCtx.clearRect(
                startPoint.X,
                startPoint.Y,
                width,
                height);
            surfaceCtx.fillRect(
                startPoint.X,
                startPoint.Y,
                width,
                height);

            whiteboard.server.draw(
                startPoint.X,
                startPoint.Y,
                width,
                height);

            currentPoint = null;
            startPoint = null;
        }
    });
```

You might have also noticed that each event handler immediately exits if the state bag does not contain a valid value for the name property. This is a quick, and maybe dirty, way to disallow drawing before connecting to the whiteboard, but for our purposes it works just fine.

5. We finish with the code that starts up the connection to the hub, shown as follows:

```
hub.start().done(function () {
    $('#join').click(function () {
        var name = $('#name').val();
        whiteboard.server.join(name)
            .done(function () {
                $('#name').hide();
                $('#join').hide();
                $('#logged').html(name);
            })
            .fail(function (e) {
                console.log(e);
                $('#logged').html(e.message);
            });
    });
});
```

When the connection is ready, we bind the `login` button to the code that calls the server-side `Join()` method, and we set up the `fail()` callback method of the returned promise to display any error message; this way, we know that the `HubException` that we throw from inside the hub in case of a duplicate user name will be displayed to the user.

We are done; now, if we launch the application and navigate to the `index.html` page from multiple browser windows, we'll be able to connect to the whiteboard with different nicknames. We can also see how shapes drawn on one window are immediately displayed on the other ones, with a specific usage of colors and text to differentiate the shapes drawn by the owner of a window from the ones received from any other. When users come in late, they receive the current status of the whiteboard as soon as they log in.

Implementing a real-time map of flying airplanes

Maps have nowadays become more and more important as a visualization tool, and real-time information often has a geographic component that can be displayed on the maps. In this recipe, we'll illustrate how we could present a flight map that shows us a set of airplanes and follow their position while they're flying to their destinations. What's interesting about this example is the fact that the coordinates of the displayed objects are constantly changing, and we have to update them on the map as quickly as possible. The other interesting thing is that **time** is a main component of the problem here. The information does not get into our system driven by any user's activity, but by the changes in time of the state of some external component.

From SignalR's perspective, this is a very simple application, and to develop it, we'll just need the following features:

> ▸ Calling the methods on a hub from the client
> ▸ Triggering client-side callbacks from the server

This sounds too basic, but that's exactly what's interesting about this sample, because building something as reactive as this with just the basics of SignalR makes us appreciate its power.

On the other hand, simulating the continuous change of state of observable things in an expressive way is less simple, but it's also something that's at the heart of many real-time problems. This is why we decided to spend some time on it in conjunction with SignalR.

Getting ready

Our application will consist of the following:

> ▸ A `Hub` instance called `FlightsHub`, which will be used to notify the movement of the planes in real time and to subscribe to the specific planes in order to get notifications about their take-offs and landings.
> ▸ A page for the client part, called `index.html`, with a Google Map on it.
> ▸ A JavaScript file called `flights.js` that contains the client-side logic around the SignalR interaction and the manipulation of the map.
> ▸ A styles sheet called `flights.css`.
> ▸ Some more stuff to put things together (the `Startup` class, proper references, and so on).

In order to proceed, you'll have to build a new empty web application and call it `Recipe49`.

How to do it...

First of all, we add a reference to the `Microsoft.AspNet.SignalR` NuGet package to have everything that we need to run SignalR in our application. We'll also use a Google Map widget, which requires a personal API key that you'll have to create unless you do not already have one available. We will not spend any time on these details; in case you need more understanding on them, please refer to the online documentation at `https://developers.google.com/maps/documentation/javascript/tutorial`. Let's proceed with the following steps:

1. We first add an `index.html` page to our project, and we put what we need on it, shown as follows:

```
<!DOCTYPE html>
<html>
```

```html
<head>
    <link href="Styles/flights.css" rel="stylesheet" />
    <script src="Scripts/jquery-2.1.0.js"></script>
    <script src="Scripts/jquery.signalR-2.0.2.js"></script>
    <script src="https://maps.googleapis.com/maps/api/js?
key=YOUR_API_KEY&sensor=false"></script>
    <script src="/signalr/hubs"></script>
    <script src="Scripts/flight.js"></script>
</head>
<body>
    <div id="map"></div>
    <div id="messages">
        <button id="start" style="display: none">
            Start</button>
        <ul></ul>
    </div>
</body>
</html>
```

As usual, we start with a reference to a CSS file, which, in this case, is named
`flight.css`. We'll add it to the project later. Then, we reference the JavaScript client
libraries that we always need for our SignalR applications whose versions will have to
match the ones that we got from NuGet when we referenced the SignalR package.

The new thing here is the reference to the **Google Maps JavaScript API**; for more
details about its usage, please refer to its documentation. Please pay attention to the
`key` parameter in the URL; in your code, you'll have to replace the `YOUR_API_KEY`
placeholder with a valid key that you are entitled to use.

Finally, we add the reference to the dynamic hubs endpoint (`/signalr/hubs`) and
a reference to the `flights.js` file that we'll create shortly to host our application
logic.

The content of the page's body is very simple; it consists of just a couple of `div`
elements to host the surface of the map, a button to start the flights, and an
unordered list to display the live notifications that we'll receive.

2. Let's add some styling directives to get things to behave properly on the page by
adding the `flights.css` file that we mentioned earlier inside a folder called
`Styles`. The following will be its content:

```css
html {
    height: 100%;
}

body {
```

```
        height: 100%; margin: 0; padding: 0;
}

#map {
        height: 100%; z-index: 1;
}

#messages {
        z-index: 10; position: absolute;
        top: 0; right: 0; width: 400px;
        text-align: right;
        margin-top: 20px; margin-right: 20px;
        padding: 10px;
        font-family: "Helvetica"
}
#messages ul {
        list-style-type: none;
}

li {
        width: 100%; position: absolute;
        background-color: yellow; opacity: 0.5;
        margin: 3px;  padding: 2px;
}
li.subscribed {
        background-color: lightgreen;
}
```

Nothing special here; we are just placing a right-hand side notifications bar on top of our fullscreen map. Please note just the `height:100%` directives on the `html`, `body`, and `#map` selectors; these are necessary to correctly display our Google Map widget fullscreen.

Let's move to the server side of the application. As already mentioned, we need a way to generate real-time information about how planes are moving, and we need to push that information to the connected clients, but first, we need to have some information about the actual planes that we are managing, such as their code and some details about their routes. Ideally, that would be the responsibility of an external system, and we have already been illustrating how to properly hook an external service inside a hub and how to have such a service refer to a hub's context. For this recipe, we'll keep things very basic and we'll have everything inside our hub; we leave the task of decoupling these aspects as an exercise for the reader. Let's proceed with the following steps:

1. We first create the bootstrapping `Startup` class using the corresponding Visual Studio template that will add `OwinStartupAttribute`, and we'll add to it the standard `Configuration` method's body:

    ```
    public void Configuration(IAppBuilder app)
    {
        app.MapSignalR();
    }
    ```

2. Then, we move on to the `FlightsHub` class for the next few steps. We first create it and change its code, as shown:

```
using System;
using System.Collections.Generic;
using System.Diagnostics;
using System.Drawing;
using System.Linq;
using System.Threading.Tasks;
using Microsoft.AspNet.SignalR;
using Microsoft.AspNet.SignalR.Hubs;

namespace Recipe49
{
    [HubName("flights")]
    public class FlightsHub : Hub
    {
        . . .
    }
}
```

3. As we said, we'll be managing everything from inside `FlightsHub`, including the generation of real-time information about the flights. To make things more easily observable, we'll have a specific method, named `Go()`, to make all the flights take off. We'll just want to guarantee that this specific method can have an effect just once, so we'll take care of that with some static fields:

```
private static bool Flying;
private static readonly object Locker =
    new object();

public void Go()
{
    if (Flying) return;

    lock (Locker)
    {
        if (Flying) return;

        Flying = true;

        . . .
    }
}
```

We use the `Flying` static `Boolean` field to mark when the flights have actually started and another static field called `Locker` to allow the operation of starting the flights to just the first call on it. This code is pretty basic and not scalable, but it's good enough for our purposes.

4. Let's now gradually fill the rest of the `Go()` method. We start by adding the following geographic context to our sample:

```
var towns = new Dictionary<string, PointF>
{
    {"Turin",      new PointF( 45.2008018F,  7.6496301F)},
    {"Berlin",     new PointF( 52.3800011F, 13.5225F)},
    {"Madrid",     new PointF( 40.4936F,     -3.56676F)},
    {"New York",   new PointF( 40.639801F, -73.7789002F)},
    {"Istanbul",   new PointF( 40.9768982F, 28.8146F)},
    {"Paris",      new PointF( 49.0127983F,  2.55F)},
    {"Cape Town",  new PointF(-33.9648018F, 18.6016998F)},
};
```

These are the coordinates of the towns that our planes will be flying to or from.

5. Then, let's define our flights, shown as follows:

```
var flights = new[]
{
    new
    {
        Code    = "LH100",    Color   = "red",
        From    = "Turin",    To      = "Berlin",
        Speed   = 10,         Period  = 500,
    },
    new
    {
        Code    = "AZ150",    Color   = "blue",
        From    = "Turin",    To      = "Madrid",
        Speed   = 8,          Period  = 1500,
    },
    new
    {
        Code    = "XX150",    Color   = "green",
        From    = "New York", To      = "Istanbul",
        Speed   = 30,         Period  = 400,
    },
    new
    {
        Code    = "AA777",    Color   = "orange",
        From    = "Paris",    To      = "Cape Town",
        Speed   = 35,         Period  = 2000,
    }
};
```

Each of the flights has a code, a color to be used on the map for the corresponding marker, outbound and inbound towns, a speed value (the custom unit of measure that we use for speed here is *latitude degrees per hour*), and a transponder period that indicates the number of milliseconds between each signal that comes from the plane to notify us of its current position. Hence, each plane will have a different speed and will push the information at a different rate.

6. To make events on the map easier to observe, we accelerate the time using a correction factor:

```
const int simulationFactor = 20; //1 hours = X seconds
```

This number will determine how many seconds will be used to represent an actual hour of time; this way, we can compress time and see things happening faster. We set up a value of 20, which will make one hour pass in just 20 seconds (!).

Now, we get to the complex part: how to make things happen over time. We could have applied a few different approaches, but we decided to use the **Rx** framework, which we can download from NuGet by adding the Rx-Main package. Rx works around the duality between the concepts of **enumerable** and **observable**, and makes working with `IObservable` as easy as using `IEnumerable` the way we do with **Linq**. It also adds a lot of infrastructure to compose observable sequences and to add scheduling features to the picture. This is really like adding time as a first-citizen component of our streams, making them available to the Linq environment as sequences. The only noticeable difference is that, in this case, the sequences are pushing information towards us instead of being pulled by us, as it happens with `IEnumerable`. This is why Rx and SignalR are technologies that go along well; both of them are about pushing information and therefore, they can be used together in very effective ways.

With Rx in place and the addition of the `using System.Reactive.Linq;` directive, we can start writing the generation of our flights' streams of data, which will actually fit in a single Linq query expression! Our goal is to enumerate every flight that we defined earlier to make it generate information about what is its position at specific points in time.

Each plane will move repeatedly back and forth between the towns specified with the `From` and `To` properties, flying at the indicated speed and taking a break of a constant duration between each leg; our expression will have to express it correctly. Let's proceed by performing the following steps:

1. Let's start the declaration of our query expression using the following code:

```
var signals =
    from flight in flights.ToObservable()
```

The first necessary step is to use the `ToObservable()` extension method from Rx to take our collection of flights and push it into the realm of observables where it will be composed with other push streams.

2. For each flight, we calculate some geometric information:

```
let f        = towns[flight.From]
let t        = towns[flight.To]
let dx       = t.X - f.X
let dy       = t.Y - f.Y
let d        = Math.Sqrt(
                    Math.Pow(dx, 2) + Math.Pow(dy, 2))
```

Here, we are using the `From` and `To` properties to get the coordinates of the two points each flight will be flying across, and we use them to calculate the absolute distance and its latitudinal and longitudinal components, expressed in latitude degrees.

> This is *not* how real planes fly. We are treating the problem as if the Earth was flat, but it's not, and we shouldn't use the Pythagoras theorem to calculate the shortest path. Nevertheless, this approximation will work fine for our goals, and it will allow us to concentrate on aspects that are more relevant to this book. At the same time, the Google Map widget uses a flattening projection of the Earth, so in our example, the planes will be traveling along straight lines. This, again, is not how a real flight would look like on a projective map, but that's not an issue for us.

3. Let's start doing some time-related computations, shown as follows:

```
let time     = d / flight.Speed
let sampling = (double)1000 / flight.Period
let steps    = (int)(sampling*simulationFactor*time)
               + 1
let sx       = dx / steps
let sy       = dy / steps
```

We first calculate the time required for each flight to complete, then we calculate the frequency of the transponder (normalized to *samples per seconds = Hertz*) that we use to determine how many times a plane would notify its position for each leg that it runs (that's `steps`, and we add 1 to the total to take both the starting and destination points into account). The `simulationFactor` constant is used to correct the number of steps. Finally, we measure how much space will separate each transponder signal on both the longitudinal and latitudinal components.

4. We also want to know how many times the transponder will send signals while the plane is down on earth waiting to take off again:

```
let paused   = (int)(0.5 * simulationFactor * sampling)
```

For simplicity, we make each stop half an hour long, and therefore, the number of signals is easily computed, including the correction factor.

5. We are ready to define the actual trajectory of each flight, starting with the `outbound` leg, shown as follows:

```
let outbound = from i in Enumerable.Range(0, steps)
               select new
               {
                   Index   = i,
                   Landed  = false,
                   Touched = i == steps-1,
                   Town    = flight.To
               }
```

It's pretty simple, we generate as many samples as the number of steps that we calculated earlier, and for each of them, we indicate the following:

❑ The index of the step, which also indicates its current position on the straight line on which it's running (if we imagine to divide that line by the number of steps)

❑ Whether the plane has landed

❑ Whether it's the last sample

❑ Its destination

6. We do something similar to generate the information to push when the plane is waiting to take off again, shown as follows:

```
let delay1  = from i in Enumerable.Repeat(steps,
                  paused)
              select new
              {
                  Index   = i,
                  Landed  = true,
                  Touched = false,
                  Town    = flight.To
              }
```

Here, we use the `paused` expression to determine how many signals to send while waiting. For this sequence, the `Index` value will always be equal to the `steps` value, which indicates that for all the time we're waiting, we're at the end of the calculated trajectory.

7. We repeat the last two points for the `inbound` leg, shown as follows:

```
let inbound = from i in Enumerable.Range(0, steps)
              select new
              {
                  Index   = steps - i,
                  Landed  = false,
```

```
                      Touched = i == steps - 1,
                      Town    = flight.From
                  }
    let delay2    = from i in Enumerable.Repeat(0, paused)
                  select new
                  {
                      Index   = i,
                      Landed  = true,
                      Touched = false,
                      Town    = flight.From
                  }
```

Notice the `Index` value. For the `inbound` sequence, this is decreasing to go back to the starting point, and for the `delay2` sequence, it is always 0 to indicate that the signals are coming out from the place where the flight first took off.

8. Now that we have the four components of a whole flight, we just concatenate them in a single sequence, from which we then generate an array because later we'll access its components by its position, as shown in the following code snippet:

```
    let route     = outbound.Concat(delay1)
                          .Concat(inbound)
                          .Concat(delay2).ToArray()
```

9. We're now ready to introduce the time component, and for that, we just join our flights and the related sequences we just produced with a sequence generator from Rx, shown as follows:

```
    from st in Observable.Interval(
        TimeSpan.FromMilliseconds(flight.Period))
```

`Observable.Interval` generates an infinite stream whose values are pushed down to the consumers at a defined frequency in time. In our case, of course, this will be the period of the transponder for each plane. Whoever will subscribe to this sequence will actually be free from any activity until `Observable.Interval` will wake it up with a new signal. How things are actually implemented behind the scenes to introduce this efficient, concurrent, and asynchronous behavior is out of scope here, but it's definitely one of the main reasons you should put Rx in your tool belt.

10. From now on, it's as if the rest of our expression will be executed at regular intervals; we just need to link the periodic samples to the information about the actual position of the plane in order to produce what we need to push to the clients, as shown in the following code snippet:

```
    let w         = route[st%route.Length]
    let s         = w.Index
    let x         = f.X + sx * s
    let y         = f.Y + sy * s
```

```
      let landed   = w.Landed
      select new
      {
          flight.Code,
          w.Touched,
          w.Town,
          Landed   = landed,
          X        = x,
          Y        = y,
          Color    = landed
                   ? "black"
                   : flight.Color,
      };
```

We first normalize our infinite stream of indices (st) towards the actual length of each route, and then everything becomes quite straightforward, with a final select statement producing all the necessary details that we need to send to the clients for each sample. A landed plane will be shown in black. Otherwise, the color specified with its definition will be used.

11. We're almost done; we just need a single consumer to actually make the generation of signals happen, and the way we built the Go() method will guarantee us that only one subscriber will be in place, shown as follows:

```
signals.Subscribe(
    flight =>
    {
        Clients.All.sample(flight.Code,
            flight.X, flight.Y,
            flight.Color, flight.Landed);
        if (!flight.Touched) return;

        Trace.WriteLine(
            string.Format("Notifying {0}...",
                flight.Code));
        Clients.Group(flight.Code).touched(flight.Code,
            flight.Town,
            DateTime.Now.ToLongTimeString());
    });
```

The `Subscribe()` method allows us to define a consumer of `signals`. Each time one of the signals will be pushed to the subscriber, all of its details will be collected and notified to the connected clients by calling the `sample` callback on `Clients.All` dynamically. If the plane has landed, we'll trigger a further notification using the `touched` callback, targeting anybody who has subscribed to a group called after the flight's code.

Please observe that the lambda expression used to define the subscriber will be fully executed at each sample; this means that the `Clients` members will be processed each time; therefore, both sets of the currently connected clients and the connections that belong to the previously mentioned group will always be up to date; this way, late connections will catch up with the current positions on the first signal that is received.

12. Before leaving the `Go()` method, we eventually notify everybody that all the planes have started flying, as shown in the following line of code:

```
Clients.All.started(Flights);
```

The `Go()` method is now complete, and with that, the generation of the live stream of data about the flights is complete as well, although a hub's method wasn't strictly necessary in this case. More suited to a hub method is the task of exposing to the users a way to register their interest in receiving notifications about the state of a single airplane.

13. Let's add a `Notify()` method to the hub to ask for notifications:

```
public Task Notify(string code)
{
    Trace.WriteLine(
        string.Format("Asking to notify {0}", code));
    return Groups.Add(Context.ConnectionId, code);
}
```

The implementation uses the code of the flight to subscribe the caller to a group that is named after the flight. This code matches what we saw earlier in the `Subscribe` call to notify these subscribers.

14. We complete `FlightsHub` with an `OnConnected` handler, which will tell every new client whether the flights are flying already or not:

```
public override Task OnConnected()
{
    Clients.All.started(Flying);

    return base.OnConnected();
}
```

We can now move to the client-side code located in the `flights.js` file. We need to perform some manipulations on the map to react on clicks on the markers that represent the planes, in order to subscribe for notifications from them. Of course, we'll also need to set up the SignalR callbacks and start the connection. The following steps show us the code, with just a few brief comments, because most of it is plumbing code that is not strictly related to SignalR:

1. We start by defining some useful variables and functions, shown as follows:

```
$(function() {

    var hubs = $.connection.hub,
        flights = $.connection.flights,
        markers = {},
        subscribed = {},
        map = new google.maps.Map($("#map")[0], {
            center: new google.maps.LatLng(45, 8),
            zoom: 2
        }),
        buildIcon = function(color) {
            return {
                path: google.maps.SymbolPath.CIRCLE,
                scale: 8,
                strokeColor: color
            };
        };

    ...

});
```

2. We then define SignalR's callbacks, starting from `sample`. Here, we add code to perform the following steps:

   ❑ Add a marker for each plane the first time a signal arrives from it.

   ❑ Move the marker at every subsequent signal.

   ❑ Attack a `click` handler on each marker to subscribe to the notifications from it.

   The following is a code snippet that shows us all this:

```
flights.client.sample = function (
    code, x, y, color, landed) {
    if (!markers[code]) {
        markers[code] = new google.maps.Marker({
            icon: buildIcon(color),
            map: map,
```

```
                    title: code
                });
                google.maps.event.addListener(
                    markers[code], 'click',
                    function () {
                        var li = '<li class="subscribed" />';
                        if (!subscribed[code]) {
                            flights.server
                                .notify(code)
                                .done(function () {
                                    var $li = $(li)
                                        .text('Watching ' +
                                            code);
                                    $('#messages ul')
                                        .prepend($li);
                                    subscribed[code] = true;
                                });
                        }
                    });
                } else if (markers[code].landed !== landed) {
                    markers[code].setIcon(buildIcon(color));
                    markers[code].landed = landed;
                }
                markers[code].setPosition(
                    new google.maps.LatLng(x, y));
        };
```

3. The next callback is `touched`, as shown in the following code snippet, which is triggered each time a plane touches land, and reaches each client who subscribed to that particular plane. This is used to fill the list of notifications about each plane the user has subscribed to:

```
flights.client.touched = function (code, town, time) {
    var m = code + ' landed in ' + town + ' @ ' + time;
    $('#messages ul').prepend($('<li/>').text(m));
};
```

4. The last callback to implement is `started`, as shown in the following code snippet, which is received by each client when it first connects and when the flights start flying. We use it to decide whether the `Start` button should be displayed or not:

```
flights.client.started = function (flying) {
    $('#start').toggle(!flying);
};
```

5. Finally, we use the usual code to start the connection:

```
hubs.start().done(function () {
    $('#start').click(function () {
        flights.server.go();
    });
});
```

When the connection is ready, we bind the Start button to a click event handler, which will ask FlightsHub to start the generation of the signals from the flights.

We're ready to test our application. We build the project, launch the application, and navigate to the index.html page, which will display a map of the world and a Start button to make the flights move. As soon as we click on it, a few circular markers will start moving on the map, each one representing a different plane. We'll see how they change color according to the state that a flight flies over, and we'll be able to click on them to receive notifications whenever they touch land. We can also open multiple tabs pointing at the same address and appreciate how all of them are updated in real time.

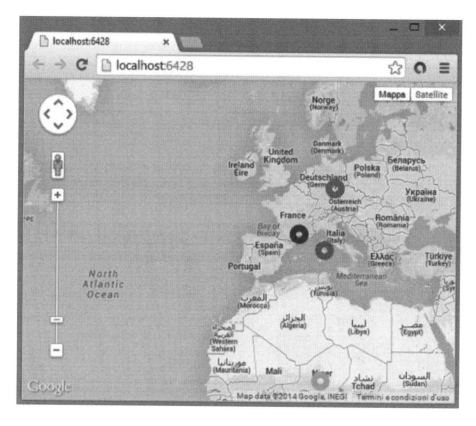

The code of this recipe was pretty complex; however, the SignalR features that we've been using were basic ones, which clearly demonstrate that, with SignalR, real-time messaging features are not the most complex part of our application anymore.

Implementing a "pets finder" application

The previous recipe showed us how a map can be used to display live information, updated at a relatively high frequency, in a scenario where the user is passive in practice and just observes what a server is broadcasting. In this recipe, we want to explore a much more interactive scenario, where the information displayed on the map is provided by the users.

This application can be used to place the name and a picture of a pet that has been lost on a map. These details will be added to other users' maps in real time. Anybody observing the map could drag-and-drop any marker on a different position to notify that the pet was there. Finally, the user who first raised an alarm about a specific lost pet can declare that he/she found it, and this action will correspond to the removal of the markers related to that specific animal from all the connected maps. This is illustrated in the following screenshot:

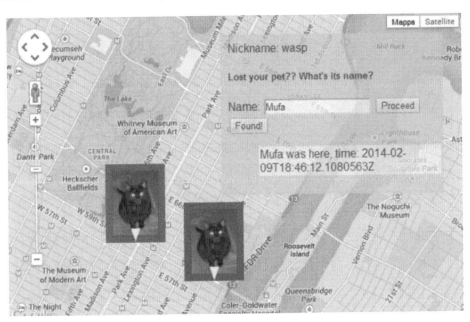

From a SignalR's perspective, we'll use the following features:

- Calling methods on a hub from the client
- Triggering client-side callbacks from the server
- Dependency injection
- Custom authorization workflow

- Services' extensibility (replacing a default service)
- Custom query string parameters

This example is quite interesting because it puts together a consistent amount of features that we've been analyzing throughout the book.

Getting ready

Our application consists of the following:

- A `Hub` called `PetsFinderHub`, which will be used to notify about lost pets' sightings in real time and to subscribe to specific pets in order to get notifications about their movements.

- A custom service defined by the `IPetsFinder` interface, with a proper implementation and a couple of supporting types. This will be the core of the application, with the responsibility of storing information about the pets and supplying it back to `PetsFinderHub` when required.

- An authorization attribute called `AuthorizeLoggedAttribute`.

- A custom implementation of `IUserIdProvider`.

- A page for the client part, called `index.html`, with a Google Map on it.

- A JavaScript file called `pets.js` that contains the client-side logic around the interactions with SignalR and the Google Map, plus some extra bits to manipulate images.

- A style sheet called `pets.css`.

- Some more stuff to put things together (the `Startup` class to set up dependencies and start SignalR, proper server and client references, and so on).

In order to proceed, you'll have to build a new empty web application and call it `Recipe50`. Before proceeding, you should be aware of the fact that this sample uses the new HTML5 `FileReader` API to read the content of an image file that is dropped onto a `div` element. Only modern browsers support it, and therefore, this sample cannot work on older browsers. Please check `http://caniuse.com/filereader` to check whether your browser will support this sample.

How to do it...

First of all, we reference the `Microsoft.AspNet.SignalR` NuGet package to have everything that we need to run SignalR in our application. We'll also use a Google Map widget that requires a personal API key; for more details about it, please refer to the previous recipe. Let's proceed with the following steps:

1. We first add an `index.html` page to our project, with the following content:

```html
<!DOCTYPE html>
<html>
<head>
    <title></title>
    <link type="text/css"
        href="/Styles/pets.css"rel="stylesheet"/>
    <script src="Scripts/jquery-2.1.0.js"></script>
    <script src="Scripts/jquery.signalR-2.0.2.js"></script>
    <script src="https://maps.googleapis.com/maps/api/js?
key=YOUR_API_KEY&sensor=false"></script>
    <script src="/signalr/hubs"></script>
    <script src="/Scripts/pets.js"></script>
</head>
    <body>
        <div id="map"></div>
        <div id="panel">
            <div id="login-panel">
                <label>Nickname:</label>
                <input type="text" id="user"/>
                <button id="login">Log in</button>
            </div>
            <div id="logged-panel">
                <label>Nickname:</label>
                <span id="nickname"></span>
            </div>
            <div id="lost-panel">
                <div id="lost-panel-name">
                    <h5>Lost your pet??
                        What's its name?</h5>
                    <label>Name:</label>
                    <input type="text" id="name" />
                    <button id="proceed">Proceed</button>
                </div>
                <div id="lost-panel-photo">
                    <h5>Drop its photo here...</h5>
                    <div id="photo"></div>
                </div>
                <div id="lost-panel-location">
                    <h5>...and locate it on the map</h5>
                    <p>
                        Position your map in the right
                        area, when ready click on the
                        'Locate it!' button and then click
```

```
                                        on the right position on the map.
                            </p>
                            <button id="lost">Locate it!</button>
                    </div>
                </div>
                <button id="found">Found!</button>
                <ul id="messages"></ul>
            </div>
        </body>
    </html>
```

The page starts with the usual references to JavaScript libraries, plus a reference to the Google Maps endpoint and to a file called `pets.js`, which we'll add to the project shortly. The body section of the page contains the `div` element for the map and a series of panels that will be displayed or hidden according to the specific actions that the user will perform on the application. It's pretty long, but there is nothing worth any specific comment.

2. The page is styled using a file called `pets.css`, placed in the `Styles` folder:

```css
html {
    height: 100%;
}
body {
    height: 100%; margin: 0; padding: 0;
}
#map {
    height: 100%; z-index: 1;
}

#panel {
    z-index: 10; position: absolute;
    top: 0; right: 0; width: 300px;
    margin: 30px; padding: 10px;
    font-family: "Helvetica";
    background-color: lightgreen; opacity: 0.7;
}
#messages {
    list-style-type: none;
}
#messages li {
    background-color: yellow;
    width: 100%; margin: 3px; padding: 2px;
}
```

```
#photo {
    width: 240px; height: 240px; margin: 3px;
    background-color: red; border: 5px dotted lightgrey;
    z-index: 2;
}
#lost-panel, #logged-panel, #lost-panel-photo,
#lost-panel-location, #found {
    display: none;
}
```

Enough with markup and styling; let's move on to see how the server-side portion of the application is actually designed.

1. Our code will be built around the concepts of **pet** and **location**. We add a file called `Pets.cs` to the project, where we'll add all the types involved in the implementation of the business rules of the application. Inside `Pets.cs`, we first add the `Location` and `Pet` types, which are straightforward and do not need any particular explanation:

    ```
    public class Location
    {
        public Location(DateTime when, PointF where)
        {
            When = when;
            Where = where;
        }
        public PointF Where { get; private set; }
        public DateTime When { get; private set; }
    }

    public class Pet
    {
        private readonly ICollection<Location> _locations;

        public Pet(
            string user, string name,
            string photo, DateTime when)
        {
            User = user;
            Name = name;
            Photo = photo;
            When = when;
            _locations = new Collection<Location>();
        }
    ```

```
public string User { get; private set; }
public string Name { get; private set; }
public string Photo { get; private set; }
public DateTime When { get; set; }
public bool Found { get; set; }

public string Id
{
    get { return BuildId(User, Name, When); }
}
public IEnumerable<Location> GetLocations()
{
    return _locations;
}
public Location AddLocation(Location location)
{
    _locations.Add(location);
    return location;
}
public static string BuildId(
    string user, string name, DateTime now)
{
    return string.Format(
        "{0}#{1}#{2}", user, name, now);
}
}
```

2. We then define our service contract, shown as follows:

```
public interface IPetsFinder
{
    Pet Lost(
        string user, string name,
        PointF location, string photo);
    Pet Seen(string id, PointF location);
    void Found(string id);
    IEnumerable<Pet> GetPets();
}
```

These methods are there to notify about a new lost pet, add a new sighting, record a finding, and enumerate all the pets recorded in the application.

3. Now, let's implement the contract that we just described:

```
public class PetsFinder : IPetsFinder
{
    private readonly IDictionary<string, Pet> _pets =
        new Dictionary<string, Pet> ();

    public Pet Lost(
        string user, string name,
        PointF location, string photo)
    {
        var now = DateTime.UtcNow;
        var id = Pet.BuildId(user, name, now);

        if (_pets.ContainsKey(id)) return null;

        var pet = new Pet(user, name, photo, now);
        _pets.Add(id, pet);
        _pets[id].AddLocation(new Location(now,
            location));

        return pet;
    }

    public Pet Seen(string id, PointF location)
    {
        var pet = _pets[id];
        pet.AddLocation(
            new Location(DateTime.UtcNow, location));

        return pet;
    }

    public void Found(string id)
    {
        _pets[id].Found = true;
    }

    public IEnumerable<Pet> GetPets()
    {
        return
            from id in _pets.Keys
            let pet = _pets[id]
            where !pet.Found
            select pet;
    }
}
```

The service is simple, and it uses a dictionary to store information about the pets in the memory. A proper implementation would, of course, use a more resilient system. The rest of the code should be quite self explanatory.

Before getting to see the implementation of `PetsFinderHub`, let's quickly implement a custom and the naïve authentication and authorization system; for this, we'll override the `IUserIdProvider` service.

4. Let's add a class called `UserIdProvider` that contains the following code:

```
public class UserIdProvider : IUserIdProvider
{
    public string GetUserId(IRequest request)
    {
        return request.QueryString["user"];
    }
}
```

We already saw this approach earlier; we use a custom query string parameter placed on the SignalR endpoint by the client to transport that information about the current user at every request. It's a simplified approach, of course, but it's enough for us.

Now that the application logic is ready, let's use it from the application hub using the following steps:

1. Let's add `PetsFinderHub` to the project:

```
using System.Drawing;
using System.Threading.Tasks;
using Microsoft.AspNet.SignalR;
using Microsoft.AspNet.SignalR.Hubs;

namespace Recipe50
{
    [HubName("pets")]
    public class PetsFinderHub : Hub
    {
        private readonly IUserIdProvider _userIdProvider;
        private readonly IPetsFinder _petsFinder;

        public PetsFinderHub(
            IUserIdProvider userIdProvider,
            IPetsFinder petsFinder)
        {
            _userIdProvider = userIdProvider;
            _petsFinder = petsFinder;
        }

        ...
    }
}
```

The constructor requires a reference of both `IPetsFinder` and `IUserIdProvider` contracts, which are then stored in the instance fields. We put some dots to indicate where the remaining methods will be added.

2. We then define how we connect to the hub, shown as follows:

```
public override Task OnConnected()
{
    foreach (var pet in _petsFinder.GetPets())
    {
        Clients.All.pet(new
        {
            pet.Id, pet.User, pet.Name, pet.Photo,
            Locations = pet.GetLocations()
        });

    }
    return base.OnConnected();
}
```

The `OnConnected` override retrieves a list of the pets who the application has already been notified about, each one with its sightings, and sends it to the caller by triggering the client side `pet` callback.

3. When a pet gets lost, the user has to notify `PetsFinderHub` about it:

```
public void Lost(
        string name, float latitude,
        float longitude, string photo)
{
    var user =
        _userIdProvider.GetUserId(Context.Request);

    var location = new PointF(latitude, longitude);
    var pet = _petsFinder.Lost(
        user, name, location, photo);

    if (pet == null) return;

    Clients.All.pet(new
    {
        pet.Id, pet.User, pet.Name, pet.Photo,
        Locations = pet.GetLocations()
    });
}
```

We first ask the `_userIdProvider` service to resolve the name of the current user and then we supply the information about the pet who just got lost to the `_petsFinder` service, which will properly store it. If everything goes fine, we notify all the connected clients about this new lost animal using the `pet` callback.

4. If someone has a chance to see one of the lost pets somewhere, he/she can notify the application about its new position using the following code:

```
public void Seen(
    string id, float latitude, float longitude)
{
    var location = new PointF(latitude, longitude);
    var pet = _petsFinder.Seen(id, location);

    Clients.All.pet(new
    {
        pet.Id, pet.User, pet.Name, pet.Photo,
        Locations = pet.GetLocations()
    });
}
```

After having contacted the _petsService service with the information related to the new position of a specific pet, we notify all the connected clients about it, triggering the client-side pet callback.

5. Eventually, and hopefully, a lost pet will be found, and the Found() method, shown in the following code snippet, will allow us to notify the application about this event:

```
public void Found(string id)
{
    _petsFinder.Found(id);
    Clients.All.found(id);
}
```

Similar to the previous methods, the connected clients will be notified about the finding by the found callback.

6. The only bits that we are still missing are the ones that are needed to bootstrap the application in the Startup class. We use the dependency injection strategies that we learned earlier in *Chapter 7, Analyzing Advanced Scenarios*, to put all the components together, as shown in the following code snippet:

```
public void Configuration(IAppBuilder app)
{
    GlobalHost.DependencyResolver.Register(
        typeof(IUserIdProvider),
        () => new UserIdProvider());

    var petsFinder = new PetsFinder();
    GlobalHost.DependencyResolver.Register(
        typeof(IPetsFinder),
        () => petsFinder);
    GlobalHost.DependencyResolver.Register(
        typeof(PetsFinderHub),
```

```
        () => new PetsFinderHub(
            new UserIdProvider(), petsFinder));

        app.MapSignalR();
    }
```

Now that we are done with the server-side portion of the application, let's move back to the client side to add the `pets.js` file to the `Scripts` folder and fill its content. We'll use the following steps to do this:

1. We first add some useful variables:

```
$(function () {

    var hub = $.connection.hub,
        pets = $.connection.pets,
        map = new google.maps.Map($("#map")[0], {
            center: new google.maps.LatLng(
                40.760976, -73.969041),
            zoom: 14
        }),
        params = {},
        locations = {};


        . . .
})
```

Among other things, here, we center the map on a specific location and set its initial zoom level.

2. We add a few `click` event handlers to the buttons that are displayed over the map:

```
$('#login').click(function() {
    params.user = $('#user').val();
    hub.qs = { user: params.user };
    hub.start()
        .done(function () {
            $('#nickname').text(params.user);
            $('#login-panel').toggle();
            $('#logged-panel').toggle();
            $('#lost-panel').toggle();
        });
});
$('#proceed').click(function () {
    params.name = $('#name').val();
    $('#lost-panel-photo').toggle();
});
```

```
$('#lost').click(function () {
    params.adding = true;
});
$('#found').click(function () {
    pets.server.found(params.id);
});
```

The only interesting line here is from the `login` button, where we use the `qs` member of the `hub` variable to set the `user` member just before we start the connection. This way, we guarantee that its value will be sent to the server at every request, allowing the `UserIdProvider` method, which we defined earlier, to work as expected.

3. When we are in the process of notifying about a new lost pet, one of the steps consists of providing its picture by dropping an image file on a `div` element called `photo`. The following is how this can be set up:

```
$('#photo')
    .on('dragover', function () { return false; })
    .on('dragend', function () { return false; })
    .on('drop', function (s) {
        var e = s.originalEvent;
        e.preventDefault();
        drop(e.dataTransfer.files);
        $('#lost-panel-location').toggle();
    });
```

Later, we'll see the `drop()` function in detail; here, we just underline the fact that we can easily send images back and forth with SignalR using their **inline Base64-encoded representation**, which is what we do here.

 At the moment of this writing, there are some limitations to this technique. In particular, strings passed to a hub cannot exceed a limit in size whose value might depend on the transport strategy. Inline images can easily exceed this limitation, and therefore, before taking architectural decisions on this feature, you should carefully verify its limitations.

4. We then need to handle the `click` events on the map, which are used to mark where a pet got lost:

```
google.maps.event.addListener(map, 'click',
function (me) {
    if (!params.adding) return;

    pets.server.lost(params.name,
        me.latLng.lat(), me.latLng.lng(),
        params.image);
```

```
        params.adding = false;

        $('#photo').empty();
        $('#lost-panel-photo').toggle();
        $('#lost-panel-location').toggle();
});
```

All the details that have been collected about the lost pet so far are sent to the `PetsFinderHub`, including a string that contains the Base64-encoded image.

5. We are ready to define SignalR's callbacks, starting from the one used to notify a new sighting:

```
pets.client.pet = function (lost) {
    if (locations[lost.Id]) {
        $.each(locations[lost.Id].markers,
            function(mi, m) { m.setMap(null); });
    }
    locations[lost.Id] = {
        id: lost.Id, markers: []
    };
    $.each(lost.Locations, function (li, location) {
        var image = new Image();
        image.src = lost.Photo;

        var marker = new google.maps.Marker({
            icon: framed(image, li ? 'green' : 'red'),
            map: map,
            title: lost.name,
            draggable: true,
            position: new google.maps.LatLng(
                location.Where.X, location.Where.Y)
        });
        google.maps.event.addListener(marker,
            'click', function () {
                var m = lost.Name +
                    ' was here, time: ' +
                    location.When;
                $('#messages')
                    .append($('<li/>').text(m));
                $('#found').toggle(
                    lost.User == params.user);
                params.id = lost.Id;
            });
```

```
            google.maps.event.addListener(marker,
                'dragend', function(me) {
                    pets.server.seen(lost.Id,
                        me.latLng.lat(),
                        me.latLng.lng());
                });
            locations[lost.Id].markers.push(marker);
        });
    };
```

For each location provided along the detail of the pet, a new custom marker is created on the map. The custom marker will contain the picture of the pet, which was built using the `framed()` function that we'll see later, and it will allow users to interact with it in a couple of ways:

- **Click**: This interaction will register the current user to receive notifications about new events regarding the pet whose picture was clicked on. Such notifications will be listed as text messages on the right-hand side of the map.

- **Drag-and-drop**: A marker can be dragged around on the map and then dropped on a new position in order to notify a new location where the corresponding pet was last seen. The drop event will trigger a call towards the `Seen()` server-side method.

6. The `found` callback will remove all the markers of the rescued pet from the map:

```
    pets.client.found = function (id) {
        $.each(locations[id].markers, function (mi, m) {
            m.setMap(null);
        });
        locations[id] = {};
    };
```

7. Finally, we quickly list the helper functions that we used earlier:

```
    function drop(files) {
        var reader = new FileReader();
        reader.onload = function (event) {
            var image = new Image();
            image.src = event.target.result;
            params.image = resized(image);
            image.src = params.image;
            $('#photo').append(image);
        };
        reader.readAsDataURL(files[0]);
    }
```

```
function resized(img) {
    var canvas = document.createElement('canvas'),
        maxWidth = 180,
        maxHeight = 180,
        size = {
            width: img.width,
            height: img.height
        };
    size = size.width > size.height
            ? size.width > maxWidth
              ? {
                  height: Math.round(
                      size.height *
                      maxWidth / size.width),
                  width:  maxWidth
                } : size
          : size.height > maxHeight
            ? {
                width: Math.round(
                    size.width *
                    maxHeight / size.height),
                height: maxHeight
              } : size;

    canvas.width  = size.width;
    canvas.height = size.height;
    var ctx = canvas.getContext("2d");
    ctx.drawImage(img, 0, 0, size.width, size.height);
    return canvas.toDataURL("image/jpeg", 0.7);
}
function framed(image, color) {
    var canvas = document.createElement('canvas'),
        size = {
            width: image.width / 2 + 20,
            height: image.height / 2 + 20
        };

    canvas.width = size.width;
    canvas.height = size.height;
    var ctx = canvas.getContext("2d");

    ctx.beginPath();
    ctx.fillStyle = color;
    ctx.rect(0, 0, size.width, size.height);
```

```
ctx.fill();
ctx.drawImage(
    image, 10, 10,
    size.width - 20, size.height - 20);

ctx.fillStyle = "yellow";
ctx.beginPath();
ctx.moveTo(size.width / 2, size.height);
ctx.lineTo(size.width / 2 + 7, size.height - 20);
ctx.lineTo(size.width / 2 - 7, size.height - 20);
ctx.closePath();
ctx.fill();

return canvas.toDataURL("image/jpeg", 0.7);
}
```

The `drop()` function is interesting because it uses the new HTML5 `FileReader` API to read the content of the image file dropped onto the `div` element named `photo`. The `resized()` and `framed()` functions leverage the Base64-encoded image format and the `canvas` capabilities to process the pictures in order to both send them to `PetsFinderHub` on the server and use them to create custom map markers on the client.

We are done and are now ready to test the application by building the project and opening the `index.html` page in multiple windows. From each of these windows, we can log in to the system and use the simple submission wizard to notify about a lost pet. We can drag-and-drop markers around to let the application know about the new positions, and the owner of the pet can eventually declare the pet as found. This way, its markers will be removed. All these actions are constantly propagated to every connected map in real time. Clicking on a marker will subscribe the user to text messages that alert about a new sighting related to the corresponding pet.

Implementing a custom backplane

This recipe will be slightly different from the other ones used in this chapter. We'll not show you any fancy application; instead, we will demonstrate how we can build a brand new custom backplane and hook it into SignalR's pipeline.

The idea of a backplane is to support SignalR's broadcasting feature in scenarios where we need to scale out the broadcast over multiple servers. We've already described the backplanes made available out of the box with SignalR, but here we show you how we can create our own backplane to distribute messages on top of a broadcasting system that we should know very well by now SignalR itself!

As explained in *Chapter 7*, *Analyzing Advanced Scenarios*, a backplane has to support several instances of the same SignalR server, and it has to redistribute every outgoing message from one of those instances to every server that it supports. This mechanism makes message broadcasting work well even behind a load balancer, regardless of which concrete server a client is connected to. In the end, what a backplane has to do is actually very similar to what SignalR has been created for: broadcasting messages. This is why SignalR looks like a realistic candidate for a backplane.

Such a backplane could be a good fit in the cases where speed, and not resiliency, is the most important feature that we need from our backplane. Whenever our frontend servers have to bear a relevant total traffic but the portion generated by SignalR is relatively small, such a backplane could be an option, and we would be confident that we are not just moving the problem *as is* on a different server. That said, this backplane should be seen as an exercise and not as a solution, as is the case with other recipes in this book. This is an interesting idea to develop in order to build a solid and production-ready component.

The following are the SignalR features that we'll leverage:

- The .NET client
- Calling methods on a hub from the client
- Triggering client-side callbacks from the server
- Registering new components into the hub's pipeline
- The `ScaleoutMessageBus` component as the base class of our brand new backplane

Getting ready

Our sample will consist of the following three different projects:

- `Recipe51`: This is a simple SignalR-based sample web application that we want to scale out. We'll need to create a new empty web application for this one.
- `Recipe51.Backplane`: This is a generic SignalR-based broadcasting web application that we can use to publish a stream of bytes that we want to redistribute across frontend servers. We'll need to create a new empty web application for this one.
- `Recipe51.SignalRBackplaneMessageBus`: This is a class library that contains reusable components that can be used from any frontend application in order to connect to our SignalR's backplane. We'll need to create a new class library project for this one.

How to do it...

Let's describe the three projects in the same order in which we listed them previously.

Recipe51 is just a target sample application that we want to scale out. We need to add a reference to the Microsoft.AspNet.SignalR NuGet package in order to have everything that we need in order to use SignalR.

The actual details of this application are not so important; any code would do. You might either want to add a basic EchoHub with some dummy method, a client page that uses it, and a Startup class with a standard bootstrap sequence, or, you might get some inspiration from any previously written sample application. You might even directly reuse one of these; it's not relevant. When the backplane code will be ready, we'll come back to this project to make use of it from the Startup class.

The second project is called Recipe51.Backplane, and it's the actual implementation of the backplane system. Again, we need to add the Microsoft.AspNet.SignalR NuGet package, and after that, we'll add a hub called BackplaneHub and a Startup class with a standard bootstrap sequence.

The code of our BackplaneHub will have to expose a couple of methods; the first one will receive an array of bytes and will broadcast it to every connected client, the second one will generate a unique numeric identifier each time it's called. Let's take a look at it:

```csharp
using Microsoft.AspNet.SignalR;
using Microsoft.AspNet.SignalR.Hubs;

namespace Recipe51.Backplane
{
    [HubName("backplane")]
    public class BackplaneHub : Hub
    {
        private static long _id = 0;
        private static readonly object Locker = new object();

        public void Publish(byte[] message)
        {
            Clients.All.Broadcast(message);
        }

        public long GetId()
        {
            lock (Locker)
            {
                return ++_id;
            }
        }
    }
}
```

There is nothing special to be explained; we just notice the `Broadcast` callback triggered on the `Clients.All` member. We handle the generation of unique identifiers with a static member and a critical section; we are assuming that this backplane will run on a single instance, and therefore, such a strategy will be good enough for our sample. Everything else is trivial, and it reaches its goal of blindly redistributing every received message to any connected observer, which is what a backplane is supposed to do.

We are ready to discuss the third and last project of this recipe, which is its real core, `Recipe51.SignalRBackplaneMessageBus`. This assembly will contain the implementation of `IMessageBus`, which will allow our client project to use the backplane that we previously prepared.

Writing the actual (and simplified) backplane system was easy, but writing a sound implementation of `IMessageBus` is more difficult. This is why SignalR offers us several useful starting points to make things simpler. Let's proceed with the following steps:

1. We start by adding a class called `SignalRBackplaneMessage` to the project. Its goal is to represent a `scaleout` message by exposing a couple of fields that contain a unique identifier and the actual body of the message:

```
using System;
using System.Collections.Generic;
using System.IO;
using Microsoft.AspNet.SignalR.Messaging;

namespace Recipe51.SignalRBackplaneMessageBus
{
    public class SignalRBackplaneMessage
    {
        public ulong Id { get; private set; }
        public ScaleoutMessage ScaleoutMessage
        { get; private set; }

        ...

    }
}
```

2. The `SignalRBackplaneMessage` class will need to be serialized and de-serialized; therefore, we add a couple of static helper methods to handle this concern. These methods will use byte arrays, standard .NET types, and code usually involved in these kind of operations:

```
public static byte[] ToBytes(
    long id, IList<Message> messages)
{
    if (messages == null)
    {
```

```
                    throw new
                        ArgumentNullException ("messages") ;
                }

                using (var ms = new MemoryStream ())
                {
                    var binaryWriter = new BinaryWriter (ms) ;

                    var scaleoutMessage = new
                        ScaleoutMessage (messages) ;
                    var buffer = scaleoutMessage.ToBytes () ;

                    binaryWriter.Write (id) ;
                    binaryWriter.Write (buffer.Length) ;
                    binaryWriter.Write (buffer) ;

                    return ms.ToArray () ;
                }
            }

            public static SignalRBackplaneMessage FromBytes (
                byte [] data)
            {
                using (var stream = new MemoryStream (data))
                {
                    var binaryReader = new
                        BinaryReader (stream) ;
                    var id = (ulong)binaryReader.ReadInt64 () ;
                    var count = binaryReader.ReadInt32 () ;
                    var buffer = binaryReader.ReadBytes (count) ;

                    return new SignalRBackplaneMessage
                    {
                        Id = id,
                        ScaleoutMessage =
                            ScaleoutMessage.FromBytes (buffer)
                    } ;
                }
            }
```

3. The second class of this library is `SignalRBackplaneConfiguration`, which will be used to represent the configuration details that we'll need in order to initialize our backplane:

```
        public class SignalRBackplaneConfiguration :
            ScaleoutConfiguration
        {
            public string EndpointAddress { get; set; }
        }
```

We derive it from `ScaleoutConfiguration` to easily expose what's usually needed while configuring scale-out scenarios, and we add a string property called `EndpointAddress` to represent the address of the backplane that we want to connect to.

4. The real heart of a backplane is its `IMessageBus` implementation, which we call `SignalRBackplaneMessageBus`. In order to simplify a task that could be daunting, SignalR exposes a base class called `ScaleoutMessageBus`, which we'll be using here. The following is its skeleton:

```
using System.Collections.Generic;
using System.Threading.Tasks;
using Microsoft.AspNet.SignalR;
using Microsoft.AspNet.SignalR.Client;
using Microsoft.AspNet.SignalR.Messaging;

namespace Recipe51.SignalRBackplaneMessageBus
{
    class SignalRBackplaneMessageBus : ScaleoutMessageBus
    {
        private readonly HubConnection _connection;
        private readonly IHubProxy _hub;


        ...

    }
}
```

Once instantiated, a message bus will have to keep a connection towards the actual backplane system; in this case, this is represented by one reference to `HubConnection` and one to `IHubProxy`, both pointing to our SignalR-based backplane.

5. Let's add a constructor for our type, shown as follows:

```
public SignalRBackplaneMessageBus(
    IDependencyResolver dependencyResolver,
    SignalRBackplaneConfiguration configuration)
    : base(dependencyResolver, configuration)
{
    _connection =
        new HubConnection(
        configuration.EndpointAddress);

    _hub = _connection.CreateHubProxy("backplane");
```

```
_hub.On<byte[]>("Broadcast", m =>
{
    var message =
        SignalRBackplaneMessage.FromBytes(m);
    OnReceived(0,
        message.Id, message.ScaleoutMessage);
});

_connection.Start().Wait();
}
```

The `ScaleoutMessageBus` base class does not have a default constructor, and therefore, we have to adapt to what's available. We declare two arguments of type `IDependencyResolver` and `SignalRBackplaneConfiguration` because both are allowed to be passed to the base class constructor; in fact, the latter works too, because it inherits from `ScaleoutConfiguration`.

What we do in the constructor is simple but vital for a fully working message bus:

- We first create a `HubConnection` that points to the right URL that comes from the configuration.

- We create a hub proxy for `backplane`, which is the friendly name of `BackplaneHub`.

- We declare a callback on it called `Broadcast`, which matches the name of the callback that the backplane system is calling for each message it receives. The callback receives a serialized message, which is first unpacked using the `FromBytes` helper method and is then forwarded to the `OnReceived()` method that is inherited from `ScaleoutMessageBus`, whose implementation does what's needed to actually trigger the necessary calls on the target hub or persistent connection.

- We finally start the connection and wait for it to be established before exiting the constructor.

6. We're almost done; we just need to override the two available overloads of the `Send()` method to define how to forward any incoming messages to the backplane, shown as follows:

```
protected override Task Send(
    int streamIndex, IList<Message> messages)
{
    return Send(messages);
}

protected override Task Send(
    IList<Message> messages)
```

```
    {
        if (_connection.State !=
            ConnectionState.Connected)
            return Task.FromResult(false);

        var newId = _hub.Invoke<long>("GetId").Result;

        var data = SignalRBackplaneMessage
            .ToBytes(newId, messages);

        return _hub.Invoke("Publish", data);
    }
```

The first override is simply forwarded to the second one because, in our simplified implementation, we deal with just one logical stream of messages. The second override returns a completed task whenever a message comes in when no connection to the backplane is available. If that's not the case, it first asks the backplane for a new unique ID, which is then used to generate a new backplane message along with the list of incoming messages. The task that results from the asynchronous invocation of the `Publish()` method on the remote hub is then returned to the caller.

7. The last missing bits are needed to wire our new message hub into SignalR's pipeline:

```
using Microsoft.AspNet.SignalR;
using Microsoft.AspNet.SignalR.Messaging;

namespace Recipe51.SignalRBackplaneMessageBus
{
    public static class DependencyResolverExtensions
    {
        public static void UseSignalRBackplane(
            this IDependencyResolver resolver,
            string endpointAddress)
        {
            resolver.UseSignalRBackplane(
                new SignalRBackplaneConfiguration
                {
                    EndpointAddress = endpointAddress
                });
        }

        public static void UseSignalRBackplane(
            this IDependencyResolver resolver,
            SignalRBackplaneConfiguration configuration)
```

```
            {
                resolver.Register(
                    typeof(IMessageBus),
                    () => new SignalRBackplaneMessageBus(
                        resolver,
                        configuration));
            }
        }
    }
```

These extension methods for `IDependencyResolver` allow us to register a factory method to inject an instance of our `SignalRBackplaneMessageBus` into SignalR's pipeline as the `IMessageBus` to be used. We just need to call one of them from the `Configure()` method of the `Startup` class used in the application that we want to scale out.

Our projects are almost ready to be tested. At this point, we just need to reference `Recipe51.SignalRBackplaneMessageBus` from our sample application, `Recipe51`, and inside the `Startup` class, call the `UseSignalRBackplane()` extension method to plug the new backplane into it, shown as follows:

```
GlobalHost.DependencyResolver
    .UseSignalRBackplane("http://localhost:7526");
```

The URL that we are specifying points to our `Recipe51.Backplane` application; this means that now `Recipe51` uses it to deliver SignalR messages. If we launch it now, we'll see that whatever implementation it contains works as expected.

Now, we can extend the test by having `Recipe51` hosted by multiple **IIS Express** instances running on different ports (as we repeatedly did in *Chapter 7, Analyzing Advanced Scenarios*, when talking about backplanes). This way, we'll appreciate how clients connected to different servers will still be able to exchange messages as if they were connected to the same endpoint, thanks to the backplane that we hooked into it.

There's more...

Of course, building a production-ready backplane is not an easy task, and our implementation does not have such a level of reliability. There are issues to be handled; for example, how to recover missing messages in case of a disconnection and reconnection, which might need better strategies. Nevertheless, we just demonstrated that it's doable, and the source code available from SignalR's repository on GitHub is a huge source of ideas in this area too. Check it out at `https://github.com/SignalR/SignalR`.

Implementing a real-time error notification system

A real-time notification system is often useful, if not necessary, to handle unexpected events in order to make humans or their automated counterparts aware of what's going on while things happen. An **unhandled exception** could well be one of those scenarios where such a system could become interesting. In this recipe, we'll see how we can set up a sample application so that it can intercept unhandled exceptions in a single central place and post them to a monitoring system that will then use SignalR to broadcast the details about the errors it receives to its users.

We will not need many features from SignalR; actually, the only feature that we'll really need is the capability to invoke a client-side callback from outside any hub's method, thanks to the hub context.

Getting ready

Our sample will consist of the following two different projects:

▶ `Recipe52`: This is a simple and traditional sample web application with just one page that raises an exception. In this application, we'll add a global exception handler, and from there, we'll collect information about the error to post to the `Recipe52.Errors` web application. We'll need to create a new empty web application to build this one.

▶ `Recipe52.Errors`: A generic SignalR-based web application that we can use to publish errors that come from monitored applications. Also, in this case, we'll start by creating an empty web application.

How to do it...

Let's describe the two projects in the same order in which we listed them previously.

`Recipe52` is just a sample application that generates errors; let's quickly illustrate the steps that are needed to build it:

1. We start by adding a single page called `index.cshtml`, which will always throw an exception:

```
@using System
@{
    throw new Exception("Something went wrong!");
}
```

We use a **Razor Web Page** (.cshtml) in order to easily trigger a server-side exception; therefore, we need to enable **Web Pages** support by adding the following configuration key to our web.config file:

```
<appSettings>
  <add key="webpages:Version" value="2.0" />
</appSettings>
```

2. We then add a global.asax file, removing all the plumbing code added by the Visual Studio template except for the Application_Error() method, which will be triggered every time an unhandled exception will be thrown on the application:

```
protected void Application_Error(
    object sender, EventArgs e)
{
    HttpContext.Current.Error.Post(
        "Recipe52",
        new Uri(
        "http://localhost:15852/PostError.axd"));
}
```

We are invoking an extension method called Post() on the Error member of HttpContext.Current, which contains the last exception thrown on the current request's thread. The goal of this method is to provide a way to post information about the error to an external application. The method is supplied with a string that contains the name of the throwing application and a target URL to which the details of the error will be posted.

3. Of course, the Post() method we just used does not exist yet, so let's define it:

```
public static class ExceptionExtensions
{
    public static void Post(this Exception error,
        string application, Uri destination)
    {
        using (var wc = new WebClient())
        {
            var descriptor = new NameValueCollection
            {
                { "Application", application },
                { "Error", error.Message }
            };

            try
            {
```

```
            wc.UploadValues(destination,
                descriptor);
        }
        finally
        {

        }
    }
  }
}
```

Its implementation prepares a collection of key-value pairs that contain the name of the application received as a parameter and the `Message` property of the exception the method is invoked on. The collection is then posted to the destination URL using the `WebClient` type and its `UploadValues()` method.

The source of errors is ready. Of course, in a real-world scenario, the `Post()` method would probably belong to an external and reusable library, and maybe, it would post errors in an asynchronous way, but the way we did this is enough to illustrate the concept.

Let's now move on to `Recipe52.Errors`, the actual monitoring application where, of course, SignalR is a necessary component. As usual, we add it through the `Microsoft.AspNet.SignalR` NuGet package before starting to add the components of the application. Perform the following steps to do so:

1. We start by adding a **persistent connection** called `ErrorsConnection`, whose content will be extremely simple, as shown:

   ```
   public class ErrorsConnection : PersistentConnection
   {
   }
   ```

   The client page of our monitoring application will connect here, and then it will have the `receive()` method of the `connection` object called whenever the server will send data to them. We'll be using `ErrorsConnection` on the server side shortly.

   We could have used a simple `Hub` and, if the monitoring application would need more features, it would've been the most sensible option. However, in this case, the implementation is so simple that we decided to use a persistent connection to illustrate its usage in a real-world sample.

2. We also need, as usual, a `Startup` class that is generated using the corresponding template and whose implementation is a simple bootstrap sequence for persistent connection (exposed on the `"/errors"` endpoint), as shown in the following code snippet:

   ```
   public void Configuration(IAppBuilder app)
   {
       app.MapSignalR<ErrorsConnection>("/errors");
   }
   ```

3. The interesting code of this recipe happens in an **ASP.NET Handler** called `Errors`, which we are going to add to the project using the template Visual Studio provides for its creation, as shown in the following screenshot:

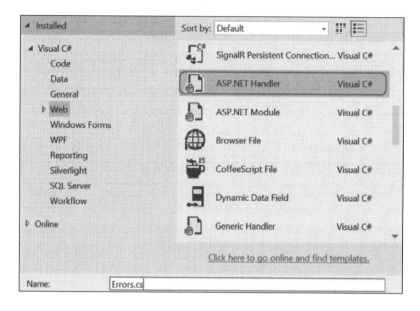

This handler can be targeted by any external application to post information about their errors to the monitoring system. We just need to expose it by registering it in the `web.config` file:

```
<system.webServer>
  <handlers>
    <add name="PostError" verb="POST"
        path="PostError.axd"
        type="Recipe52.Errors.Errors" />
  </handlers>
</system.webServer>
```

This new entry in the `handlers` section declares that an instance of our `Errors` type will be invoked any time a client reaches an endpoint called `PostError.axd` with an `HTTP POST` request.

4. After having seen how to create and wire the new handler, let's take a look at its code, which is as follows:

```
public class Errors : IHttpHandler
{
    public bool IsReusable
    {
```

```
            get { return true; }
        }

    public void ProcessRequest(HttpContext context)
    {
        var post = context.Request.Params;

        var application = post["Application"];
        var error       = post["Error"];

        var connection = GlobalHost.ConnectionManager
            .GetConnectionContext<ErrorsConnection>()
            .Connection;
        connection.Send(
            new ConnectionMessage(
                connection.DefaultSignal,
                new
                {
                    application, error
                }));
    }
    }
}
```

Just like any other ASP.NET Handler, `Errors` implements `IHttpHandler`; therefore, it has to provide a property called `IsReusable`, which, in our case, can simply return `true` and a method called `ProcessRequest`, which will be invoked every time an HTTP request reaches it. The content of `ProcessRequest` is quite simple and is as follows:

- It first extracts the two fields that we are expecting in the POST payload from any client that contacts these handlers: `Application` and `Error`.

- Then, it gets an instance of `ConnectionManager` from `GlobalHost`, and from there, it retrieves a **connection context** related to our `ErrorsConnection` type, which is eventually used to send data to every connected client in the form of an anonymous type instance that contains the application name and the error message that comes from the posting application.

We're almost done; now, we just need a simple client page that will receive all incoming errors posted to our monitoring application in real time.

We create a page called `index.html` and add the following content:

```html
<!DOCTYPE html>
<html xmlns="http://www.w3.org/1999/xhtml">
<head>
    <title></title>
    <script src="Scripts/jquery-2.1.0.js"></script>
    <script src="Scripts/jquery.signalR-2.0.2.js"></script>
    <script>

        $(function() {

            $.connection('errors')
                .received(
                    function (e) {
                        var message =
                            e.application +
                            ' failed with error: ' +
                            e.error;
                        $('#errors')
                            .prepend($('<li/>').text(
                                message));
                    })
                .start();

        });

    </script>
</head>
<body>
    <ul id="errors"></ul>
</body>
</html>
```

The code is very simple; it just contains the necessary JavaScript references, an unordered list in the body section of the page, and a piece of script to open a SignalR connection after having registered a `receive` callback that will be invoked for every error descriptor broadcasted by the server-side `Errors` handler. The callback will build a simple string with some detail about the error, and it will prepend it to the unordered list on the page.

In order to test the monitoring application we have to build the `Recipe52.Errors` project, launch it, and then navigate to its `index.html` page. While we keep that browser instance around, we build and launch `Recipe52`, we navigate to its `index.cshtml` page, and we observe the **Yellow Screen Of Death** (**YSOD**) that appears because of the exception it raises. At the same time, on the browser window we opened earlier pointing at the `Recipe52.Errors` application, we should see a message describing the same error and displayed at the same time the error happens on `Recipe52`.

There's more...

With this sample, you should have a general idea about how to build such a monitoring system to notify errors in real time, but it's also true that there are a lot of details to take care of if you want to provide a full-fledged solution to the problem. In case you are interested, a similar solution already exists and is basically built on the same ideas that we just saw. It's called **ElmahR** (`http://elmahr.apphb.com/`), and it's a real-time error-monitoring dashboard that can be configured to display live information about errors that happen on multiple monitored applications. The potential sources of errors just have to use **ELMAH** (`https://code.google.com/p/elmah/`), a very well known library to intercept unhandled exceptions and plug into it a module exposed by **ElmahR.Elmah**, which belongs to the ElmahR project. ELMAH and ElmahR.Elmah are both available on NuGet, and together, they play the same role of both the `Error` handler and the `Post` extension method from `Recipe52`, while `Recipe52.Errors` corresponds to the ElmahR dashboard. For more details, you can check its source code at `https://bitbucket.org/wasp/elmahr/wiki/Home`.

Creating Web Projects

In this appendix, we will cover the following topics:

- ► Creating an empty ASP.NET web application
- ► Creating an ASP.NET web forms application
- ► Creating an ASP.NET MVC application
- ► Creating an MVC controller and a related view
- ► Creating an ASP.NET website

Introduction

Throughout the course of this book, we've been using various types of ASP.NET projects that need a few steps to be correctly created in Visual Studio. In this appendix, we'll briefly review the steps to create each one of them in case you are not yet used to it.

Creating an empty ASP.NET web application

To create an empty ASP.NET web application, ensure you have Visual Studio 2013 open; you might want to create an empty solution or open an existing one where we can put the project that we'll create. Let's prepare the ground using the following steps:

1. Create a new web application by navigating to **File** | **New Project**.
2. Select **Web** after navigating to **Installed** | **Visual C#**.

3. On the central panel of the dialog box, select **ASP.NET Web Application**, give it a name, and click on **OK**, as shown in the following screenshot:

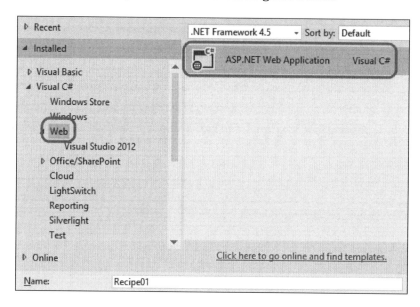

4. On the following screen, select the **Empty** application template, leave all the available options unselected, and then click on **Create Project**, as shown in the following screenshot:

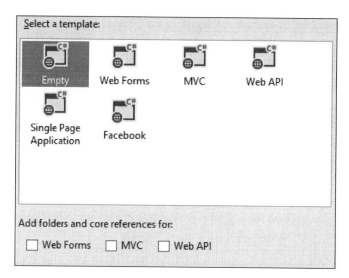

Creating an ASP.NET web forms application

To create an ASP.NET web forms application, ensure you have Visual Studio 2013 open; you might want to create an empty solution or open an existing one wherein to put the project we'll create. Let's prepare the ground by performing the following steps:

1. Create a new web application by navigating to **File | New Project**.

2. Select **Web** after navigating to **Installed | Visual C#**.

3. On the central panel of the dialog box, select **ASP.NET Web Application**, give it a name, and click on **OK**, as shown in the following screenshot:

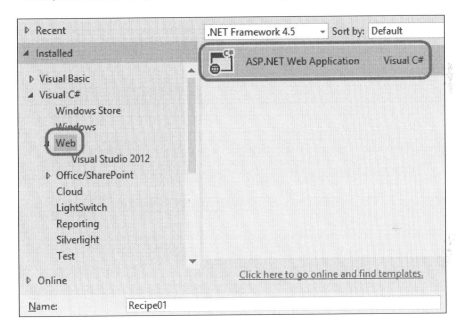

4. On the following screen, select the **Empty** application template, activate the **Web Forms** option, and then click on **Create Project**, as shown in the following screenshot:

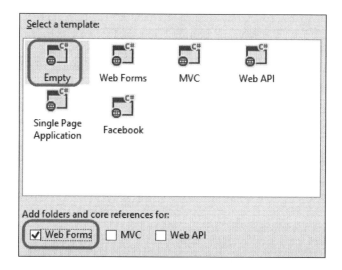

Creating an ASP.NET MVC application

To create an ASP.NET MVC application, ensure you have Visual Studio 2013 open; you might want to create an empty solution or open an existing one wherein to put the project we'll create. Perform the following steps:

1. Create a new web application by navigating to **File | New Project**.

2. Select **Web** after navigating to **Installed | Visual C#**.

3. On the central panel of the dialog box, select **ASP.NET Web Application**, give it a name, and click on **OK**, as shown in the following screenshot:

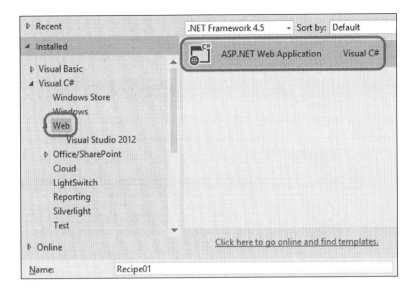

4. On the following screen, select the **Empty** application template, activate the **MVC** option, and then click on **Create Project**, as shown in the following screenshot:

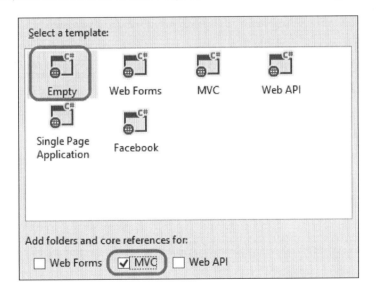

Creating an MVC controller and a related view

Let's add a default controller by opening the context menu on our MVC web application and then navigating to **Add | Scaffold...**. From there, let's select the **MVC 5 Controller – Empty** option and give it a name, as shown in the following screenshot:

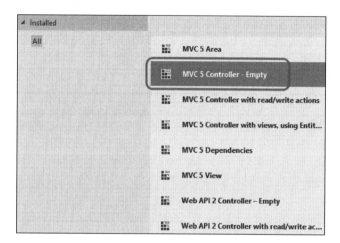

Our controller will have an `Index()` method; for our recipes, we'll just need to add a view for that method in the same way we would do for every other controller action (we'll name it `index.cshtml`), as shown in the following screenshot:

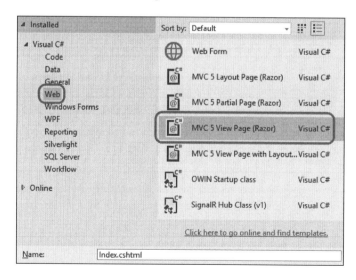

Visual Studio will create the specified file with some basic HTML content.

Creating an ASP.NET website

To create an ASP.NET website, ensure you have Visual Studio 2013 open; you might want to create an empty solution or open an existing one wherein to put the project we'll create. Perform the following steps:

1. Create a new website by navigating to **File | New Web Site**.

2. Select **Web** after navigating to **Installed | Visual C#**.

3. On the central panel of the dialog box, select **ASP.NET Empty Web Site**, give it a name, and click on **OK**, as shown in the following screenshot:

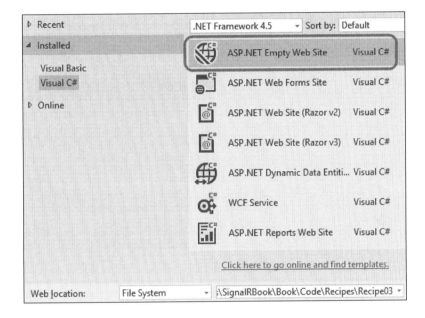

Visual Studio will create the specified file with some basic HTML content.

B
Insights

In this appendix, we will cover the following topics:

- ▶ Transport strategies
- ▶ Asynchronous programming and SignalR

Transport strategies

As briefly mentioned a couple of times in this book, when a connection is started, SignalR chooses a transport strategy to provide the logical persistent connection on top of which every feature we described is made available. SignalR decides which strategy to use according to the environment it runs on. The connection process starts with a traditional HTTP connection, and from there the available options are checked in sequence until the best available option is determined and used.

The first two strategies checked are based on HTML5 and are as follows:

- ▶ **WebSocket**: This is an HTML5-related protocol that provides full duplex communication channels over a single TCP connection. It provides the most complete set of features and the best performance, but has strict requirements. This option is available in modern web browsers only, and requires Windows Server 2012 or Windows 8, and .NET Framework 4.5. For more details about WebSocket, you can refer to `http://www.websocket.org`.

- ▶ **Server Sent Events**: This strategy is based on `EventsSource` HTML5 support, which allows a server to stream messages to connected clients. An `EventSource` instance can be created from JavaScript, making it target a remote endpoint that can then stream messages on the opened connection. Event handlers can be defined on the `EventSource` instance to receive the messages pushed by the server. For more details, you can check out `http://www.w3.org/TR/eventsource`.

When HTML5 is not available, two more strategies, commonly known as Comet, are checked. More details about the Comet web application model are available at `http://en.wikipedia.org/wiki/Comet_(programming)`. The two strategies are as follows:

- **Forever Frame**: This is a strategy based on the use of a hidden iframe where the **Chunked Encoding HTTP** feature is used to send an indefinitely long stream of bytes. It allows a server to start sending a response before knowing its total length, therefore supporting incremental delivery of content.

- **Long Polling**: This is a basic technique that involves opening a connection and keeping it artificially alive to create the illusion of a persistent connection. Asynchronous requests are initiated and kept open until data is available to be sent to the client, or a timeout occurs. In both cases, a new connection is immediately opened when the previous one ends; that's why the term polling can be used to describe this technique. This is a generic description, but there are actually several ways to implement this strategy.

In *Chapter 3*, *Using the JavaScript Hubs Client API*, and *Chapter 4*, *Using the .NET Hubs Client API*, we illustrated the fact that developers can alter the probing sequence, making it possible to have SignalR make different choices. That said, most of the times this is not the recommended approach because the sequence is already optimized to guarantee the best features and performance available for a given environment. What's important here is to actually understand how and why a specific strategy is chosen, and then how such a strategy works so that you might be able to diagnose and fix issues you might find in specific scenarios.

More details about connection management in general, and about how that relates to specific transport strategies, can be found at `http://www.asp.net/signalr/overview/signalr-20/hubs-api/handling-connection-lifetime-events`.

Asynchronous programming and SignalR

This book has no ambition of being an architectural one, and it does not go too deep into technological issues because those would take a lot of space and distract the content from its direct goal of delivering straightforward solutions to common problems. Nevertheless, the fully asynchronous nature of SignalR deserves a couple of words and some reference material for those interested in digging into it.

The trend in programming in the last few years has been pretty clear: asynchronicity rules. Whether you are building a modern and reactive UI, a database-intensive backend, or a distributed system, you want to optimize resources, and the first logical choice to achieve that is avoid holding them if you don't use them. In other words, you never want any code to be stuck waiting for something else, because blocked code does nothing while still holding precious computational power that could be used for good in different ways.

This brings complexity, because it's clearly harder to know when a result is ready if we do not wait for it anymore. Computer scientists have been working on these problems for a long time, but it's just recently that mainstream platforms started supplying programming models more sophisticated than classical callbacks, which do their work fine but inevitably lead to intricate and unreadable code.

Nowadays, we have easy access to several better approaches that allow us to manage asynchronous code better. One of those is the idea of a **promise**, or **future value**. This is an object that represents a value that will be ready at *some point in the future*, and its availability will happen asynchronously with respect to the logical thread of code that has a reference on the promise itself. The great advantage of this model is the fact that *promises can be composed*, leading to more natural and readable programs that end up looking sequential even if they are totally asynchronous.

JavaScript does not support promises natively, but there are several libraries implementing the pattern. One of those is the **jQuery Deferred Object**, which we have mentioned here because it's the one used by SignalR. Another quite popular one is the **Q** library (`https://github.com/kriskowal/q`).

On the .NET side, the **Task** API, available since Version 4.0, is an implementation of the promise pattern that allows the usage of the **Task-based Asynchronous Pattern** (**TAP**), and the **async/await** syntax from C# 5.0 greatly simplifies the composition of promises. What's important here is the fact that most of the networking infrastructure available with .NET is fully asynchronous and implements TAP.

SignalR, on the one hand, leverages and embraces such support from the networking infrastructure, and on the other exposes itself the very same way, making sure things are done the most efficient way possible behind the scenes while clients are enforced to do the same by the model. On the server, methods are invoked when corresponding low-level messages become asynchronously available, resulting in a highly scalable messaging framework. On the client, the connection and hub's proxy objects expose methods that return composable promises, leading developers to write clean and efficient code.

This is an incredibly vast topic we just wanted to briefly introduce; you can find a lot of material about it on the Web for your investigations. The following are a few helpful links:

- **Futures and promises**: `http://en.wikipedia.org/wiki/Futures_and_promises`
- **jQuery Deferred Object**: `http://api.jquery.com/category/deferred-object/`
- **Task-based Asynchronous Pattern**: `http://msdn.microsoft.com/en-us/library/hh873175(v=vs.110).aspx`

▶ **Continuation Passing Style and Asynchrony in C#** (blog post series by Eric Lippert):

- ❏ `http://blogs.msdn.com/b/ericlippert/archive/2010/10/21/` `continuation-passing-style-revisited-part-one.aspx`
- ❏ `http://blogs.msdn.com/b/ericlippert/archive/2010/10/28/` `asynchrony-in-c-5-part-one.aspx`

Index

J

JabbR
  URL 203
JavaScript client
  SignalR Hub, connecting from 18, 19
JavaScript Hubs Client API
  client-side method, adding on proxy 71-73
  client-side method, calling from server 71-74
  connection transport strategies,
     setting up 66, 67
  errors, managing across complex
     asynchronous workflow 74-78
  Hub connection, starting 62-65
  server-side Hub method, calling 68-71
JavaScript proxies
  static files, generating for 136
jQuery Deferred Object 269
JSON.Net library 111
JsonProperty attribute 150
JSONP support
  enabling 130

K

KeepAlive value 121

L

lifetime, of connection
  controlling 119-125
Linq 218
Login() method 199
Logout() method 199
Long Polling technique 66, 268

M

MapSignalR() method 12, 156, 174
maxConcurrentRequestsPerCPu
     parameter 152
messages, Persistent Connection API
  exchanging, between server and JavaScript
     client 111-114
  exchanging, between server and .NET
     client 114-117
  sending, from server 104-107
  sending, to server 108-111

messaging systems application 194
MVC controller
  creating 264

O

observable 218
OnConnected() method 102, 122
OnDisconnected() method 122
on() method 167
OnReceived() method 110
OnReconnected() method 122
Open Web Interface (OWIN) 12
Owin hosting infrastructure
  URL 146

P

Persistent Connection API
  about 99
  adding 100-103
  messages, exchanging between server and
     JavaScript client 111-113
  messages, exchanging between server and
     .NET client 114-117
  messages, sending from server 104-107
  messages, sending to server 108-111
  registering 100
  requests, authorizing 142-145
  working 104
PersistentConnection class 106
persistent cookie 126
pets finder application
  implementing 227-242
property bag 125
proxy-less connections
  establishing 165-168

R

Razor Web Page 252
real-time error notification system
  implementing 251-256
  Recipe52 251
  Recipe52.Errors 251
real-time map of flying airplanes
  implementing 212-227

Thank you for buying
SignalR Real-time Application Cookbook

About Packt Publishing

Packt, pronounced 'packed', published its first book "*Mastering phpMyAdmin for Effective MySQL Management*" in April 2004 and subsequently continued to specialize in publishing highly focused books on specific technologies and solutions.

Our books and publications share the experiences of your fellow IT professionals in adapting and customizing today's systems, applications, and frameworks. Our solution based books give you the knowledge and power to customize the software and technologies you're using to get the job done. Packt books are more specific and less general than the IT books you have seen in the past. Our unique business model allows us to bring you more focused information, giving you more of what you need to know, and less of what you don't.

Packt is a modern, yet unique publishing company, which focuses on producing quality, cutting-edge books for communities of developers, administrators, and newbies alike. For more information, please visit our website: www.packtpub.com.

About Packt Open Source

In 2010, Packt launched two new brands, Packt Open Source and Packt Enterprise, in order to continue its focus on specialization. This book is part of the Packt Open Source brand, home to books published on software built around Open Source licences, and offering information to anybody from advanced developers to budding web designers. The Open Source brand also runs Packt's Open Source Royalty Scheme, by which Packt gives a royalty to each Open Source project about whose software a book is sold.

Writing for Packt

We welcome all inquiries from people who are interested in authoring. Book proposals should be sent to author@packtpub.com. If your book idea is still at an early stage and you would like to discuss it first before writing a formal book proposal, contact us; one of our commissioning editors will get in touch with you.

We're not just looking for published authors; if you have strong technical skills but no writing experience, our experienced editors can help you develop a writing career, or simply get some additional reward for your expertise.

SignalR: Real-time Application Development

ISBN: 978-1-78216-424-1   Paperback: 124 pages

Utilize real-time functionality in your .NET applications with ease

1. Develop real-time applications across numerous platforms.

2. Create scalable applications that are ready for cloud deployment.

3. Utilize the full potential of SignalR.

ASP.NET 3.5 Application Architecture and Design

ISBN: 978-1-84719-550-0   Paperback: 260 pages

Build robust, scalable ASP.NET applications quickly and easily

1. Master the architectural options in ASP.NET to enhance your applications.

2. Develop and implement n-tier architecture to allow you to modify a component without disturbing the next one.

3. Design scalable and maintainable web applications rapidly.

Please check **www.PacktPub.com** for information on our titles

[PACKT] open source*
community experience distilled
PUBLISHING

ASP.NET Site Performance Secrets

ISBN: 978-1-84969-068-3   Paperback: 456 pages

Simple and proven techniques to quickly speed up your ASP.NET web site

1. Speed up your ASP.NET website by identifying performance bottlenecks that hold back your site's performance and fixing them.

2. Tips and tricks for writing faster code and pinpointing those areas in the code that matter most, thus saving time and energy.

3. Drastically reduce page load times.

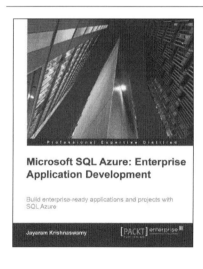

Microsoft SQL Azure: Enterprise Application Development

ISBN: 978-1-84968-080-6   Paperback: 420 pages

Build enterprise-ready applications and projects with SQL Azure

1. Develop large scale enterprise applications using Microsoft SQL Azure.

2. Understand how to use the various third-party programs such as DB Artisan, RedGate, ToadSoft, and so on developed for SQL Azure.

3. Master the exhaustive Data migration and Data Synchronization aspects of SQL Azure.

Please check **www.PacktPub.com** for information on our titles

18809548R00165

Made in the USA
San Bernardino, CA
03 February 2015